JESUS CHRIST AND CHRIS
AND MISSI
(Gospel Commentaries)

To my very good friend Leah Santiago

Isaac Olamp

JESUS CHRIST AND CHRISTIANITY

HIS LIFE AND MISSION
(Gospel Commentaries)

DR. ISAAC OLANIYI

KISOL PUBLISHERS

British Library Catalouging in Publication Data.
A catalogue record for this book is available from the British Library.

ISBN 1-904382-04-5

First Published in 2003 by Kisol Publishers Limited
24, View Close
Biggin Hill
Westerham
Kent.

Typeset by Kisol Publishers Ltd
Kent.

CONTENTS

INTRODUCTION

THE aim of this work is to examine the life of Jesus Christ, both in a historical and a spiritual sense, and also the political, economic and religious settings that surrounded His Birth, Mission and Death.

The historical setting before His Birth is especially important, so also His Teaching and His influence on the formation of the Christian Church. Much has been written about the historical and the Christian Jesus, and many people have tried to detach the historical Jesus from the Christian one. It is difficult to judge to what degree they have succeeded in achieving this.

This work is not just a historical chronicle and a discussion of the political setting under which Jesus accomplished His Mission, it is also an analytical one, but not analytical in the accepted sense. An intellectual analysis and examination of the nature of Jesus, His Work or His accomplishments is bound to fail for quite obvious reasons.

Jesus was spiritual in all He did, and in order for us to understand Him, we are obliged to use a similar implement to examine His words. This implement is the intuitive perception, which belongs to the spirit. Our failure to understand Jesus and His Work in the past has stemmed from the inability of many of us to do just that. The failure to use our intuitions to examine the life and the works of Jesus.

The life of Jesus will not be the butt of scholarly diatribes. He who fails to use his intuition will only run around in circles, and in the end will be forced to attempt to debase the Word of Christ in order to understand Him. He would have to drag the Word of Jesus into the dust of the intellect. We are the ones to lift ourselves high through the use of our spirits, and then perhaps we will be in a position to understand Him better, instead of the pitiable attempts over the centuries to debase this Figure.

1

PART I

HISTORY AND GEOGRAPHY

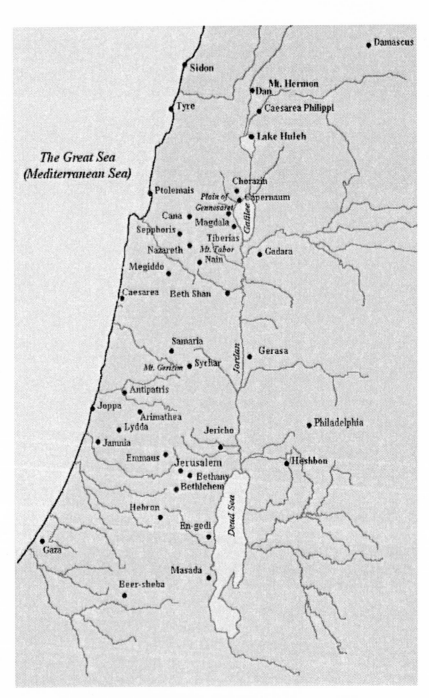

MAP OF PALESTINE DURING JESUS' TIME

1

Geographical Background

JESUS was born in Palestine, which for centuries was known as the crossroads of the world. It is situated strategically between two continents and became an important transcontinental trade route.

The area known as Palestine at that time was bounded to the north by Mount Hermon, to the south by the Negev desert, to the west by the Mediterranean Sea and to the east by the Syrian Desert.

There are two large bodies of water: to the north is Lake Galilee and to the south is the Dead Sea. The river Jordan joins the two in an almost absolutely straight line from north to south. The two countries to the north are Syria and Phoenicia (modern day Lebanon) and to the south was the Idumaean kingdom from where king Herod the Great hailed.

The country itself was divided into three regions: Galilee to the north, Samaria in the middle and Judea to the south. Most of Jesus' ministry was concentrated around the Lake Galilee and its environs in the north.

2

Historical Background

THE patriarch Abraham's covenant with God made the Jewish people a called people, destined to receive spiritual tidings and spread it among the Gentiles. All that they had to do was to upkeep the Laws of God. This upkeep guaranteed continued earthly and spiritual success. Through a succession of prophets, they were always reminded of their great destiny. Among them a Messiah was to be born who would free the world.

The sufferings engendered by the captivity in Egypt kept the flame of the longing for God pure and allowed the Jewish people to outstrip all other races in their spiritual development and recognitions. Through Moses, and when the time was right, they were given the Ten Commandments and eventually led into the Promised Land by Joshua. Here, they were meant to put into effect the full workings of the Laws of God as revealed in the Ten Commandments. They hardly kept these Commandments however, and disaster followed.

First came leadership through the Judges and then King David, followed by his son Solomon. The moral fibre of the society deteriorated, however, with the reign of Solomon with his concubines and the infusion of foreign customs through these people. The worship of foreign idols made an appearance during this time and the consequences of this was not only the spiritual but also the earthly decline of the nation.

With Solomon's death, the decline of the nation of Israel which had already begun was finally completed. The kingdom was split in 928BC and divided between his two sons: the kingdom of Israel itself and that of Judah. This split, with the inevitable weaknesses made both kingdoms open to attack and plunder by foreign powers.

As is the fate of weak nations in those times, Israel was attacked and defeated by the Assyrians in 722BC, whereas Judah had since become a vassal state to the same Assyrians. The status of Judah did not last for long, however, as it too came under the dominion of the Babylonians in 587BC. This conquer was followed by extensive depopulations, deportations and exile in what has become popularly known as the Babylonian exile and captivity. The Temple of Solomon was destroyed and thus ended the so-called First Temple period of Jewish history.

The Israelites were kept in Babylon for about 50 years until their captors were themselves defeated by the Persians in 539BC. The Persian king Cyrus the Great was very benevolent and allowed the Jews to return to their country. Thus started the first wave of returnees from exile. They were also allowed religious autonomy and in the space of a few years, the first returnees, in concert with those who had stayed behind in Israel rebuilt the Jerusalem Temple, thereby marking the beginning of the Second Temple period.

First under the leadership of Ezra, and then Nehemiah, the Pentateuch was canonised, several religious reforms were introduced and the lives of the Israelites were rededicated to the worship of God. The office of High Priest was created, which office came to play a pivotal role in the lives of Israelites until the Romans came. The occupier of this office was the de-facto head of state of Israel. It could be argued that the creation of this office, while it was very crucial that it be created, led directly to the further moral decline of the Israelite leadership, as we shall see.

Alexander the Great

The Persians were defeated by Alexander the Great and hellenization of the Jews began in earnest. Trade and commerce and everything else came to be conducted in the Greek language. It was inevitable that this culture found its way into the homes of ordinary Jews, especially the upper and the middle classes. The adoption of the Greek culture, especially by the priestly aristocracy led to a gradual decline in Jewish identity and inevitably with time, the entire Jewish people would have been thoroughly assimilated. Fate, however, had other plans for the Jewish people, as we shall soon see.

The sudden death of Alexander the Great in 323BC led to in-fighting among his generals, which eventually led to the division of his empire among them. For our purposes, two of these divisions are of especial interest: the Ptolemaic and the Seleucid. Egypt and its environs, including Palestine went initially to the former while Syria, Turkey and Persia went to the latter. Several years later, the Ptolemaics lost Palestine to the Seleucids. The former were benign rulers and allowed some degree of religious autonomy, but with the latter, hellenization was more thoroughly advanced.

Hasmonaean rule

As mentioned earlier, the Seleucids, who now had jurisdiction over Judaea thoroughly promoted hellenization and under their rule, and especially with the connivance of the upper and middle classes, the religion of Israel and a whole way of life would have disappeared forever. This, however, was not to be.

Antiochus IV Epiphanes, a Seleucid was ruler by the time the Maccabaean revolt started. During all this time, the high priests had come from the descendants of Aaron as a hereditary post with no outside interference in the choice for this office. Everything changed, however, with Antiochus Epiphanes as the position suddenly ceased to be hereditary. Jason, who was brother to Onias III, the high priest bribed Antiochus IV Epiphanes and was made high priest while Onias was exiled. Jason was thoroughly pro-Hellenic and increased still further the pace of hellenization. He himself was later deposed by a certain Menelaus, also with the help of Antiochus IV Epiphanes. A dangerous precedent had been set. There were now three people contending the post of high priest.

Some years later, having been defeated in Egypt, Antiochus IV Epiphanes returned to discover that Jason in his absence had returned to depose his protégé Menelaus. Outraged, he besieged the Temple and massacred all those who refused to co-operate with him. He banned all manner of Jewish religious worship in the country and ordered that all shall worship the Greek gods. To make matters worse, he ordered that a pagan altar be built upon the existing altar of burnt offering in the Temple. This action, known as the "abomination of desolation" was the last straw for the majority of Jews who saw no other way out of this desecration but to resist. The Maccabaean revolt had begun.

The Maccabaean revolt started with a local Jewish priest called Mattathias and his five sons. Instead of obeying the order of a local officer to offer pagan sacrifices, they refused and killed the officer. They later gathered other people around them in their open revolt against the Seleucid rule. When Mattathias died, Judas, one of his sons took his place and was especially famous for his victories against the Seleucids and for his appellation *the Maccabee*. Judas succeeded in instituting some degree of normalcy and managed to rededicate some of the Temples that had been desecrated to the pure worship of God.

Judas, however, had to wage a bitter struggle against some of his own people who were pro-Hellenic. Most of these people had been deposed by him and as such they sought an opportunity to revenge themselves against him. This opportunity came in the persons of Alcimus, a pro-Hellenic local priest and a new ruler by the name of Demetrius I Soter. Alcimus and his supporters sent a representation to Demetrius I Soter complaining bitterly about how they had been treated by Judas and his supporters. Alcimus was appointed high priest and was installed by force of arms. In the ensuing struggle, even Judas the Maccabee lost his life.

Judas was succeeded by his brother Jonathan, but eventually he fell and was succeeded by another one of the brothers Simon. With Simon now as high priest and political head of state, the rule of the Hasmonaean had begun. Simon achieved total independence for his country from the Seleucids and was declared as Prince, and his position was made hereditary by an act of law.

A series of successions followed, not by any means peaceful until we reach the time of Antigonus, the last Hasmonaean ruler. The time of Antigonus unfortunately coincided with that of Herod the Great, who after having been declared king of Judaea by Caesar Augustus took arms against Antigonus and eventually defeated him. This completed his installation as king of the Jews in Jerusalem, even though he hailed from Idumaea, a country to the south of Judaea.

Roman rule

Before Antigonus, the power struggle among the Hasmonaeans eventually allowed the great Roman general Pompey to lay siege to Jerusalem and take the city. After Simon Maccabbeus came his son John Hyrcanus I and a time of relative prosperity followed. He was succeeded by his eldest son Aristobulus, a cruel and despotic leader. He had his mother tortured and killed and his brothers imprisoned but died suddenly after a very short reign. He was succeeded by his widow and one of his brothers Alexander Jannaeus.

It seemed no one had learnt any lessons and this ruler was just as cruel, if not more so than Aristobulus. His rule was so despotic that the Pharisees and others asked the Seleucid king for help. The battle against Alexander Jannaeus was almost won when most of his opponents switched sides, thereby handing him an easy victory. What followed in terms of the terrible revenge he exacted on his enemies is not difficult to imagine.

Alexandra Salome, his wife succeeded him as political ruler and appointed her son John Hyrcanus II as high priest. When she died however, the power struggles started all over again, now in the form of two brothers; John Hyrcanus II and Judas Aristobulus II his younger brother. After many a battle Judas Aristobulus II defeated John Hyrcanus II and installed himself as the king of the Jews and high priest.

Antipater, the Idumaean king was not happy with this and plotted with John Hyrcanus II and some outside forces to depose Judas Aristobulus II, which they promptly did. Pompey, the great Roman general happened to have been in the area at the time. He, also like Antipater supported John Hyrcanus II against Aristobulus II laying siege to the Temple of Jerusalem in the process. John Hyrcanus II was reinstated as high priest. Even after the Roman civil war, which saw the defeat of Pompey by Julius Caesar, his position was again confirmed as high priest and leader of the Jewish people.

Judas Aristobulus' son Antigonus was, however, not happy and sought to take revenge for the deposition of his father. In collusion with the Parthians, he invaded the country and installed himself as high priest. As mentioned earlier, he later fell out with Antipater's son Herod. By this time, Judaea had become a vassal state to Rome. The position of high priest could only be maintained with the help of Rome through Herod the Great who was a client of Rome.

Idumaean control

The power of Idumaea, a country to the south of Judaea started to rise with Antipater. He was shrewd enough to know who to support among the Roman generals since Rome held the real power in the region. He supported John Hyrcanus II against Judas Aristobulus II because he felt that the latter might prove to be too powerful for him. His son Herod was just as shrewd if not more so. First, he supported Mark Antony and was nominated tetrarch by him and then later switched sides to Caesar Augustus, who confirmed his position and actually made him king of Judaea. It was with this confidence in the support of the emperor of the Roman Empire that he attacked Antigonus and defeated him in 37BC, thereby setting himself up as the undisputed ruler of Judaea and king of the Jews. Herod's rule was despotic to say the least and he had most of his close associates, including members of his own family killed.

He vigorously promoted Roman culture and embarked on grand architectural projects among which was the reconstruction of the Jerusalem Temple on a very grand scale, which took over forty years to complete. All these he did in his attempt to gain support among his Jewish subjects. He also built amphitheatres, hippodromes and so on to impress his masters in Rome.

Herod the Great died at about 4BC and the country was divided up among his sons: Herod Antipas was made tetrarch of Galilee; Archelaus was given Judaea, Idumaea and Samaria and Herod Phillip was given an area on the eastern shore of Galilee. Archelaus' rule was marked by terrible despotism and was deposed in 4BC and direct rule was established by the Romans.

Herod Phillip was the most benevolent and was well liked by his subjects. Herod Antipas was also very despotic and was responsible for the death of John the Baptist in collusion with his wife Herodias. The direct Roman rule imposed on Idumaea, Samaria and Judaea meant that Roman procurators were appointed with headquarters in Syria. A succession of procurators followed the deposition of Archelaus until the time of Pontius Pilate, the procurator at the time of the trial of Jesus.

Roman yoke

Roman rule was characterized by extensive taxation which included among others, a poll tax, crops tax and a levy on the transportation of goods. Apart from this, there was also the tax that was to be paid to the Jewish internal government which took the form of a temple or religious tax, which is primarily meant for the upkeep of the temple. This eventually led to a very great acquisition of wealth in the temple.

This double taxation eventually led to the impoverishment of many families, with many selling off their land to become serfs, or even to become hired labourers. This evidently is not acceptable and the resentment felt by the people began to show in the various riots and revolts that characterized this period. With this unrest also arose the expectation of a deliverer from this yoke. A messiah, who perhaps would be able to destroy the Romans and free them from their oppressive will.

This desire for a messiah and the expectation grew so high that many would-be leaders took the opportunity and some declared themselves messiahs and kings and led the people to senseless revolts against the Romans which almost always led to a massacre of the Jews culminating in the eventual destruction of the Jerusalem temple and the final exile of the Jews in 135AD.

PART II

JEWISH RULE

1

Jewish Internal Rule

THE Hasmonaean rulers combined the role of kingship with that of the high priest. This was also the case before this rule under the Persians and Alexander the Great. This figure was the most important ruler of the entire Jewish people until the end of the Hasmonaeans and the imposition of Herod the Idumaean as king of the Jews. Herod took political power away from the high priests and actually appointed the high priests himself.

Successors to Herod saw no reason to change the status quo and hence a succession of high priests followed who were evidently pawns in the hands of their political kings. The prefecture of the Romans also continued to maintain the status quo. Nevertheless, this role of high priest continued to be very powerful largely because of the enormous religious clout this figure commanded, but also because of the enormous wealth he controlled since the keys to the temple vaults were in his hands.

The high priest was the head of a general council of religious officials called the Sanhedrin which consisted of three groups: members of the high-priestly family, lay elders and scribes who were religious and legal experts. The post of the high priest was often filled by people from wealthy Sadducean families, who were often known to give bribes to the Roman prefects to secure their position. Their main aim, apart from being a religious one is to keep the Jewish people under control.

They were very unpopular among the people as they were seen as collaborators. At the same time, the people resented their wealth. They were allowed to arrest Jews who were deemed to be breaking the law. They could pass sentences but were not really allowed to carry them out but to hand over offenders to the Romans. This further decreased their popularity among the people.

2

Groups

THE people were divided even among themselves as to the best way to practise their religion. This was complicated by the Hellenic influence they had been subjected to and also the ever increasing Roman influence. The upper classes were Roman collaborators and had absorbed the Hellenic influence most of all. At the same time, they also happened to be the ruling classes amongst whose ranks the high priesthood came to be chosen. Which way to interpret the law? Is it going to be the way of the ruling aristocracy who wanted nothing more than to preserve their own positions? Or is it going to be in the way of the common people who over time had come to resent these leaders?

Out of this turmoil arose three principal groups: the Sadducees, the ruling aristocracy; the Pharisees who were closer to the common people and who argued for a stricter observance of the law and the scribes who were mostly scholars attached to the temple, whose main aim was to encourage the common people to pay their tithes, and attend the temple festivals three times a year. Other groups emerged aside from the above. Among these were the Zealots who broke off from the Pharisees because of the disagreement as to the degree of cooperation to be given to Rome. Moderate Pharisees urged restraint, while the more aggressive decided to form their own party in open or internecine guerrilla warfare with the occupying forces. Therefore, the Zealots were a resistance force who used whatever in their means to fight for political freedom.

Another group, whose activity had become the focus of attention especially since the discovery of the Dead Sea Scrolls was the Essenes. These were separatists who preferred the ascetic life and had withdrawn themselves from the corruption of the outside world. They also demanded, as the Pharisees, a strict interpretation of the law.

Sadducees

Said to be the descendants of the priest Zadok, the chief priest during the first temple period. Subsequently all Sadducean priests had been able to trace their lineage directly to Zadok. Throughout the first and second temple periods, the position of high priest came from their ranks. They advocated a literal and strict interpretation of the written Torah and rejected the oral interpretations brought in by the Pharisees. One of the most important differences between this group and the Pharisees is the latter's belief in resurrection of the dead. This often was a point for quarrels and contentions as demonstrated in the Bible when Paul exploited this knowledge in his trial at Caesarea.

They were the most thoroughly hellenized of all the groups and have been known, as indicated above to be collaborators with all the occupying powers whether Greek or Roman. Apart from their rejection of the oral interpretative tradition of the Pharisees, they also differed in terms of how they interpreted the written Torah. Altogether, they were not as strict as the Pharisees in the requirement of the common people to obey the Torah. They were, however, always the minority and their base was the temple. When this was destroyed, they vanished and left the Pharisees to develop what today is known as Rabbinic Judaism.

Pharisees

These were in the majority and were the most popular of the groups. Their aim was to interpret the Torah in the most literal way and they demanded a strict observance of the Mosaic Law. Apart from the Torah itself, they composed a huge number of what has become known as the 'unwritten law', the oral interpretation of the Torah, which has been collected in the Talmud and the Mishnah.

They also formed a group in the Sanhedrin and were quite ready to accept the priestly authority of the Sadducees as long as they were left alone with their own interpretation and understanding of the law.

They were very rigorous in their demands and were felt to be laying heavy burdens on the shoulders of the people in terms of requiring them to obey mundane laws which really had no basis for them in the written Torah. They have also been described as hypocrites, people who preached one thing and did another.

They, in spite of all this had a large following among the people and when the temple was destroyed and with the disappearance of the Sadducees that had to follow this since the latter depended solely on the existence of the temple, they were responsible for the continuation of the Judaism as we know it today.

Scribes

These were closely associated with the temple and their main function as has been mentioned above was to circulate among the people, explaining temple procedures, making sure or encouraging the people to pay their tithes and also encouraging them to attend the festivals in the Jerusalem temple thrice a year.

They were closely connected with the Sadducees and would have helped in temple worship and sacrifices. They also would have helped in maintaining the various aspects of temple work, such as the library. They have been regarded as teachers, theologians, lawyers and expounders of the Jewish law.

Into all this turmoil, the social and political struggles both with the occupying forces and among themselves was born Jesus of Nazareth. Amid the riots, revolts, the massacres and the expectation of a Messiah, or a deliverer from the Roman yoke, Jesus had to grow and develop and also had to develop a clear sense of mission, a clear sense of why He was here and what He had to do. What was His Mission? Was He to be the one to lead Israel from the bonds of their oppressors? Crush Rome and give the people the political freedom that they had been yearning for? Or perhaps He was to be another kind of leader?

Perhaps the expectation of the people was wrong. In expecting a Messiah to deliver them from an earthly bondage, they forgot the much more important desire for the deliverance from a spiritual bondage. It was this misunderstanding that led to the tragedy, the importance of which most mankind has not even after two thousand years begun to understand.

PART III

THE LIFE OF JESUS

1

The Birth of Jesus

Jesus was born in Bethlehem of Judea between 6 and 4BC. His birth was preceded by the Annunciation in which an Angel appeared to Mary and prophesied the birth of a son and commanded her to name Him Jesus. Whether the massacre of the Innocents is historically true or not as has been claimed by some scholars, what then followed was the escape to Egypt by Joseph, Mary and her son. We can assume that Jesus was probably about a few months old at the flight to Egypt.

Historically, we do not have the records of how long Jesus was in Egypt with His parents but it can safely be assumed that they came back when he was still a child because we have reports of Joseph going to the Jerusalem Temple every year and that Jesus Himself according to the custom was taken to the Temple when he was twelve.

Going back to when Jesus was born; His birth was preceded by the Annunciation and also by the appearance to Joseph of an Angel reassuring him not to be alarmed at the state of Mary. This is an interesting development because the question here was that Mary was suddenly found to be pregnant by Joseph, who was her betrothed and according to the custom was already considering breaking his vow to her. He was, however, prevented from doing this by the Angel who reassured him that this was no ordinary pregnancy but one that was holy.

The question of the Annunciation, however, and the purpose of it was different. Mary was approached by the Angel even before she got pregnant and was promised that she would bear a child and was to call the child Jesus. After the visitation by the Angel, we are told that Mary offered the Magnificat in which there was praise to the Lord and a heartfelt gratitude for being deemed worthy of such Divine Grace.

According to the book "In the Light of Truth: The Grail Message" by

Abd-ru-shin, the purpose of the Annunciation was to prepare Mary spiritually for the events that were to follow. The event (the Annunciation) was so stupendous that it became the most important in her life and allowed her to occupy herself more with spiritual matters, which made all base thoughts and feelings disappear. Her intuitions were so pure at this stage that it provided a soil upon which an immaculate conception could occur.

If an earthly woman was chosen to carry the Divine Spirit, she must be seen to carry within herself the basis for this in terms of purity of thoughts and intuitive perceptions. The soil therefore was prepared in Mary for an entrance of a part of God. In fact, it is only on such a soil that a part of God can enter.

At that time, we are told that there was a census going on and has recently been confirmed that Caesar Augustus deemed that a census be carried out for the sake of proper tax estimations. Therefore, Joseph, who normally lived and worked in Nazareth as a carpenter journeyed with his wife, Mary, who was heavily pregnant with child. Joseph was a direct descendant of king David and as such had to go to Judaea for the census, since the law demanded that each return to their ancestral land for this. Because of the overcrowding there, however, there was no inn for them to stay in so much so that when Mary went into labour, they could only find space in a stable.

She gave birth to Jesus in *Bethlehem of Judea* in a stable. It is interesting to note that one of the reasons advanced by the priestly aristocracy for rejecting Jesus was that as far as the writings of the prophets were concerned, no Messiah was supposed to arise from Galilee. The general supposition then was that Jesus could not be the Messiah because it was thought that He was born in Nazareth, in Galilee whereas it had been predicted that the Messiah was to have been born in Bethlehem. We now know historically that Jesus was born in Bethlehem.

It is at this point appropriate to take a brief look at the events surrounding the Birth of Jesus, using the Scriptures. Matthew's aim, because of the peculiar condition in Israel where genealogy was most important was to attempt to trace Jesus back Abraham. It would have been difficult otherwise without this to accept the authenticity of Jesus. Lineage was most important and if Jesus was to be accepted as Lord, His lineage had to correspond to what apparently had been predicted in the Scriptures. The Gospel of Luke took a similar line.

Let us take a look at the Annunciation:

Luke 1:26-38 In the sixth month the angel Gabriel was sent from God to a city of Galilee named Nazareth, (27) to a virgin betrothed to a man whose name was Joseph, of the house of David; and the virgin's name was Mary. (28) And he came to her and said, "Hail, O favored one, the Lord is with you!" (29) But she was greatly troubled at the saying, and considered in her mind what sort of greeting this might be. (30) And the angel said to her, "Do not be afraid, Mary, for you have found favor with God. (31) And behold, you will conceive in your womb and bear a son, and you shall call his name Jesus. (32) He will be great, and will be called the Son of the Most High; and the Lord God will give to him the throne of his father David, (33) and he will reign over the house of Jacob for ever; and of his kingdom there will be no end." (34) And Mary said to the angel, "How shall this be, since I have no husband?" (35) And the angel said to her, "The Holy Spirit will come upon you, and the power of the Most High will overshadow you; therefore the child to be born will be called holy, the Son of God. (36) And behold, your kinswoman Elizabeth in her old age has also conceived a son; and this is the sixth month with her who was called barren. (37) For with God nothing will be impossible." (38) And Mary said, "Behold, I am the handmaid of the Lord; let it be to me according to your word." And the angel departed from her.

This is the Annunciation announced by the Angel Gabriel. The purpose of this has been explained above but it suffices to say here that the Child's name was given as Jesus which means "the Lord saves". This is in contrast to the name given by Matthew who called Him Imanuel, which means "God with us". This is very significant because here we have only Matthew's word for this. Not even the Angel called the Child Imanuel. The Angel *instructed* that the Child be called *Jesus*. Even when the Angel appeared to Joseph he also was consistent in asking that the Child be called Jesus. Matthew 1:20-21 **But as he considered this, behold, an angel of the Lord appeared to him in a dream, saying, "Joseph, son of David, do not fear to take Mary your wife, for that which is conceived in her is of the Holy Spirit; (21) she will bear a son, and you shall call his name Jesus, for he will save his people from their sins."** Matthew was always looking for the fulfillment of prophecies and on *his own* assumed that the Child that Mary was to have, whom the two Angels demanded be named Jesus was the same Child that Isaiah prophesied called Imanuel. Through this, He confused two very different fulfillments requiring *two separate* births. This error unfortunately has been carried on to this day and has prevented many people from recognizing the nature of this *second* Child.

Matthew went on to say: Matthew 1:22-23 **All this took place to fulfill what the Lord had spoken by the prophet: (23) "Behold, a virgin shall conceive and bear a son, and his name shall be called Emmanuel" (which means, God with us).**

These are Matthew's words, not the Angel's. They are his *own* assumptions. He did not even notice that the names are different and that their meanings differ. Jesus means "the Lord saves" and Imanuel means "God with us". It is obvious that the Angels in their appearances to both Joseph and Mary would have mentioned this if this was meant to be so. The fact that on two different occasions they were consistent with the name of the Child goes to prove that the Child that Mary gave birth to was not Imanuel, but Jesus. We will be considering the birth of Jesus in more detail later.

2

Childhood of Jesus

There is no evidence to assume that Jesus did not live a normal life like any other child. There are quite a number of writings, notably the Gospel of Thomas, that have painted fanciful pictures of the childhood of Jesus in their attempts to make Him appear great. There have been reports of Him moulding images of birds from clay, and these images spontaneously coming to life. These are obviously the writings of very imaginative individuals, who, instead of enhancing the allure of Jesus do damage to it. These people obviously meant well, and it was done in an attempt to win more adherents to Christianity at that time.

As mentioned above, it is safe to assume that Joseph went back with his family to Israel when Jesus was a child and that he went to Nazareth, which was his hometown, and where he was already established as a carpenter. Obviously, here Jesus must have undergone instructions like other children of his age in any one of the schools because we know that He was quite educated in the laws as attested to by His numerous quotations from them.

We also know that Joseph, his father was a very religious man and he made several trips to the temple in Jerusalem at least once a year probably for the most important Jewish festival, which is the Feast of the Paschal Lamb. When Jesus reached maturity, which was about the age of twelve, He was taken to the Temple in Jerusalem, at the time of the high priest Annas. We must emphasize that His going to the temple at this age is the custom in Israel at that time. All children, when they reach this age are taken to Jerusalem for a rite of passage, so to speak.

It is to be assumed that He probably joined His father Joseph after some time in the trade of carpentry and for many years was assistant to him until his death. It is also safe to assume that upon Joseph's death,

Jesus assumed the master carpenter's role. This He continued to do until He heard that John was baptizing at the river Jordan and He felt an urge within Himself to find him.

3

Jesus' Baptism

JOHN the Baptist had been born several months before Jesus and had started his mission much earlier. He preached near the river Jordan and baptized those whom he felt were worthy to receive baptism. Through this act, he was able to transmit spiritual power to those who were open to it. He has been generally regarded, and he himself regarded himself as the forerunner of Jesus. He was meant to soften the soil upon which Jesus, the Son of God was meant to work. He was meant to loosen the souls of men so that it would be easier for the Word of the Lord to penetrate into them, consequently making the Work of Jesus much easier.

Through the spiritual turmoil, which must have characterized the early life of Jesus, especially as He reached adolescence, as He began to ask Himself questions as to His origin, the purpose of life and His own purpose in life, there must have arisen the conviction that He needed to see John and perhaps receive the baptism which would bring Him the final clarification as to Who He really was.

Through the baptism, as the account in the Bible showed, He came to recognise Himself, His Origin and His Mission. Through this act, He could consciously enter into His Mission on earth. With this realisation, which would have been tremendous, He withdrew into the wilderness to gain and receive more strength for this Mission. It is not unknown for those who had been chosen by God to withdraw into solitude for further maturing and the receipt of their full powers.

On His return, however, He was fully ready for His Mission, He had received His full Powers and the clarification of what He had to do. He could now go among the people to proclaim the Word of which He was a part.

4

Jesus' Temptation

JESUS, being the embodiment of the Love of God wanted to approach human beings with this Love which could conquer everything. At the same time, while He was still maturing in the wilderness, and while He had not received His full Powers, He was vulnerable to the possibility of misusing this Power in His Love for mankind, and also in His enthusiasm for His Mission.

Lucifer knew this and wanted to use this period of vulnerability, which was actually the only opportunity and window left to him. It is inconceivable that Lucifer would have wanted to help the work of the Light with these schemes. In fact, this is the reason these are called temptations. Schemes which are intended to do maximum harm if yielded to. To take just one example, Lucifer told Jesus to jump down from a height, saying that the Angels would bear him in their arms and save Him. If He had jumped and indeed had been rescued by Angels, then the people more than ever would have flocked to Him, and His Mission would have been easier to accomplish. This, however, was not the intention of Lucifer. If Jesus had jumped He would have harmed Himself, and probably would have been killed, thereby thwarting His Mission even before the start.

The same applies to the other temptations. They were meant to do incalculable harm. He meant to induce Jesus into doing something that must prove impossible for Him, thereby either harm Him physically, or diminish His influence among the people, or even make Him begin to doubt the potency of His Powers, if these things failed as He tried to do them. Whatever the case, incalculable harm would have been done and a very terrible blow would have been dealt the Work of Redemption right at the very start.

His pure noble intuition would not allow this however, and this simplicity of intuition allowed Him to prevail over what would otherwise have been catastrophic, allowing Him to easily overcome them and begin His Mission in earnest. Let it be said that it is impossible to jump from heights without suffering some physical injury of some sort. Jesus, by incarnating on earth subjected Himself voluntarily to the physical laws of His Father and would have been harmed if He had yielded to that temptation. The same goes for turning stones to bread. This is simply impossible and it was a ploy to make Jesus lose confidence in the potency of His Powers and to make Him become confused about when and how to use them.

5

Jesus' Mission

The question here is how conventional Christianity has interpreted the Mission of Jesus and the significance of His death. There are varying interpretations of what He said, or even whether He said some of the things that we read in the Bible. There are many words that we can with confidence attribute to Jesus, and there are some which can be comfortably excluded. What is important is to be able to examine in detail these words of Jesus and their meaning and to compare them to the way Christianity is understood today.

Later, we will also be examining the letters of the Apostles and the history of early Christianity to see how this influenced the teachings of Christ, and not just early Christianity but what has become known as middle Christianity. In terms of doctrinal change, the impact of middle to late Christianity was probably greater. Also important is today's influence and the way each pastor and each Church interprets the words of Christ and the Apostles. The greatest deviation therefore, or the greatest point of difference from the true words of Jesus is today's interpretations which take place in thousands of Christian churches everyday.

The best way to approach this is to attempt to resolve what we think the true Mission of Jesus really was. Did He incarnate just to die and carry all our sins on His shoulders? Or did He have a Message which He advised us to adhere to and strive to keep to? The question is that of *works* against the letter of safe passage that we see preached everywhere today. We will need to examine several verses of the books of the New Testament in order for us to be able to establish this. We will also need to be able to examine what the words of the Apostles have to offer here in clarifying matters taking into consideration the fact that these Apostles did not fully understand their Master, as can be attested to by various verses of the Bible.

We will also need to take a look at what the early Christians had to tell us and in what milieu they worked and under what extreme circumstances they had to profess their beliefs. This will sometimes require a verse by verse examination of these most important issues.

PART IV

THE MISSION OF JESUS

1

Mission

Iᴛ is true that Jesus died for our sins, but the meaning of this is different from what has been hitherto believed. Jesus obviously brought a Message and it can be argued that almost all His time, if not all was spent in giving this Message. He explained to people how it really was in the Kingdom of God. He also explained in parables or other means what the mechanisms or the Laws of Creation were and how we were meant to adjust ourselves to them.

There is no place in the Bible where He said that the main purpose of His coming to this earth was solely to die, and through this automatically carry the sins of the world on His shoulders. There is not a single statement to this effect, not even by His apostles. Though, they made various references to the death of Christ and indeed to the saving grace afforded by His Blood, no place will one find this clearly stated as the main purpose of Christ's sojourn on earth.

There are numerous verses that one could quote, but the conclusion to be drawn from an objective reading of the Scriptures is the fact that His Teaching undermined the influence of the religious authorities on the people. This led to hatred and the hatching of a plan to be rid of Him. They eventually found an instrument in Judas who was willing to betray his Master.

There are many places where Jesus said that we should reap whatever we sowed, and that we should be as perfect as the Father, pointing to the importance of personal efforts in the salvation of each individual. In the apostles' writings, the same tone is set in their constantly adjuring people to make the effort to be better human beings and strive to improve themselves. If only we would take the time to read the Scriptures ourselves and not listen to conventional interpretations by people who would like nothing better than to lull us to sleep telling us that all we need to do to get into the Kingdom of Heaven is to become a member of a Church, and that they could become intermediaries on the way thereto.

After all, each one is responsible for his or her own spiritual well-being and indeed we must make the requisite efforts to save our own spirits from the Wrath of God and His Judgment. In promoting indolence, these people attract more believers to themselves, they get stronger and richer, but in so doing, they allow the believers to lose valuable time. Time that they would otherwise have used to improve themselves, strive to become better human beings and avoid the Judgment of God.

By their ready-made explanations, they prevent people from really examining the Scriptures themselves and realising that there is much more vitality than the dull message which they hold out to be the message of Christ Jesus. We allow these religious leaders to quote convenient passages to us instead of taking the messages of the apostles as a whole. Since there is absolutely nothing of the Word of Jesus that they can use to support their suspicious doctrine, they selectively quote the Apostles' writings, which they use to their purposes.

Apart from some doubtful interpretations in the letter to the Hebrews, the authorship of which is in dispute, there is not a single place in the New Testament where it is stated that the main mission of Jesus was solely to come to the earth and die. The question now should be why did He die? What is the meaning of it and what are the consequences of it and just as important what are the factors that led to His death.

As mentioned above, the religious situation, and indeed the political situation in Palestine was precarious during the time of Jesus. They were an oppressed people, weighed down by extreme poverty, and in the midst of all this were those amongst them who were apparent collaborators with the oppressors who had everything. In the midst of this grinding poverty was a desire for a deliverer from the yoke of the oppressors, and indeed there had been would-be deliverers who had led the people astray and got many of them killed in several futile attempts to overthrow the Roman domination.

Also to be considered is the question of the prophecy from God of a

Messiah, which apparently had been misinterpreted by the people of Israel. When God makes a prophecy of a messiah, He does not mean an earthly messiah, He does not mean a messiah to deliver people from an earthly bondage. Indeed, a little reflection would allow us to arrive at the conclusion that what God meant was a spiritual messiah. A messiah to free the people from their spiritual bondage, which led to their earthly bondage in the first place.

It is obvious that God would never promise a messiah for the sole purpose of deliverance from an earthly affliction. It must be a spiritual messiah, because all earthly afflictions have arisen first from a spiritual imperfection. The spiritual aspect of all matters must first of all be addressed and if this is done, then, it is automatic that the earthly aspects will follow. However, the Jewish people misunderstood this prophecy and placed all their expectations on the appearance of an earthly messiah. It was then not surprising that when the *Messiah* appeared, they failed to recognise Him since they were looking in the wrong place. All those they placed their hopes in led them to destruction, because these people had nothing else to offer. They should have first learned to recognise themselves through their faults. They should have first striven to free themselves spiritually, after which their earthly freedom will follow as a matter of course.

Because of this lack of recognition by the leaders of the Jewish community and indeed the majority of the Jewish people, it was easy for His enemies to attack Him, oppose Him and to seek to destroy Him. After so many years of agitating against Him, they finally succeeded in killing Him. So His death was nothing more than a political assassination. The priestly authorities saw Him as a threat to their established doctrine which saw their firm hold on the people begin to weaken.

There are several verses in the Bible where He had differences with the way the religious law of the people of Israel was being interpreted. He felt that the real Law of God had been ignored, and in its place were external ordinances which really had nothing to do with the ascent of the spirit. He felt that the people were being made to adhere to what did not matter in the true ascent of the spirit, was immaterial to it. This He pointed out so many times and this brought Him into conflict with the religious leaders.

With His Teaching, He was winning away people, thereby undermining what they felt was an ancestral tradition in the interpretation of the law. Eventually, when they could really find nothing concrete to accuse Him of, Caiaphas, now said that it was better for one man to die for the peace of the nation. More like his own peace of mind! What logic?! It did not matter whether He was innocent or guilty. He just had to die because He was troublesome.

There are people who say that God must have sanctioned it for Him to have been killed. God sanctioned nothing! Jesus was sent as a Messiah to the Jewish people, and in the law of the free will they could accept or reject Him. He could not unfold His Mission among other peoples, because He was sent specifically to the Jewish people. The condition of the fulfilment of His Mission required that He completed It amongst them. He could of course have left or fled, but then He would not have fulfilled His Mission. Among the Israelites, He was to find a people who were meant to understand His Message best, since this people had the requisite maturity for this. Elsewhere, He would have been like a Stranger, with no connection to the people. All His helpers and His disciples incarnated among this people. All the prophecies indicated that He was meant to come to this people and work amongst them. We must realise that Jesus was not just another human prophet. Being out of God, the Laws apply to Him even more strictly and there was no question of a deviation from this.

To have fled would have ruined His reputation and to have denied His Origin when Caiaphas asked Him if He was the Son of God would have done irreparable damage to His Mission. It was the darkness' last trump card. However, it did not work. He sacrificed Himself so that His believers would continue to have the authority of His Word. To have fled or to have denied all He stood for at the threat of physical suffering would have completely undermined everything, and Jesus today would have been nothing more than a footnote in history, and our Salvation would have been lost. There would have been no possibility of progress for mankind, and we would have been lost to the darkness. As it is, we could cling to the Message of Jesus, the love He preached, and the power He gave to us through the Holy Spirit. This is what has sustained humanity, believe it or not for two thousand years.

That was His Sacrifice. Not that He had to, but He was forced to make it out of love for mankind to prevent a final descent into darkness. In the face of this realisation to now say that He came specifically to die is to deny the magnitude of this most important Sacrifice.

We must realise that by the time Jesus came, mankind was in total darkness, with no possibility whatever of Salvation. We would irretrievably have been destroyed in the darkness, even before the Judgment. That is how bad the downward spiral of mankind was. His coming therefore, should be regarded as a measure designed to arrest a rapid decline into destruction, which would otherwise have been the case. That is the Sacrifice, and that is what we should thank the Creator for.

2

His Disciples

THE disciples of Jesus came from among the common people because it was just this soil which still remained healthy. They still remained true to their Jewish roots and had rejected unhealthy foreign customs. Aside from this, these people still maintained a purity of intuitive perception which was rarely to be found among the more cultivated and educated.

The latter had destroyed their spirits through the overexertion of their intellects. They had closed the door to spiritual activity for themselves, and as such were not found worthy to be disciples of Jesus. It was the common people who still bore the possibility of understanding the Message of Christ within themselves. The understanding for His Words required a mobility of the spiritual intuition which very few people still possessed, and certainly not the priestly aristocracy whose entire lives, as has been revealed have been spent on scheming about how to maintain their position of influence, but never on pondering spiritual matters.

With this action of not choosing His disciples among the lettered,

Jesus showed that erudition, and the intellectual interpretation of the Laws of God had nothing to do with how one stood spiritually, or on how one was viewed by God. It is the degree to which one has allowed one's intuition to flourish that determines one's spiritual standing, nothing else. Just as it was then, so it is today. Intellectual study and examination of scriptural work has nothing to do with the real knowledge of God. God does not demand that people go to university in order for Him to be understood. In fact, it is just such influence which is contrary, and makes the understanding of God very difficult.

It is the *uninfluenced* intuitive perception which can understand God. Since God is Divine, and His Power Spirit, it is those who use this same implement of spirit that are best placed to understand Him. This is neither acquired at universities nor awarded by the Church. Such people already have fully developed within themselves the understanding for spiritual matters, and already have sharpened intuitive perceptions for the absorption and understanding of God's Word.

Israel's higher classes over centuries, as their history suggests, had spent all this time in adopting alien cultures and disregarding its own. It had forgotten how to truly practise its own religion. All it was concerned about was self-preservation and the maintenance of the status quo.

The others, called the scribes or the Pharisees were no better. The former were associated with the priestly aristocracy and held more or less the same opinions. They were happy with their privileges and were not prepared to subject their beliefs and any interpretations thereof to any examination.

The latter had become so intellectualized in the way they interpreted the Law of Moses that nothing of the original brilliance and quality remained. They made rigid earthly rules to which the common people were supposed to adhere and bound the people up in shackles. Through their interpretations, they had lost the mobility of the spirit needed for an understanding of the Words of Jesus. Who then was left? Where was the human material that Jesus was to work with? The rich and the powerful and the educated had become corrupted. He could do nothing with them. They had become pernicious, and were nothing but obstacles to the true deliverance of the people from spiritual bondage. In their abnormal spiritual condition, it was easy for the Adversary, Lucifer to use them to try to thwart the Mission of Jesus.

Jesus therefore, not surprisingly resorted to the only soil that was still healthy and the only soil that perhaps was still loose for the penetration and germination of His Words. He chose His disciples from among the common people.

Even though these disciples were the best that Israel could offer, they showed by their questions that they did not fully understand their Master. Jesus often lamented this lack of understanding. Now, if these showed a great misunderstanding for the Words of Jesus and were meant to be the most spiritually open that He could rely on, we can then begin to get an understanding of the enormously difficult task that Jesus faced in bringing the Word of God close to mankind's understanding. How was He then to extend His Word to the not so spiritually quick?

How was He to explain the meaning of His overall Mission? The generality of the people, including the disciples expected or wanted an earthly Messiah. They wanted someone to deliver them from the yoke of the hash rule of the Romans. They had lost everything. They had no land, and they were still being taxed heavily. Deliverance out of this earthly servitude was, as far as they were concerned of more importance.

Seeing Jesus' miracles, many became convinced that He was the Messiah, but as is often the case, the hopes in Him had to merge with their expectations. He who could do such works, obviously was the one sent to them to deliver them from earthly suffering. From this, we can see that even with the most healthy soil (the common people), the notion as to the true Mission of Jesus was misplaced. After all, they were the ones feeling the effects of the double taxation, they were the ones who had lost their lands, they were the ones forced to take up manual labours for their creditors.

As for the middle and upper classes, they simply loved the status quo, and would like nothing better than for things to continue in the old way. Jesus was an inconvenience Who had come to threaten their authority, and was even winning adherents to Himself. If allowed, the majority of the people, who had begun gradually to understand Him would begin to see through the shallow structure that they had built up and would turn against them. Something had to be done.

Within the ranks of the disciples too, for the majority, understanding for the true Mission of Jesus had begun to dawn on them. They began to realise that He did not come to set them free from earthly bondage, but to set them free from the more terrible spiritual darkness. Only one of them still clung to the idea of Jesus as the earthly Messiah.

Judas Iscariot had observed Jesus. He had noticed the effect that He had on people. He had witnessed His miracles and had become convinced of His messianic status. He was often frustrated that Jesus, with all that He had never sought to exploit the situation to His advantage. Why not use this power and declare Himself king of the Jews. Who was to stop Him? With a wave of His hand He could destroy the entire Roman legion.

What was wrong with this man who refused to allow Himself to be crowned king? Judas alone failed to understand at the end the true nature of the Mission of Jesus and only saw it as an earthly fulfilment in the deliverance of the Jews from an earthly bondage. This proved disastrous. For in him there developed someone who felt that all his efforts in crowning Jesus and in his plans with resistance leaders had come to naught. The flame of his injured vanity was fanned to the uttermost by the darkness and in a moment of brooding confusion committed an act of betrayal against the Son of God.

3

His Teaching

IT is perhaps appropriate for us to examine the Words of Jesus from an objective standpoint and through that glean an idea of the real reason for His Coming. It is reasonable to assume that by examining His Words ourselves, we will be able to arrive at a reasonable conclusion as to the true nature of His Mission.

As mentioned earlier, Jesus went into the wilderness at a particular point in His Life to gain more clarification as to the nature of His Mission and also as to the nature of His origin. After gaining clarification, He went among the people to fulfil His Mission. It is, however, this Mission and its nature that most people have not understood. The true Mission of Jesus, many have asserted, was just to come to earth, die and carry the sins of mankind on Himself without further ado.

In fact, this is the prevailing conception, and no one has thought for thousands of years to challenge this notion. It has been accepted as the norm in spite of all the evidence to the contrary. It is better if we take nothing for granted but make the effort to examine Jesus' Word to see if perhaps His sole intention was to die and carry humanity's sins on His shoulders. This calls for a sentence by sentence examination of the Word of Jesus, something akin to a commentary.

4

Gospel of Matthew

The Beginning of Jesus' Mission

FROM Matthew 4:17 we read **"Repent, for the Kingdom of Heaven is at hand."** From the first words that He uttered, He set the tone that was to characterize His Mission. It was to be a mission to teach people, to admonish and adjure them to change for the better. Here, He was telling the people of Israel and for that matter anyone who cared to listen to change for the better. To become better human beings, because the Kingdom of God, which is akin to a Judgement was at hand, was near. This was like a warning to the people to make haste before a terrible Judgement overtakes them. No place here do we hear anything even close to the taking on of anyone's sins. We were to repent and change for the better, if we wanted to see the new Kingdom of God.

Matthew 4:23-25, **"And Jesus went about all Galilee, teaching in their synagogues, and preaching the gospel of the kingdom, and healing all**

manner of sickness and all manner of disease among the people. (24) And his fame went throughout all Syria: and they brought unto him all sick people that were taken with divers diseases and torments, and those which were possessed with devils, and those which were lunatick, and those that had the palsy; and he healed them. (25) And there followed him great multitudes of people from Galilee, and from Decapolis, and from Jerusalem, and from Judaea, and from beyond Jordan."

This paragraph speaks for itself; Jesus taught in synagogues and was preaching the good news of the Kingdom. He complemented these teachings with the healing of the sick. Here, we must realise that the miracles that Jesus performed were an adjunct but a necessary one to His Teaching. It was meant to instil belief and faith in the power of God still further in the people. Seeing the miracles, the people were meant to ponder over these events and come to a conclusion that only someone who worked in Divine Power could accomplish such deeds. So He walked among the people, taught them and healed the ailing. He announced to them that the new Kingdom of God was to be established on earth, but that in order for them to see this Kingdom, they would have to change for the better. They would have to be pure at heart. They would have to make the efforts themselves if they were to make it. The miracles that He performed, and the Power in His words attracted people from diverse areas, from the north of the country, which is Galilee to the east comprising the Decapolis, which is a region of ten Hellenistic cities; to the south as far as Jerusalem, and also to other countries as far as Syria.

The Beatitudes

Matthew 5: 3-12 **"Blessed are the poor in spirit, for theirs is the Kingdom of Heaven.**
Blessed are those who mourn, for they will be comforted.
Blessed are meek, for they will inherit the earth.
Blessed and those who hunger and thirst for Righteousness, for they will be filled. Blessed are the merciful, for they will be shown mercy.
Blessed are the pure in heart, for they will see God.
Blessed are the peacemakers, for they will be called sons of God.

Blessed and those who had persecuted because of Righteousness, for theirs in the Kingdom of Heaven.
Blessed are you when people insult you, persecute you and falsely say all kinds of evil against you because of me. Rejoice and the glad, because great is your reward in Heaven, for in the same way the persecuted the prophets who were before you."

The Beatitudes show the overriding Message of Jesus. They are words of encouragement for those who are already on the right path. A word of encouragement for the poor in spirit, those perhaps who are about to give up the spiritual struggle. A word for those who are spiritually alive enough to feel the suffering of others and also who possess enough love within them to actually feel the loss of a loved one. He also offered a word of encouragement for the meek, those who have retained the simplicity of their spirits. These are actually the ones who will remain when all the arrogant and proud have passed away.

If you show mercy, mercy will also be shown to you. This is reminiscent of the Lord's Prayer "Lord forgive us our trespasses as we forgive those who trespass against us". This is a prerequisite. We must show mercy to others if we are expected to receive any merciful dispensations from God. This is actually a Law that we must learn to obey. He who fulfils this Law is on the right path.

Those who seek after righteousness are those who seek to know the Laws of God and adjust their lives to these Laws. To be righteous has nothing to do with arrogance or vaingloriously looking down on our neighbours, thinking that we are better than him. It is the condition of consciously making the spiritual effort to be better human beings through the *knowledge* of the Laws of God. It is the conscious decision to adhere to the Laws of God through the deed. Those who are too indolent to seek after righteousness will never come to know these Laws of God, and as a result will never come to know how to adjust themselves in this Creation.

Through the beatitudes, Jesus gave us directions as to how to live from then on in order to be pleasing to God. We have to be simple (meek); we have to be merciful, and we must hunger and thirst after righteousness. We must seek knowledge, but not the hitherto intellectual knowledge that mankind has enslaved itself to, but a different kind of knowledge. We must seek *spiritual knowledge*. It is this knowledge that is wholly lacking in mankind of today, and has led to the disaster that we see before us.

The pure in heart are those people who have made the effort to keep their intuitions pure. Those who have refused to engage in evil thoughts, words or deeds. To be pure in heart as we also know is to be pure within, to be pure in spirit. This has nothing to do with physical chastity. What good will it do if we keep the physical body chaste by avoiding sexual intercourse but engage in evil thoughts, words or actions. We will obviously never be able to enter the Kingdom of Heaven in such a state. This therefore, is another commandment from Jesus adjuring us to keep our hearts, our spirits pure by making the effort to be good, to avoid evil in our thoughts, words or deeds. He said that blessed be those who are pure in heart. This blessing is the reward for those who obey this commandment. This is similar to what Jesus later told the disciples about the fact that what defiles a man is not what he consumes but what comes out of him in the form of his thoughts, words or deeds. We get defiled because our thoughts, words and deeds are realities which shape themselves according to the nature of the thought or deed. If evil, they are ugly and dark and are attached to our spirits, thereby burdening the spirit and dragging it down. If good, they are light and they beautify the garment of the spirit.

Because God is Purity, such pure persons are admitted to His vicinity, and will be permitted to witness things which will forever be closed to those not so pure. It is obvious then from this that if our goal is to enter the Kingdom of Heaven, we must make the effort to be pure in heart. No other route leads to the proximity of God. The impure are confined to the lower regions corresponding to their natures, and will never be able to participate in the purity that animates Paradise.

Given the situation prevalent in the world today, it is inconceivable that war or conflict is the solution to anything. The blessings of God can only flourish in a peaceful environment, and those who work to promote this peace shall be adopted as children of God. In fact, the ultimate goal of the human spirit is this adoption. Working so that peace reigns for all mankind in small and in great things is one of the most important duties that we can be engaged in, because by so doing, we promote and provide a suitable soil for the gradual establishment of the Kingdom of God on earth. The blessings of God will not be anchored on a soil riddled with terror and ravaged by conflict. We must see to it that peace reigns. It is our duty.

Again the importance of seeking after righteousness, that seeking to improve oneself spiritually is pointed out by Jesus. Not only that, but we must not allow ourselves to be diverted from the chosen path, even when persecuted because of our beliefs and because of our efforts to be different from others in our willingness to adhere ourselves to the Laws of God.

There will be detractors, and there will be persecutors, but we are adjured to persevere and bear it all. It is nothing new. It is always the case that those who cannot bring themselves to make the effort to adhere to the Laws of God will scoff and attempt to hurt in ways often unexpected. It is our duty not to let ourselves weaken as a result of their attacks. The reward is great. What is a short time on earth compared to the eternal life, which adherence to the Laws of God bestows?

Warning to believers

He went further Matthew 5:13-16 **"Ye are the salt of the earth: but if the salt have lost his savour, wherewith shall it be salted? it is thenceforth good for nothing, but to be cast out, and to be trodden under foot of men. (14) Ye are the light of the world. A city that is set on an hill cannot be hid. (15) Neither do men light a candle, and put it under a bushel, but on a candlestick; and it giveth light unto all that are in the house. (16) Let your light so shine before men, that they may see your good works, and glorify your Father which is in heaven."**

Those who adhere to the Laws of God are the best of mankind. Because of their closeness to spiritual heights, they will be given abilities which only they can have. These abilities set them apart and allow them to accomplish great things among men. People are meant to take notice of such people, who are meant to be examples for all mankind. God accomplishes great deeds through them, and men are to learn to recognise God through their actions. Through their activities, these gifted ones are to bring men to God. Men will come to see the greatness of God through them.

Such people should also proclaim God boldly. They should never hide their talents. They should be conscious of it and use it for the benefit of mankind while at the same time recognising that all blessings come from God. There is also a note of warning to these blessed ones. They must exert themselves to maintain their positions. The slightest deviation from a continued adherence to the Laws of God will lead to a downfall, whereby they lose all that they were privy to. They lose all their privileges and they no longer stand before mankind as examples. In fact, they become useless with no more roles to play in the further upliftment of mankind. Such people will be cast out.

Fulfilment of the Laws of God

Matthew 5: 17-20 **"Do not think that I have come to abolish the Law or the prophets; I have not come to abolish them but to fulfil them. For truly, I say to you, till Heaven and earth pass away, not an iota, not a dot, will pass from the Law until all is accomplished. Whoever relaxes one of the least of these commandments and teaches men so, shall be called least in the Kingdom of Heaven; but he who does them and teaches them shall be called great in the Kingdom of Heaven. For I tell you, unless your righteousness exceeds that of the scribes and Pharisees, you will never enter the Kingdom of Heaven."**

Many people have misinterpreted the first two lines as meaning that here Jesus was saying He had come to fulfil the prediction concerning His death when He said that he had not come to overthrow but to fulfil the laws. This, however, is not the case. The laws that Jesus was referring to was the Laws of God as they manifest in this Creation. He who enters Creation, be it even a Son of God has to place himself voluntarily under these Laws. Nothing can go beyond the ambit of the Laws of God. Jesus, by incarnating on earth voluntarily submitted to the Laws of God *as they manifest here*. He was part of these Laws, and it would not have occurred to Him to think of going beyond or against them. The question of the prediction of His death is an entirely different matter to which we shall come presently.

He who takes on a physical body is subject to all the Laws to which this body is subject. It will hunger, thirst, tire and feel pain. It will also not be able to descend from the cross without physical assistance. If we have wrong expectations as to the operability of the Laws of God, then the blame must lie with us, for we have never really concerned ourselves with knowing them. The Laws of God will not adjust themselves to our ignorance. The Laws of God as they operate in the Universe will not be contravened by Jesus, as He was a part of these Laws. He went further in what can be seen as a warning to mankind, in that the Laws of God do not allow of any omissions. We will account for everything and every evil that we have put into the machinery of Creation. We will receive every retribution, no matter how small. Every careless word, thought or deed will have to be accounted for by the individuals responsible for committing these deeds. There can be no exception. What, then, is this theory of a propitiatory sacrifice that without further ado simply washes away mankind's sins? It is time to wake up! There is no such thing! Jesus Himself testifies to the impossibility of such a happening.

He went further to threaten that anyone who breaks the Commandments and teaches men to do the same shall be called least in the Kingdom of Heaven. He shall suffer the consequences, but whoever adheres to the Commandments shall have their reward. These are clear words. Why have we never bothered to read them? They do not even require any interpretations.

He went further to say that unless the effort that we make as regards our salvation exceeds those of the Pharisees and scribes, we will never enter the Kingdom of Heaven. No clearer words could be uttered as to the importance of making personal, constant, unwavering efforts, otherwise, we will never make it into the Kingdom of Heaven. No stricter rule could have been laid. Here, it is not just a question of the external observance of the Laws of God, which actually is of no consequence, it is the inward spiritual absorption of the Word of God into our hearts and the resolution to adhere and adjust our lives accordingly.

The scribes and Pharisees paid more attention to externals and observances, which in reality had nothing to do with the ascent of the spirit. Jesus called it "the weightier matters of the law". These weightier matters were ignored by these scholars and instead rigorous external practices were introduced which bore no relation to what will advance the people spiritually.

The simplicity in the laws of Moses had been replaced by oral interpretative laws, which no one but themselves could understand. Through this, the cheerfulness and the mobility of spirit of the people had been debased. The laws consisted of a set of rigid dos and don'ts which no one could adhere to. More is demanded of the human spirit by the Laws of Creation than adhering to a set of rules. We are to live vitally in this Creation, seeking to understand our God. There is no room for blind adherence. We must do more. This is why Jesus said that we will never be able to get by through such blind rules and regulations. Such observances never touch the core of man, which is the spirit. The latter never participates in such rigid observances. The spirit demands constant movement.

We can only serve God and as such enter the Kingdom of Heaven through the activity of our spirits. This means through exercising good thoughts, words and deeds. Working vitally in Creation, and always seeking to bring harmony to our environments through our deeds. A series of dos and don'ts will not suffice.

The New Law

Matthew 5: 21-26 **"Ye have heard that it was said by them of old time, Thou shalt not kill; and whosoever shall kill shall be in danger of the judgment: (22) But I say unto you, That whosoever is angry with his brother without a cause shall be in danger of the judgment: and whosoever shall say to his brother, Raca, shall be in danger of the council: but whosoever shall say, Thou fool, shall be in danger of hell fire. (23) Therefore if thou bring thy gift to the altar, and there rememberest that thy brother hath ought against thee; (24) Leave there thy gift before the altar, and go thy way; first be reconciled to thy brother, and then come and offer thy gift. (25) Agree with thine adversary quickly, whiles thou art in the way with him; lest at any time the adversary deliver thee to the judge, and the judge deliver thee to the officer, and thou be cast into prison. (26) Verily I say unto thee, Thou shalt by no means come out thence, till thou hast paid the uttermost farthing."**

Here it was not just a question of paying attention to the great sins but we are advised also to pay attention to the small things. The little things that we do that inconvenience our neighbours but have never really paid attention to. We must learn tolerance and get into the habit of forgiving those who offend us. These are all words that point to the absolute importance of righteousness, a constant working on ourselves to become better human beings. These are Commandments that we have been told to follow. If we fail to pay attention to the little things, we run the risk of perdition. The little things can accumulate and weigh our spirits down, especially when there are so many of them. Only the observance of all these guarantees entrance into the Kingdom of Heaven. There is no mention of His carrying our sins on His shoulders, giving us a letter of safe conduct without our working on ourselves. No such imbalance and imperfections exist in the Laws that proceed from the Godhead.

Matthew 5: 27-30 **"Ye have heard that it was said by them of old time, Thou shalt not commit adultery: (28) But I say unto you, That whosoever looketh on a woman to lust after her hath committed adultery with her already in his heart. (29) And if thy right eye offend thee, pluck it out, and cast it from thee: for it is profitable for thee that one of thy members should perish, and not that thy whole body should be cast into hell. (30) And if thy right hand offend thee, cut it off, and cast it from thee: for it is profitable for thee that one of thy members should perish, and not that thy whole body should be cast into hell."**

Every single thought or feeling that we generate takes on a form that corresponds to the nature of the thought. Lust, being a feeling is no exception. It takes on a form and moves towards the object, in this case the woman. This thought is capable of tainting the spiritual surroundings of the woman. Nothing physical may have been done but a desire has already been sent in the direction of the woman. Such thought-forms, depending on how powerful they are, are capable of attracting similar forms. These thoughts are impure and in the final analysis soil the ethereal garment of the person concerned, and can even confuse the intuitive perceptions of those who have become the object of their attentions.

In this Creation, the spiritual always precedes the physical in their manifestations. It is therefore the case that a sexual intercourse with a woman first of all takes place through the generated thoughts and feelings, even before the physical act itself. Any physical action, no matter how trivial is always preceded by either a spiritual volition or a thought process, and has already become a deed spiritually or ethereally. The physical manifestations are nothing but a consequence of the preceding thought process. If I intend to do evil, I would have initially thought about it, or felt it within before I carry out the action. I may indeed decide not to proceed with the action but the generated thought is there, has been brought into being, and continues to be active. The action has already become deed in the ethereal, even though the effects are not yet manifest on earth. They may never manifest, but more often than not they do.

These thought-forms seek to attach themselves to other people who generate similar thoughts, and they can attach to the brains of these people and goad them to act in ways desired by these thought-forms. We all at one time or the other have felt waves of thoughts approaching our brains, whether lust, or something else and have often wondered where these thoughts come from.

So if I lust after a woman and desire to have a physical relation with her, then I have indeed already had that relation with her ethereally. If I make further efforts, I may indeed work towards bringing it about physically. I have thought about it, I have imagined it and the deed has been done. Whether it manifests physically or not is immaterial. The principle that every single earthly action is always first preceded by a creative thought-process is applicable in all cases, even in the so-called impulse actions. Something stronger is even at play here; whereby the force of some intuitive volition seizes the individual and entirely bypasses the conscious intellectual brain. Some forms of impulse actions can also seize the brain and then consequently recruit muscle groups for some action or the other. No matter in which category, the action has been preceded by some form of thought action or spiritual volition.

The other sentences of Jesus about severing members of the body if they cause us to sin emphasizes the temporal nature of our earthly existence, and forces us to begin to acknowledge what is important in our earthly lives for spiritual ascent and what only serves earthly purposes.

Jesus here was not asking us to literally remove our physical eyes and cut off our hands. What He was saying was that nothing, no matter what it is should be deemed so important that it stands in the way of our spiritual progress. No earthly matter, family, friends, loved ones, wealth, no matter what it is should ever be placed on the same pedestal as the pure worship of God and the desire to enter the Kingdom of Heaven.

In this Jesus was saying that we must obey the First Commandment utterly, which in any case He declared to be the greatest of the Commandments "I am the Lord thy God, thou shall have no other gods but Me". If loved ones or whatever else, no matter how important they are to us stand in the way of the true worship of God, and the desire to enter the Kingdom of Heaven, then these things must be done away with. No matter how important we deem these things to be, whether family, spouses or friends, the gods of love of money and so on; if they prevent us from obeying the First Commandment to the fullest extent then, we must cut them off. Earthly relationships are only temporary, very rarely do they last into the Beyond, but here it is a question of the eternal existence of the spirit.

Therefore Jesus, with these few words tried to bring us to the realisation of what is truly important for a human being while he is here on this earth. There are things on earth that only serve to facilitate life on earth. We can never take these things with us into the Beyond. There are other things, however, that can be taken with us into the Beyond. It is the latter that we must pay more attention to. We only have to think a little to realise what these things are and be able to easily differentiate.

He emphasised that it was better to cut off these things now, even if they cause us enormous pain than to have to face the pain of eternal torment in hell. The pain that we will feel on earth when we do away with our propensities will only be felt for a short period of time compared to the much greater pain caused by running the risk of spiritual death which is eternal. These words are not to be taken lightly.

Matthew 5:31-32 **"It hath been said, Whosoever shall put away his wife, let him give her a writing of divorcement: (32) But I say unto you, That whosoever shall put away his wife, saving for the cause of**

fornication, causeth her to commit adultery: and whosoever shall marry her that is divorced committeth adultery."

It is obvious here that unless there are genuine reasons, it would be difficult to justify a separation from a spouse. Separation, however, can be inevitable if for some reason or the other genuine love no longer exists between the two. In such a case, it would even be immoral to continue such a relationship. Such relationships, more often than not are kept going only for the sake of appearances. Here, Jesus was referring to situations where one or the other person uses one excuse or the other to do away with the other person without adequate spiritual grounds. It was to prevent a situation which existed during His time, and which still exists today in some cultures where husbands could simply declare that they no longer wanted to be married to their wives and that was it. On a whim, the husband could declare that he wanted a divorce and there was really nothing that the woman could do about it.

There are obviously no adequate spiritual grounds for the separation, and such a man forces the woman out alone on her own and leaves her with no choice but to look for another partner in often very unhealthy circumstances. This is the situation where he forces the woman to become an adulteress. This applies to both sexes however, because unless there are real spiritual grounds for a demand for a divorce or separation, either by a man or woman, then it is difficult to justify it.

Matthew 5:33-37 **"Again, ye have heard that it hath been said by them of old time, Thou shalt not forswear thyself, but shalt perform unto the Lord thine oaths: (34) But I say unto you, Swear not at all; neither by heaven; for it is God's throne: (35) Nor by the earth; for it is his footstool: neither by Jerusalem; for it is the city of the great King. (36) Neither shalt thou swear by thy head, because thou canst not make one hair white or black. (37) But let your communication be, Yea, yea; Nay, nay: for whatsoever is more than these cometh of evil."**

It is inconceivable that in spite of these clear words, States which purport to be Christian still require that we swear oaths, whether it be in a court of law, or in allegiance to some head of state, or to the State itself. The conclusion can be drawn that as human beings we can choose to ignore the Words of Jesus when these do not suit us and selectively apply the ones that we find agreeable. No human being should be required to swear an oath, whether that of an allegiance, or in any court of law. His words stating that he will perform his duties to the best of his abilities, or that he will speak the truth in a court of law should be sufficient. If it is then found out that he had uttered a lie, then he could be made responsible for this. We should hallow God's Name in such a way that prevents us from ever dragging It down into earthly insignificant affairs.

The reference to "Let your 'Yea' be sufficient" is an adjuration to keep our speech simple. We should not indulge in loquaciousness. He who works with his intuition will never be able to make many words. Loquaciousness is an indication that the individual is a slave of the intellect and that he has a distorted intellect which has choked up the spirit and prevents it from truly functioning as it should. Lucifer uses the intellect as his tool, and as such all those who submit unconditionally to the intellect in the making of all their decisions are only using what to Lucifer is the keenest weapon.

Since everything that goes beyond the simple in speech comes from the intellect and the intellect is Lucifer's tool, it stands to reason that such speech merely proceeds in reality from him. We should therefore guard against loquaciousness, as the words never proceed from our spirits. They come from the intellect and all that is earthly. They shape forms which do not uplift. They weigh us down. Besides, loquaciousness does not allow enough reflection, which is an activity of the intuition. We thereby never really receive anything from our spirits. We are never quiet enough within ourselves to listen to the voice of the spirit. We rule out spiritual activity for ourselves.

Lucifer has chained us down through inducing us to overdevelop the intellect at the expense of the spirit. In this way, he has ruled out spiritual activity for this mankind. The way to God therefore has been cut off. The way to God requires that we use our spirits since we can never understand God through intellectual activity. God lies beyond the capacity of the intellect and as such attempting to use the intellect to discover God is bound to fail for this simple reason.

The intellect is an earthly instrument suitable for all earthly activity. Whatever goes beyond the earthly requires that we use a similar, homogenous instrument to investigate it. It is exactly in this that mankind has consistently failed. Attempting to investigate the spiritual world with intellectual studies will not get us very far. Therefore, we have been earthbound through the intellect. It is in this that we must change first if we want to understand God.

Matthew 5:38-42 Ye have heard that it hath been said, An eye for an eye, and a tooth for a tooth: (39) But I say unto you, That ye resist not evil: but whosoever shall smite thee on thy right cheek, turn to him the other also. (40) And if any man will sue thee at the law, and take away thy coat, let him have thy cloke also. (41) And whosoever shall compel thee to go a mile, go with him twain. (42) Give to him that asketh thee, and from him that would borrow of thee turn not thou away.

This is a reaffirmation of the Commandment in the Old Testament which states that "Vengeance is Mine, I will repay". The Laws of God are responsible for meting out reward and punishment for any action. By not taking revenge, we may even help in changing the other person for the better. Not taking revenge is not a sign of weakness; it is a demonstration of our confidence in the Laws of God. The desire for revenge forms a thread which binds the two persons to each other. It is impossible to proceed spiritually until this thread has been severed. We retard our spiritual development, and we actually go to where the other person has been drawn to in the Beyond. If the other person is an evil person, and has been drawn to an evil place in the Beyond as a result of his nature, our desire for revenge will drag us with him to his nether region, which otherwise we would have avoided, and we could run the risk of perdition as a result of this.

This Commandment from Jesus is therefore given out of love as a protection against such happenings. In addition, in taking revenge, we perform an evil deed, which we will have to account for in any case. The Laws of God do not see the action as an act of revenge or justice. It is simply another evil act which must be fully redeemed. The "eye for an eye" in the Old Testament does not refer to human to human interaction at all, as some might believe. It applies only to the activity of one of the Laws of God called the Law of Reciprocal Action. This Law returns to every individual the results and the fruits of all their activities. Therefore, this law returns an eye for an eye. After all, we cannot sow rice and receive rye. It returns the same fruit as the seed. It does not direct that we should take revenge on our fellow human beings. It simply states that it will return the *same kind* of fruit as the seed to each individual. But as always, we human beings have distorted the concept and have as a result burdened ourselves with enormous guilt by always trying to seek revenge, thinking that we are doing the Will of God as a result.

Matthew 5:43-48 Ye have heard that it hath been said, Thou shalt love thy neighbour, and hate thine enemy. (44) But I say unto you, Love your enemies, bless them that curse you, do good to them that hate you, and pray for them which despitefully use you, and persecute you; (45) That ye may be the children of your Father which is in heaven: for he maketh his sun to rise on the evil and on the good, and sendeth rain on the just and on the unjust. (46) For if ye love them which love you, what reward have ye? do not even the publicans the same? (47) And if ye salute your brethren only, what do ye more than others? do not even the publicans so? (48) Be ye therefore perfect, even as your Father which is in heaven is perfect.

More is demanded from those who want to follow the Laws of God. Perfection of spirit is demanded of them, perfection of being. They must have absolutely no fault of character and no weaknesses. These are all clear from Jesus' words. The prerequisite to entrance into the Kingdom of God is this perfection of being and the effort required to achieve this. It is just this effort that the religious representatives of today fight against.

It is clear from Jesus' words that we have to make constant and considerable efforts to enter the Kingdom of Heaven. These efforts are geared towards perfecting our spirits. All His words point in this direction and it is difficult to imagine where the current teaching of a letter of safe conduct, whereby God without further ado forgives everything, and Jesus carries all the sins of mankind on His shoulders. He clearly states that not only must we be prepared to forgive all who trespass against us, we must go further in such a way to see if we could influence the other person to change for the better. We must go the extra mile in caring for the well-being of the soul of our neighbours, even if in our judgment they are bad. He went on to say that of what use is it to do the minimum, what reward have we if we greet those who are friendly to us; even sinners and thieves do that. We are meant to be different. We are meant to be examples for humanity. This requires the efforts to perfect our spirits. Here, we are not talking about intellectual perfection because there is nothing of the sort; we are talking about not having any spiritual faults or weaknesses.

Avoiding conceit, hypocrisy and spiritual arrogance

Matthew 6:1-4 **"Take heed that ye do not your alms before men, to be seen of them: otherwise ye have no reward of your Father which is in heaven. (2) Therefore when thou doest thine alms, do not sound a trumpet before thee, as the hypocrites do in the synagogues and in the streets, that they may have glory of men. Verily I say unto you, They have their reward. (3) But when thou doest alms, let not thy left hand know what thy right hand doeth: (4) That thine alms may be in secret: and thy Father which seeth in secret himself shall reward thee openly."**
This speaks for itself. All good actions are to be done for their sakes and not with any ulterior motives. Helping people should be done without the thought of any reward. All rewards comes from God through His Laws. Deliberately doing good with the expectation of gain is nothing but the result of intellectual activity. The spirit takes no part in such actions. It is all earthly and the reward can only be earthly. These deeds are not sufficient to raise the spirit higher to the level in the Beyond to which it should belong if the deeds had resulted from the activity of the spirit. All deeds, as mentioned above take on form. If a deed has arisen through the calculation of the intellect and the spirit had not vibrated in the coming into being of such a deed, though the deed may have been a good one, the returning radiation will not be able to attach to the spirit of the doer. It will find no suitable anchor within him as his spirit did not participate in the coming into being of the deed because it had not furnished any spiritual threads as starting points for the deed.

Of course men may praise the individual for all his deeds and he may indeed receive a lot of benefits of an earthly nature because of the deeds. He may become very popular and famous. Those are the only rewards that he will receive. For those whose goal is not spiritual, and who have no intention of entering the Kingdom of Heaven, these earthly benefits and rewards may be sufficient. In fact, it is what they crave.

For those, however, whose goal is of a spiritual nature and whose ultimate desire is to attain to the Kingdom of Heaven, then they should take heed to let their spirits vibrate in their good actions. They should never need to broadcast their good deeds. The vibrations of their spirits and the joy that they feel as they accomplish these deeds should be reward enough. On passing into the Beyond, it would be easy for such people to take flight into the Luminous Heights, because through their activities, their ethereal bodies have been made light, and they will journey to those heights that is rightly their due. The returning radiation of their goods deeds will beautify their spiritual environment, making it brighter and lighter, carrying them on high. The results of such good deeds are eternal and go far beyond this earth.

The decision to do good should be anchored deep in the spirit and those who feel this way never have a desire to broadcast their actions. Those who feel the need to let others know of their good deeds are using once again that tool which has led to the downfall of mankind. It is only the intellect in its scheming nature that makes such things possible. Those who submit to it unconditionally will act in this matter, and will as a result mark themselves out as Lucifer's slaves. They are intellectuals and are unable to understand anything that goes beyond the boundaries of this earth. They understand only matter. They understand only the material and are thus branded materialists. They do not understand the spiritual, and as such cannot be expected to act in any other way. He who is spiritual will act in a spiritual way, and in the same way those who are out and out intellectuals will act only in the way their intellects dictate. Hence the division of mankind into two camps.

The intellect is Lucifer's tool and it is the only way that he can reach us. Those who unconditionally use their intellects for all their decisions run the risk of being in contact only with Lucifer. They will only hear

Lucifer's voice, and unconditionally follow his directions. In following Lucifer's direction, they follow the anti-spiritual path, which leads downwards. If these do not awaken in time and change the basic distortion within themselves, it wil be too late and they will have to face the consequences, which is the fate of those who oppose the spirit.

The proper way to pray and the Lord's Prayer

Matthew 6:5-15 **"And when you pray, you must not be like the hypocrites; for they love to stand and pray in the synagogues and at the street corners, that they may be seen by men. Truly, I say to you, they have received their reward. But when you pray, go into your room and shut the door and pray to your Father who is in secret; and your Father who sees in secret will reward you. 'And in praying do not heap up empty phrases as the Gentiles do; for they think that they will be heard for their many words. Do not be like them, for your Father knows what you need before you ask him. Pray then like this: Our Father who art in heaven, Hallowed be thy name. Thy kingdom come. Thy will be done, On earth as it is in heaven. Give us this day our daily bread; And forgive us our debts, As we also have forgiven our debtors; And lead us not into temptation, But deliver us from evil. For if you forgive men their trespasses, your heavenly Father also will forgive you; but if you do not forgive men their trespasses, neither will your Father forgive your trespasses.'"**

The craving for recognition is a particular characteristic of the distorted intellect. Along the same lines as the previous passage, Jesus warned us to guard against this temptation that always wants us to crave for earthly recognition. In the same way, these men have their full reward in the satisfaction they get from being admired by men. But that is all they get. They crave admiration but this will never bring them one step closer to the Luminous Heights which should be the goal of every human being. Here, and in many other passages, Jesus warned against the evil of vanity, which is one of the excrescences of the intellect.

The full meaning of the Lord's Prayer has been discussed by Abd-ru-shin in his book "The Ten Commandments and the Lord's Prayer", but it suffices to say here that the first two lines of the Lord's Prayer already exposes the truth that this mankind will only pay lip-service to the fact that they are Christians and followers of Christ when in reality we worship only ourselves and are followers of our own vanity. The line "Hallowed Be Thy Name" means that the Name of God should be hallowed in such a way that it does not become the everyday sound that It has become with mankind of today. We should never swear oaths with It, nor should we utter the Name in a careless manner. But we are guilty of this every single minute. Every court of law requires that we take an oath in the Name of God, and the use of the Name of God is an everyday occurrence in today's language.

"Thy Kingdom come" is our asking that God establish His Kingdom on earth, and that we are ready to create the conditions for the establishment of this Kingdom. It is our duty to create these conditions. The terror and conflict and suffering which predominate today are all man-made, and these are not the conditions that will lead to the establishment of the Kingdom of God on earth. We hold back any true blossoming for this Creation through our wrong activities. God's Kingdom can only be established on soil free from war, death and conflict. We have failed so far to create these conditions and as such have held back the establishment of this Kingdom on earth.

The Will of God are His Laws which He has woven into this Creation as the guardians of the order. They proceed from Him and are perfect. The perfect spiritual beings in Paradise consciously obey this Will. They know that It is good for them. It is perfect and just. It is our duty to learn to know this Will while here on earth and seek to adjust ourselves to It. We must adjust ourselves to this Will just as the spiritual beings in Paradise adjust to the same Will in their Realm. There is only one Will that permeates the entire Creation. It is impossible for us to be happy and to belong fully to this Creation without adjusting ourselves. It is like living in a country without knowing the laws that operate therein. Sooner or later we will come into conflict with the law. We cannot live in peace in this Creation unless we know of the Laws and adjust ourselves. When we say this Prayer, we are promising that we will learn of the Laws of Creation and adjust ourselves voluntarily to them just as the perfect human spirits do in Paradise.

After we have fulfilled the condition of upholding the Will of God, then we can ask for His Blessings on our activities, but not before. We deserve to be given nothing if we do not learn to know the Laws and adhere ourselves to them. We become directly harmful and obstructive in this Creation and we deserve to be cast out.

The precondition for the forgiveness of our sins is that we have previously forgiven our neighbours. God does not lead any one into temptation, but here Jesus was saying that God should deliver us from evil by whatever means necessary. Even at the cost of some pain to us. He should forcibly restrain us from falling into temptation and evil. It should read "Let us not *fall* into temptation".

Matthew 6:16-17 **"And when you fast, do not look dismal, like the hypocrites, for they disfigure their faces that their fasting may be seen by men. Truly, I say to you, they have received their reward. (17) But when you fast, anoint your head and wash your face,"**
Whatever trials one is going through should be borne with the assurance and knowledge that it is for the best. One should never demand sympathy. One should face all difficulties and trials with a cheerful disposition, otherwise one becomes unjust to one's surroundings. If also we voluntarily decide to undertake a spiritual task, it should be taken up with joy, not calling attention to one-self and demanding that one be recognised for it. These are spiritual decisions and tasks, and it is only between the individual and his Creator.

The Spiritual comes first

Matthew 6:19-24 **"Lay not up for yourselves treasures upon earth, where moth and rust doth corrupt, and where thieves break through and steal: (20) But lay up for yourselves treasures in heaven, where neither moth nor rust doth corrupt, and where thieves do not break through nor steal: (21) For where your treasure is, there will your heart be also. (22) The light of the body is the eye: if therefore thine eye be single, thy whole body shall be full of light. (23) But if thine eye be evil, thy whole body shall be full of darkness. If therefore the light that is in thee be darkness, how great is that darkness! (24) No**

man can serve two masters: for either he will hate the one, and love the other; or else he will hold to the one, and despise the other. Ye cannot serve God and mammon."

As mentioned earlier, each spiritual volition takes on a form that corresponds to the nature of the volition. If good, the form is beautiful and if evil, it is ugly. This is an adjuration to turn away from materialism, from the materialist orientation which makes us forget the spiritual and the real purpose of our existence on earth. Obviously, if we ignore the spiritual, that is, if we do not do spiritual works, then there will be nothing spiritual whatsoever awaiting us when we pass on into the Beyond. We arrive there as paupers. We may have the greatest wealth on earth but it is no longer of any use to us once we pass on. Good spiritual works lead to spiritual wealth, and this is reality. The more spiritual works we do, the richer we are spiritually. The same law applies as they do on earth.

If we ignore the spiritual and pay all our attentions solely to the accumulation of earthly wealth, then it is obvious that we must arrive in the Beyond with absolutely nothing to show for our earthly existence. This is not to say that we must ignore the earthly, no, but in tending to the earthly, we must not forget what is far more important, which is the spiritual and that the earthly only lasts for a short while. The existence of human beings moves mainly in the spiritual and ethereal realms.

The service to God encompasses everything, and we will also not be allowed to want for anything in the earthly sense if we obey His Laws. So we gain both ways. Not only will we be rich in the earthly sense, we will also be rich in the spiritual sense.

The spirit is the lamp of the body. The core of man is spirit. That is what he is. The physical body is nothing but a covering that he needs on this earth in order for him to live here. When his time here is done, he drops it and continues with his journey in the Beyond. If the human being is corrupted, then the ethereal covering around his spirit becomes darkened, and all that proceeds from him will be evil. All the thoughts, intuitive perceptions and so on will be evil. How great then is that darkness! If the spirit (eye) is good, then it is brighter and lighter and shines forth. People around will even notice this. If the human being is evil, his ethereal garment is dark and heavy.

Those who are slaves to the intellect and who as such are materialists are in reality, as mentioned earlier, Lucifer's servants and must obey Lucifer's promptings and will be used as tools in the warfare that he wages against the Will of God. Such people, without knowing it have become enemies of God. They have enthroned another master in their hearts through their decision to become out and out materialists. They will never be able to serve God without first dethroning Lucifer, changing their materialistic outlook and embracing the spirit. It is simply one or the other. It is either or. There is nothing in between.

Matthew 6:25-26 **"Therefore I tell you, do not be anxious about your life, what you shall eat or what you shall drink, nor about your body, what you shall put on. Is not life more than food, and the body more than clothing? Look at the birds of the air: they neither sow nor reap nor gather into barns, and yet your heavenly Father feeds them. Are you not of more value than they?"**

Here Jesus advises us to do first things first. The spiritual comes first. We should make the effort to seek to understand the Laws of God. Seek first of all to adhere to these Laws. That is the most important Commandment of "Thou shall have no other gods but Me". Our goals should primarily be spiritual, then other things which are material will be given to us by God Himself without too much toil on our part. He gave the example of the lilies that are very beautiful and cared for through the grace of God and these plants do not even gather or sow. Why do we spend so much time on matters that do not really count? God is the custodian of all blessings in this Creation. As long as we adhere to His Laws, He will let us have what we need for our lives on earth. What each individual needs will come on his path automatically.

Many of us in our attempts to become materially comfortable not only retard our spiritual development by spending too much time on such matters, but we also harm others in the process. If we only have the spiritual as our goal, it would be impossible for these aberrations to occur. Then, there can be no question of being burdened with guilt. We will attain to the heights that we are meant to spiritually, and we will also be cared for materially without having to harm anyone. We have everything to gain and absolutely nothing to lose.

It is a shame that the whole of mankind to a man has ignored this Commandment. The result of this we see before us. We have held back any true blossoming. It is the material first for mankind of today. We have no time for spiritual things. We have done exactly the opposite of what Jesus commanded. And yet many of us are Christians. As in all things, it is that intellect which stands in the way, always asking the question "Are you sure?" Just as we transposed the order within ourselves by overdeveloping the intellectual brain at the expense of the spiritual one, we have managed to contravene every single commandment of Jesus. We did and still do exactly the opposite of what He desires. Is there a pattern in this? Of course there is. There is an inherent distortion in the human being brought about by the condition mentioned above. As a result he must simply follow the order as dictated by his inner condition.

If his inner condition is of a particular order, then he must simply follow that order. He is simply acting according to how he has become through his own fault. Man has become wholly intellectual. He is intellectual man, not spiritual man. Is it then surprising that we find a pattern in his behaviour?

He takes a purely spiritual Commandment from God and adapts this Commandment to his nature. He transposes it. He does exactly the opposite. He is simply obeying the distortion that lies within him. We have therefore reached the core of the problem. Why has mankind always done the opposite of what he is asked to do for his own good? Why has he always failed to listen to the voice of the spirit? Until he changes himself, that is, until he recognises the distortion that he carries within, it will be impossible for him to find his way back to Paradise, his origin. He must be destroyed as he cannot be used for any upbuilding in his present distorted state. He must be cast out so as to prevent him from disturbing those newly born who will now carry the mantle for the further advancement of mankind.

The importance of self examination before criticizing others

Matthew 7:1-5 **"Judge not, that ye be not judged. (2) For with what judgment ye judge, ye shall be judged: and with what measure ye mete, it shall be measured to you again. (3) And why beholdest thou**

the mote that is in thy brother's eye, but considerest not the beam that is in thine own eye? (4) Or how wilt thou say to thy brother, Let me pull out the mote out of thine eye; and, behold, a beam is in thine own eye? (5) Thou hypocrite, first cast out the beam out of thine own eye; and then shalt thou see clearly to cast out the mote out of thy brother's eye."

It is easy to judge. The level of intolerance that we have for others and the strictness by which we measure and judge other people will be used as criteria for us by the Laws of God. If we are lenient towards our neighbours, and if we easily forgive them their trespasses against us, then the Laws of God will be lenient towards us and we will get all measure of help from these Laws.

When we notice the mote that is in the other person's eye and rave and criticise this blemish in his personality, we often fail to see the same fault which is present to a far greater degree in ourselves. This is the beam that we fail to notice. It is convenient to criticise one insignificant fault or the other in our neighbours but we will notice that if we examine ourselves keenly enough, we possess these same faults to a far greater degree within ourselves.

We should first of all make the effort to be rid of the faults that we have before we can dare to point out the faults in other people. If we notice the faults that we have, then it would be very difficult indeed to criticise others since the keen awareness of the fact that we carry similar faults within will prevent us from doing so. Leniency towards our neighbours will then come of its own accord.

Advice upon advice is what we find in Christ's words. Exaltations, adjurations to become better, to change our old ways of living and to let peace reign characterise His words. It is a pity that we have made something else out of this most important Mission.

Matthew 7:6 **"Give not that which is holy unto the dogs, neither cast ye your pearls before swine, lest they trample them under their feet, and turn again and rend you."**

The Word of God may be offered only to those who are deserving of hearing about It. This has come out from the steps of the Throne of God and must not be offered to those who would play with It or perhaps scoff at It. It is pitiable that the Love of God has been misrepresented by well-meaning preachers who teach that God is all-forgiving and lenient to the extreme. This is nothing but weakness, which has never been nor will ever be an attribute of God.

The Word of God should only be offered to those who are deserving, and it is very easy to differentiate between genuine seekers and those who are not so genuine. It is often better to allow someone to ask for It before offering It, and even then, one has to make sure that it is truly the genuine seeking for the Truth that prompts him to ask. Offering the Word of God to those who have not asked for It, or to those who are perhaps hostile to It will do no good at all. On the contrary, they may turn in anger and try to destroy the person who offered this Word.

Matthew 7:7-12 **"Ask, and it shall be given you; seek, and ye shall find; knock, and it shall be opened unto you: (8) For every one that asketh receiveth; and he that seeketh findeth; and to him that knock-eth it shall be opened. (9) Or what man is there of you, whom if his son ask bread, will he give him a stone? (10) Or if he ask a fish, will he give him a serpent? (11) If ye then, being evil, know how to give good gifts unto your children, how much more shall your Father which is in heaven give good things to them that ask him? (12) Therefore all things whatsoever ye would that men should do to you, do ye even so to them: for this is the law and the prophets."**
Jesus here did not refer to the relationship among human beings. He was referring to the relation between human beings and the Laws of God. If through the exercise of our intuitive perceptions, we pray in the right manner and we act in this Creation in a manner pleasing to God, then we receive all that we need for our earthly existence. If we seek the Creator in humble petition and if we ask God in humble petition, we will receive whatever is necessary for the continued development of our spirits. Jesus here was not one-sidedly referring to the granting of our earthly desires. He was speaking in an all-embracing way. In a way that benefits the spirit even after we shall have left this earth.

He also emphasised the great Goodness of God in saying that if we who are deemed evil know how to give good things to our children, how much more so God. All we have to do really is concentrate mainly on spiritual works. If we do the spiritual, then the material will follow as a matter of course. We should ask God for help, for strength in fulfilling our promise as human beings. Strength in overcoming our faults, strength in the love that we offer our neighbours, then we would never need to offer any special petitions for material needs. We will simply be given all these things through the workings of the Divine Laws. That is the kind of asking that Jesus was talking about. Asking for help in the development of our spiritual abilities. Then, we will be happy. Nothing is more joyful than the ability to be able to put our talents to work in the upliftment of our environments. Then, we would no longer have to ask for petty earthly things.

Matthew 7:13-14 **"Enter ye in at the strait gate: for wide is the gate, and broad is the way, that leadeth to destruction, and many there be which go in thereat: (14) Because strait is the gate, and narrow is the way, which leadeth unto life, and few there be that find it."**
The adherence to the Laws of God requires that we do not give in to temptations and this can often be very difficult. Letting oneself go, which is tantamount to giving in to temptations is the broad way that leads to destruction. Mankind, over millennia have ignored the path that leads to salvation and as a result, this path has become very thorny and difficult indeed. It was not always so.

When mankind adhered to the Laws of God, or at least when the majority did, the intuitive volitions surrounding the earth was of a light nature, and it was very easy indeed for mankind to find their way to the Light. As mankind turned to the darkness, good and light thought-forms became a rarity, and these days it is much easier to be influenced by evil than it is by good, making it especially hard for those who desire good to find any encouragement and strength for their activities. This is why those who wish to follow this road find it especially difficult. They are in the minority and would often be misunderstood by others and often be deliberately hindered in their progress by those whose goals are different.

These good people feel isolated and lonely. Surrounded as they are by evil thought-forms and deeds and also by human beings who do not share the same goals, it would be more difficult for this people to follow this path. They would have to be doubly careful and would have to always redouble their efforts to keep to the chosen path. The road to Salvation would have been broad if mankind had always walked on it. It has become narrow and thorny because very few walk on it. The same physical laws apply. If a road is not used, in time, it becomes overgrown by thorns and bushes and becomes narrower, but on the contrary, if used all the time, it is smooth, wide and easier to walk on.

What Jesus was describing was and is still is the condition of the abandoned road to salvation for mankind. It will remain narrow and difficult until more and more people walk on it, which in the final analysis will make it broader and easier to walk on again.

Matthew 7:15-20 **"Beware of false prophets, which come to you in sheep's clothing, but inwardly they are ravening wolves. (16) Ye shall know them by their fruits. Do men gather grapes of thorns, or figs of thistles? (17) Even so every good tree bringeth forth good fruit; but a corrupt tree bringeth forth evil fruit. (18) A good tree cannot bring forth evil fruit, neither can a corrupt tree bring forth good fruit. (19) Every tree that bringeth not forth good fruit is hewn down, and cast into the fire. (20) Wherefore by their fruits ye shall know them."**

By their spiritual fruits, ye shall know them. Those who belong to God shall act in ways which are desired by Him. It cannot be otherwise. Those who belong to the devil, even if they appear in the most resplendent earthly garments cannot but act in ways desired by their master. Through their activities, which is their fruit, we will be able to recognise every single one of them. It is not by outward appearance but through the nature of their being that they will be recognised. If the nature of an individual's spirit is evil, then his thoughts, deeds and words will also be evil and at a point we will be able to recognise these people even if they try to hide and pretend to be something else.

A warning here that the evil, at the time of harvest will be done away with. Anyone who at the time of reckoning is found not to belong to God will henceforth not be allowed to continue to enjoy the blessings of this Creation, which only God bestows. They will be cast off and be forced to go to their master, whom they have insisted on serving even after the unbelievable mercies and forbearance shown to them by God.

It is a question of the continual opposition to the taking root of the Will of God on earth. These people, through whatever influence or position they hold on earth have always acted in ways which oppose the Will of God and they also prevent those who would do this Will from doing so, usually through acts of force and violence. If they would only have this effect on themselves, it would not be so bad, but they are like poison which destroy all around them. This they will not be allowed to do in future.

The overwhelming importance of righteousness

Matthew 7:21-23 **"Not every one who says to me, 'Lord, Lord,' shall enter the kingdom of heaven, but he who does the will of my Father who is in heaven. On that day many will say to me, 'Lord, Lord, did we not prophesy in your name, and cast out demons in your name, and do many mighty works in your name?' And then will I declare to them, 'I never knew you; depart from me, you evildoers.'"**

This is one of the most important indictments against those people who preach against the importance of personal efforts in our attempts to enter the Kingdom of Heaven. Here, it is not just a question of saying that we declare our beliefs in Jesus and then that is it. No! It is not just a question of going to church and be seen to go to church. It is not just a question of uttering prayers by the hundred, everyday. Here, it is a question of actually *knowing* of the Will and *doing* this Will. We must learn to know the Laws of God and then adjust ourselves to them. That is what is demanded of us as human beings.

There is no letter of safe conduct into Heaven. We must walk there. It is the present state of the human spirit that counts and not what he may have achieved in the past. For the human spirit, there is only the present. Not only that, he must be seen by the Light to really be living aright. His opinions of himself count for nothing. He may have cast out a thousand demons in the Name of Jesus, but if he lacks humility and genuine desire for the Kingdom of God, and if he rests on his laurels and refuses to constantly exert himself, then he faces the risk of being disavowed by Jesus on the Day of Atonement.

We cannot adhere to the Will of God unless we first learn It. We must seek to know these Laws. The explanation of these Laws are available to us. If we seek them, we will find them. After knowing the Laws, the onus now rests on us to adjust our lives to them. No other way leads to the proximity of the Almighty. Easy and agreeable to most human spirits is the road that those who would like to increase the number of adherents to their churches paint. They lull us to sleep. We are meant to awaken before it is too late. There is no such thing as an easy blindly believing way to the proximity of God. The words of Christ point to the contrary. It is these words that must be used as a yardstick for how we organize our lives and not anyone else's interpretations.

Matthew 7:24-27 **"Therefore whosoever heareth these sayings of mine, and doeth them, I will liken him unto a wise man, which built his house upon a rock: (25) And the rain descended, and the floods came, and the winds blew, and beat upon that house; and it fell not: for it was founded upon a rock. (26) And every one that heareth these sayings of mine, and doeth them not, shall be likened unto a foolish man, which built his house upon the sand: (27) And the rain descended, and the floods came, and the winds blew, and beat upon that house; and it fell: and great was the fall of it."**
Continuing in the same vein, He advised as to the benefits of *doing*, of acting. No other way leads to the Light. Those who tell us otherwise do not have our well-being at heart. They do not love us. All they want is to paint an agreeable, easy, sweet picture, thereby exploiting the spiritual indolence which still ails all mankind. They only want us to add to the numbers of Church-goers with earthly expansion and wealth as their ultimate aim. These people are the false prophets who deliberately misinterpret the Word of God for their own purposes and ends. They are the ones who come to us in sheep's clothing but inwardly are ravenous wolves.

They do not have as their goal the salvation of their own souls and as a result do not care, would not care about what happens to ours. It must be said that they exploit what to mankind has been one of our greatest weaknesses: our spiritual indolence. Our unwillingness to work on ourselves for our own salvation. Oh how we wish that someone would come and offer us an easy way out! And they come, in droves, in answer to these our inner wishes. How we would love someone else to do the work for us, think for us and even say our prayers for us, and all we have to do is pay, attend the services, nothing more.

Obviously, we are not building a good spiritual foundation with this attitude and when we are asked to reveal our hands in the Beyond, we would discover that there is virtually nothing in them. We cannot blame the churches for misleading us as it was our desires for an easy way out that led to the proliferation of these churches. We created a milieu in which they could flourish. Once we all make the decision to examine the Word of the Lord ourselves and not always ask for interpretations, then these so-called mediators would disappear. It is after all in the final analysis the personal interpretations of the Word of the Lord that matters. How we understand this Word is what determines the level to which we ascend to in the Beyond, nothing more. The more we understand the Word and the more we apply It to our lives, the more we are able to ascend. Third party interpretations count for nothing.

We have now examined the great sermon on the mount. In no place here have we discovered it said that Jesus would carry anyone's sins on His shoulders. What we found instead are exactly the opposite of what conventional interpreters would have us believe. We will, however, continue to explore the Words of Jesus and it is hoped that at the end of this examination we would have convinced ourselves of what Jesus really demands of us and what He wanted us to do if we are to attain to the Kingdom of Heaven.

Matthew 7:28-29 **"And it came to pass, when Jesus had ended these sayings, the people were astonished at his doctrine: (29) For he taught them as one having authority, and not as the scribes."**
It has already been mentioned that the scribes had through intellectual sophistry turned the simple Commandments that Moses received into a rigid form, so much so that no one knew what to do with it. More atten-

tion was placed on externals, which had nothing to do with the real ascent of the human spirit. The people were downcast and there was no way out of their spiritual lethargy. Jesus' words was like a breath of fresh air. He brought back the mobility of spirit which was like a memory of a bygone era. He freed and liberated them from the rigid and impossible observances set up by the scholars and interpreters of the law. He spoke like one who knew what He was talking about and not the ramblings of those who thought that they knew the Laws of God. The people suddenly realised that all that they had to do to enter the Kingdom of God was to act naturally, to love their neighbours and to just be simple natural human beings. That God demanded nothing more from them than to be simple normal human beings.

No spiritual contortions were necessary. No rigorous fasting and the so many demands placed on the common people. It was revolutionary. No one had ever taught them like that. Not only the assurance with which Jesus uttered these words, but the power that emanated from Him and the words themselves. Suddenly the simplicity of the law of Moses had been revealed in an entirely new light and much more.

Matthew 8:1-4 **"When he was come down from the mountain, great multitudes followed him. (2) And, behold, there came a leper and worshipped him, saying, Lord, if thou wilt, thou canst make me clean. (3) And Jesus put forth his hand, and touched him, saying, I will; be thou clean. And immediately his leprosy was cleansed. (4) And Jesus saith unto him, See thou tell no man; but go thy way, shew thyself to the priest, and offer the gift that Moses commanded, for a testimony unto them."**
This passage shows that Jesus, quite aside from the fact that He had no intention of overthrowing the Laws of God also wished to follow the earthly laws. He did not wish to set Himself against the authorities and wished to observe the ancient religious customs of the Jewish people. His aim was to address His teaching to man himself, to the individual and then allow him to voluntarily make a decision as to the truth of His Teaching. It was meant to be a gradual transformation of man into a better being through first hearing His Teaching, weighing them up within himself, seeing that they are true and then finally making a decision to follow them.

His aim was the spiritual change in man. It was this that was His priority and in fact was the most important. If man could be healed spiritually, then all else would follow, since the earthly conditions that we have before us are but consequences of our spiritual lives. He would therefore never concern Himself with the overthrow of earthly order or authority. The change in the earthly order will come of itself when mankind had done the first things, which is spiritual. He therefore ordered the leper that He had just healed to go to the priest and offer the gift that Moses commanded.

Matthew 8:5-13 **"And when Jesus was entered into Capernaum, there came unto him a centurion, beseeching him, (6) And saying, Lord, my servant lieth at home sick of the palsy, grievously tormented. (7) And Jesus saith unto him, I will come and heal him. (8) The centurion answered and said, Lord, I am not worthy that thou shouldest come under my roof: but speak the word only, and my servant shall be healed. (10) When Jesus heard it, he marvelled, and said to them that followed, Verily I say unto you, I have not found so great faith, no, not in Israel. (11) And I say unto you, That many shall come from the east and west, and shall sit down with Abraham, and Isaac, and Jacob, in the kingdom of heaven. (12) But the children of the kingdom shall be cast out into outer darkness: there shall be weeping and gnashing of teeth. (13) And Jesus said unto the centurion, Go thy way; and as thou hast believed, so be it done unto thee. And his servant was healed in the selfsame hour."**

Israelites were regarded as a stiff-necked people, arrogant, vain and very stubborn. It is this that Jesus referred to when He said that those to whom He had been sent have rejected Him and it will be outsiders who will inherit the glory of this people. The centurion is a classic example of this. A Roman, who perhaps still worshipped his pagan gods had become so advanced spiritually as to recognise Jesus, whereas those who considered themselves so great and spiritually advanced failed to recognise Him, even though they had been prepared for centuries for His coming.

This was a bitter blow and an indictment of this people who dared to reject the Son of God and the Messiah Who had been promised, and instead dared to demand a Messiah that corresponded to their wishes and expectations. They who came first would now be last. This is actually the fate of the conceited and the vain. They always asserted that they had Abraham as their father and as such their entrance into the Kingdom of Heaven was guaranteed. Nothing could be further from the truth. There is no such thing as an inherited right to enter the Kingdom of Heaven.

With this paragraph, He already passed a judgement on that generation and the fate that awaits them in their rejection of the Word of God. This rejection will never go unpunished and to make matters worse, the atonement for the crime of the crucifixion.

Power over the forces of Nature

Matthew 8:23-27 **"And when he was entered into a ship, his disciples followed him. (24) And, behold, there arose a great tempest in the sea, insomuch that the ship was covered with the waves: but he was asleep. (25) And his disciples came to him, and awoke him, saying, Lord, save us: we perish. (26) And he saith unto them, Why are ye fearful, O ye of little faith? Then he arose, and rebuked the winds and the sea; and there was a great calm. (27) But the men marvelled, saying, What manner of man is this, that even the winds and the sea obey him!"**

The natural environment is maintained by beings which have been variously referred to as nature beings, fairies and so on and so forth. These are beings of which every culture on earth have stories about. Many have seen them and are convinced that they exist. Of course they remain hidden to these deceitful eyes of men of the intellect. They will never be able to see them because they do not deserve such honour. There are nature beings that maintain the wind, known commonly as sylphs; those that are involved with fire, known as salamanders; those involved with the earth called gnomes and those involved with the water element known as water-sprites.

Storms and the like are brought into being through the activities of such beings. They carry out such activities in accordance only with the Will of God, as these beings are unable to do otherwise. Obviously, such a One as Jesus, being directly descended from the Father could see these beings, could understand their activities and more importantly could command them. Therefore, when He ordered that the sea be calm, these beings had to obey their Master. There is nothing arbitrary in this. It is the most natural phenomenon. All creatures in this Creation come under the influence of the Power of God, and they must obey the Divine Command. The same happened in the case of Lazarus and the youth of Nain when Jesus commanded their souls to re-enter their physical bodies. This event should have induced reflection in those who observed it. It probably fortified the faiths of some of them as should be the case in all goodwilling people.

Power over evil spirits

Matthew 8:28-34 **"And when he came to the other side, to the country of the Gadarenes, two demoniacs met him, coming out of the tombs, so fierce that no one could pass that way. (29) And behold, they cried out, 'What have you to do with us, O Son of God? Have you come here to torment us before the time?.....'"**

Under the pressure of the Light that Jesus carried with Him, even unclean souls were compelled to acknowledge His presence and His Nature. When they saw Him fear seized them as they knew that their time had come to leave the body they had occupied. In the same way, these had to obey the Divine call. Earthbound, evil human spirits could from time to time, or even permanently occupy the bodies of earthmen and use it, including the brain. There are many in the lunatic asylums with really nothing wrong with them but this. They crowd out the rightful owner of the physical body.

The Divine Power to forgive sins

Matthew 9:1-2 **"And he entered into a ship, and passed over, and came into his own city. (2) And, behold, they brought to him a man sick of the palsy, lying on a bed: and Jesus seeing their faith said unto the sick of the palsy; Son, be of good cheer; thy sins be forgiven thee."**

As mentioned earlier, the healings of Jesus, apart from being acts of mercy were also meant to help fortify the faiths of those who had these miracles performed on them and also those who witnessed these miracles.

It was also meant to bring people to Him because in following up these stories of miracles, people would come upon the saving Word. It is inconceivable that anyone or any ordinary person could have performed these miracles and the people knew it. Such works had never been done before. The raising of the dead, the healing of paralytics and so on and He was now forgiving sins. This was unheard-of. The forgiving of sins by Jesus has been taken over by the church as proof that they could also do the same since they considered themselves to be envoys of God, or of Jesus. They, however, err as they are neither envoys of Jesus nor of God.

Envoys of God are those with the same inner Nature as God. This, from the outset rules out any human beings. The fact that they claim to be envoys does not in reality make them so. All we have are their claims. If Jesus could forgive sins, the question we should ask is how. It is not, however, difficult if one realises that Jesus was the Son of God and as such had the power to see into the souls of the petitioner and to determine the exact state of that soul in relation to its threads of fate.

He was able to judge whether indeed this soul had become so good and so penitent that he had indeed reached a point where he had redeemed all his guilt. Jesus was able to see this and as such could say that their sins were forgiven. Remember, He did not say this to every Tom, Dick and Harry. He said this to certain people. Some churches, however, took this as a letter of safe conduct and went about forgiving sins. They could not even see into the souls of these people thus not having the faintest idea what they were doing.

They could not tell whether the individual was truly penitent or whether the person had reached a stage in his maturity that he had truly redeemed his guilt. Jesus did not act arbitrarily. He did not forgive sins that had not already been forgiven through the actions of the inflexible Laws of God. He had seen ethereally that the threads of fate attached to these individuals had already been cut off or were about to be cut off by the elemental beings. He was using those words as an earthly anchor to inform those concerned that they could now start a new life and that their former trespasses had fallen off. He was only conveying what He saw ethereally to those concerned.

Additionally, since these people now vowed to follow the Laws of

God, then this adherence would guarantee that they stayed free from sin in the future since they would no longer act in ways contrary to these Laws, which in the first place had led to their sins.

All this the church knew nothing about. They simply went about forgiving sins and leading the masses to believe that their sins had been forgiven. These masses were forgiven nothing. It was all an utter deception and delusion which has led many millions to waste valuable time. Instead of working on themselves so that their sins would be truly forgiven through the inflexible Laws, they simply went to sleep and even added more in the assurance that all they had to do was to pay some money, and that prayer for the forgiveness of their sins will be said on their behalf, and that the church father in any case had the power to forgive sins, since he was an envoy of God. It is time to wake up.

Matthew 9:10-13 **"And it came to pass, as Jesus sat at meat in the house, behold, many publicans and sinners came and sat down with him and his disciples. (11) And when the Pharisees saw it, they said unto his disciples, Why eateth your Master with publicans and sinners? (12) But when Jesus heard that, he said unto them, They that be whole need not a physician, but they that are sick. (13) But go ye and learn what that meaneth, I will have mercy, and not sacrifice: for I am not come to call the righteous, but sinners to repentance."**

The exclusive nature of the religion of Israel was brought into sharp focus here. Those who thought themselves better than the others felt that it was in God's Law not to mix with these. Those whom society had regarded as sinners were not to be mixed with. They were to be ostracized, ignored and looked down upon. They were even to be pitied. How was anything healthy to blossom in such circumstances? It was scandalous. These were people who claimed that they knew the Laws of God. They claimed that they knew about the Love of God, yet they never practiced it. They appointed themselves guardians of the Laws of Moses, yet they showed by their actions that they had not the faintest idea of his message.

The cold calculating intellect with which these people worked exposed them the more to the searching gaze. They were not called ones; they could not be called ones, as they did not possess that quality of spirit which is a characteristic of those who had been chosen by God: love. These were self-appointed teachers, who basked in their own glory and the respect paid to them by the people. They regarded others as unclean and would never suffer themselves to sit with them, much less talk to them. How then were they meant to guide the people on to the right path?

They wanted Jesus to use the same yardstick, to apply the same rule of exclusion. They decided who was and who was not a sinner. Jesus rebuffed them by saying that He had not come for the self-righteous. He had not come to save those who already thought themselves saved. Those who thought that they had a right to demand an entrance into the Kingdom of Heaven.

He had come among the people of Israel to save those who wanted to be saved, those who knew that they were sinners, those who were humble enough to know that they were sinners and were prepared to make the efforts to change themselves.

Matthew 9:14-15 Then came to him the disciples of John, saying, "Why do we and the Pharisees fast oft, but thy disciples fast not? (15) And Jesus said unto them, Can the children of the bridechamber mourn, as long as the bridegroom is with them? but the days will come, when the bridegroom shall be taken from them, and then shall they fast."
For the first time Jesus alluded to the fact that He might not be around on earth for much longer. This is one of the verses that people quote to back up their assertions that Jesus came to die, and that the real purpose of His Mission was this death. Foreknowledge that He was going to die is not proof that He came primarily to die. In fact, Isaiah Chapter 53 is devoted to this. His death was definitely predicted, but this is not to say that it was in the Will of God, or that Jesus was happy with it. There are verses that we shall come to presently which point to the fact that Jesus did not come for the sole purpose of dying and carrying our sins on His shoulders. All that He had said so far points to the contrary.

He knew the controversy that His Teaching brought with the religious authority. It was only a question of time before they would think of ways of getting rid of Him, and that also it would only be a question of time before they would be able to convince someone to betray Him.

It was all a question of a race for time whereby Jesus would complete as much of His Mission as possible before the people who had presented themselves as Lucifer's servants would use the earthly authority that they had against Him to thwart His Mission. The prevailing evil made this outcome almost inevitable. The fact that it was predicted had nothing to do with it. A prophecy is always to be regarded as a warning of impending events. They are given so that those concerned may take heed and change their ways. If the prophecy is an unfavourable one as in the case of Jesus, then those concerned were meant to take this to heart and change their ways.

Isaiah saw what could happen to the Son of God if the prevailing evil still reigned in Israel by the time He had to come. It was seen that if mankind did not change their ways, then their hatred for anything from the Light would prompt them to offer themselves to Lucifer as executioners of the Divine Word. It was given as a warning to the people of Israel that they would be murderers of the Word of God if they continued in their evil ways. The prophecy would come to be fulfilled, if they did not change their ways.

The people of Israel should have taken a harder look at this prophecy and should have examined themselves. If they had changed for the better, then definitely this prophecy would not have been fulfilled. No prophecy is inevitably fulfilled. They depend entirely on the conditions of the souls of those involved. If the souls change, then the fulfilment of the prophecy also changes as a matter of course.

There can be no subterfuge! These people did not heed the warnings sent to them centuries before, and yet in spite of these warnings allowed themselves to be used by the hate-filled darkness. To even assert that it was in God's Will that He had to die makes us guilty of a double murder, of an indolence which prevents us from thinking matters through for ourselves. The consequences will be terrible.

The raising of Jairus' daughter

Matthew 9:18-26 **While he spake these things unto them, behold, there came a certain ruler, and worshipped him, saying, My daughter is even now dead: but come and lay thy hand upon her, and she** shall live. (19) **And Jesus arose, and followed him, and so did his disciples. (20) And, behold, a woman, which was diseased with an issue of blood twelve years, came behind him, and touched the hem of his garment: (21) For she said within herself, If I may but touch his garment, I shall be whole. (22) But Jesus turned him about, and when he saw her, he said, Daughter, be of good comfort; thy faith hath made thee whole. And the woman was made whole from that hour. (23) And when Jesus came into the ruler's house, and saw the minstrels and the people making a noise, (24) He said unto them, Give place: for the maid is not dead, but sleepeth. And they laughed him to scorn. (25) But when the people were put forth, he went in, and took her by the hand, and the maid arose. (26) And the fame hereof went abroad into all that land.**

Man is not just the physical body. His core is spirit and surrounding this core are the various layers representing each realm of Creation. Without the physical body then, what we have is the spirit as core and the various coverings around this core taken from the various layers of Creation through which this spirit has passed. Right from the Spiritual realm, which is the highest part of Creation, we have in descending order: the realm of the Animistic where the animal souls and the nature beings have their origin; then the Ethereal realm, which is part of the material world but lighter and of a different consistency than the lower lying World of Gross Matter to which the earth and the other planets that we can observe with our physical eyes and with the help of earthly aids belong.

The World of Gross Matter, like the Ethereal world is divided into three main subsections: the World of Fine Gross Matter, which is the finest part of the World of Gross Matter; the World of Medium Gross Matter, which lies between the former and the World of Heavy Gross Matter to which the earth belongs. We, as human beings on earth bear each and every one of these layers within us as we have had to pass through them on our journey to the earth for an incarnation.

When we leave the earth on our physical death, the region in which we find ourselves in the Beyond will correspond to the nature of our inner being. If we have been good, then we will find ourselves in a region corresponding to the weight of our bodies. Our nature determines how heavy our ethereal bodies will be. If we are evil, then we are heavy, because the nature of evil is dark and heavy as a natural phenomenon. If we are good, then we are bright and lighter and as a result we rise to a corresponding lighter region in the Beyond. Our ethereal bodies are made lighter as a consequence of our good volitions.

The physical body therefore is nothing but a temporary vessel which we need on this earth for the purposes of experiencing this place. It is soon discarded at our physical death, whereby we are set free to journey to those areas to which we are drawn through our natures as a natural consequence. Therefore on earth, we bear the ethereal body coming from the Ethereal world; the body of Fine Gross Matter, which we took on when we passed through that world; the body of Medium Gross Matter and then finally the physical body.

If one could imagine an onion, then we come a little bit closer in our imagination and in our understanding of the nature of man on earth. The closest body therefore to the physical one on earth is that of medium gross matter, which some people have already given the name of astral body. This body is connected to the physical one through a silver cord attached to the solar plexus. At death, there is loosening and detachment of this cord from the physical body, and after some time this cord completely degenerates.

When Jesus commanded that this young girl should rise, it was simply a question of this young girl's soul being drawn back into the physical body through the elastic silver cord. Since the animator of the physical body is the soul, then it was not surprising that all the girl's organs started functioning as before. The physical body is lifeless without the animating influence of the spirit. Without this animating influence, it would be nothing. The animation of the body is not due to the brain. The brain itself takes instructions from the spirit. The brain too is lifeless without this animating influence. When the soul re-enters the physical body, all the organs, including the brain, as mentioned earlier will start functioning again.

Every movement of the body is indeed first spiritually willed. The impulse is then passed through the solar plexus to the cerebellum and then from there to the frontal and other parts of the brain responsible for carrying out these instructions. It is now that scientists have noticed that there is an initiating factor that precedes the frontal and motor areas of the brain for the initiation of movements. Before, it was thought that everything resulted through the will of the frontal brain. The scientists are already in the right direction but they will have to look beyond the physical for them to be able to fully elucidate this initiating factor.

It was the same with Lazarus and the youth of Nain. It was all a question of the drawing back of their souls into their physical bodies.

Matthew 9:27-31 And when Jesus departed thence, two blind men followed him, crying, and saying, Thou Son of David, have mercy on us. (28) And when he was come into the house, the blind men came to him: and Jesus saith unto them, Believe ye that I am able to do this? They said unto him, Yea, Lord. (29) Then touched he their eyes, saying, According to your faith be it unto you. (30) And their eyes were opened; and Jesus straitly charged them, saying, See that no man know it. (31) But they, when they were departed, spread abroad his fame in all that country.

Humility, faith and a deep conviction in the Power of God allows this Power to stream through us and work miracles. Without simple belief and conviction, it is impossible for us to receive any help from God. This condition of faith has the quality of opening our souls and allowing the ever-present help from God to reach us. We are the ones who have over the millennia closed ourselves to this help. The Power has always been there, and the help always available, but because we thought that we knew everything better we could never really develop the humility necessary for the receipt of this Power. If these blind men had not had the trusting faith in the Power of God, it would have been impossible for Jesus to help them. His Power would not have been able to penetrate into their souls, and consequently into their bodies because they would have been undeserving of this help. The Power of God does not reach those undeserving of it. It will only work on soil which is open to It and never on soil hostile to It. Mankind receives exactly according to their level of conviction in the Power of God, no more.

The sending out of the Twelve

Matthew 10:5-10 **These twelve Jesus sent forth, and commanded them, saying, Go not into the way of the Gentiles, and into any city of the Samaritans enter ye not: (6) But go rather to the lost sheep of the house of Israel. (7) And as ye go, preach, saying, The kingdom of heaven is at hand. (8) Heal the sick, cleanse the lepers, raise the dead, cast out devils: freely ye have received, freely give. (9) Provide neither gold, nor silver, nor brass in your purses, (10) Nor scrip for your journey, neither two coats, neither shoes, nor yet staves: for the workman is worthy of his meat.**

Jesus was sent primarily to the people of Israel because these people through their advanced spiritual development possessed the ability to fully understand Him. Later, the people of Israel were to take the Message of Jesus and spread It among the Gentiles. This is the reason why Jesus would not be diverted from His insistence that the lost sheep of Israel were to hear His Message first.

He directed His disciples to go to the lost sheep of Israel and to avoid going to the other peoples. This should not be taken to mean that the Word of God was not for these other people but that at that moment, the focus of attention should be on the people who had for centuries been spiritually prepared to receive and to understand much more readily the Message of God.

When the Israelites failed in general, the Message of course went elsewhere, but we must note that the Message in any case still primarily spread through the works and efforts of Jews like Paul and the other Apostles.

Jesus incarnated in the midst of the people who were the most spiritually advanced at that time as could not otherwise be the case, as One like Him, Who was the Son of God needed to incarnate in the midst of people whose degree of understanding of the Laws of God would make it easier for Him to work amongst them.

He instructed His disciples to say that the Kingdom of Heaven was at hand meaning that the time for the establishment of the Kingdom of Heaven on earth was at hand. The establishment of the Kingdom of God ushers in a time when *only* those human beings who voluntarily adjust to the Will of God will be allowed to live on this earth. Before the establishment of this Kingdom, however, the Judgement must take place. This Judgement removes all those human beings who have been evil and who have no intention of adjusting their ways along with their works from this earth. These people are removed to where they properly belong, which is the realm of darkness. They will be prevented from incarnating again on earth unless in the meantime, while in the realm of darkness, they have become better and have been able to rise through the results of their intentions to do better, to a level where they can again incarnate.

Jesus was trying to warn the people of Israel, and also others to make haste and change now before they are overtaken by a terrible Judgement. If we do not make use of the allotted time now, we would not be able to free ourselves in time and we will pass away in the flames of the Judgment, and will not be allowed to witness the establishment of the Kingdom of God on earth.

The evil that we do is dark, heavy and clings to our spiritual bodies. This body is the body that we are left with when we depart this earth. It is the body of medium or fine gross matter. It is still a material body. This body becomes heavy and weighed down by this impurity and the concerned soul is dragged to a region in the Beyond of likewise weight. There comes a time in this Creation when every part of material Creation will have to go through its purification. When that time comes for the earth and its inhabitants and the surrounding ethereal regions of the earth and their inhabitants, we have to be so pure and light as to find ourselves in lighter regions that do not have to face this purification. Those who are left behind in these darker regions, because they could not free themselves from matter will have their fine or medium gross material bodies destroyed with the destruction which naturally occurs when the cycle closes for the realm in which they find themselves.

We should therefore work hard now so that when we pass into the Beyond, we do not find ourselves in places which are marked out for dissolution because we run the risk of also going through dissolution with these places.

When Jesus said that the Kingdom of Heaven was at hand, obviously, He was not referring to it in earthly time concepts. In spiritual terms, a thousand years are as one day, which means that what takes a thousand years to accomplish on earth takes only one day to accomplish in the Spiritual realm. But we must remember that was two thousands years ago and that what He meant by "at hand" is being enacted at the present time.

He gave His disciples the spiritual power to heal diseases and to perform all kinds of miracles so that in the same way as with Him, the people's faith may be fortified. He now felt that He could let His disciples be on their own after they had been understudying Him for a while.

He advised them not to take any gold or silver or food with them and that on their way they would be cared for. They were not to preoccupy themselves about what they would wear or eat or drink. These needs, as He had already mentioned with the lilies in the field would be taken care of. This is what He meant by "the workman is worthy of his food". They have done what was spiritually required of them and that God seeing this would provide for them in ways that they could not even imagine.

Jesus' moral strength and severity

Matthew 10:11-16 **"And whatever town or village you enter, find out who is worthy in it, and stay with him until you depart. (12) As you enter the house, salute it. (13) And if the house is worthy, let your peace come upon it; but if it is not worthy, let your peace return to you. (14) And if any one will not receive you or listen to your words, shake off the dust from your feet as you leave that house or town. (15) Truly, I say to you, it shall be more tolerable on the day of judgment for the land of Sodom and Gomorrah than for that town. (16) Behold, I send you out as sheep in the midst of wolves; so be wise as serpents and innocent as doves."**

The pride with which followers of Jesus should act is revealed here. They should show confidence and assurance in God but they are not to cast pearls before swine. If any one refuses to accept them, they are to depart in dignity and go elsewhere. They are never to go round begging people to listen to the Word of God. It is man's responsibility to seek out his God and not the other way round. Some preachers, over the centuries have perverted this notion and have fostered the erroneous beliefs among human beings that God needs them and has to run after them. Nothing is further from the truth. God will calmly abandon to the darkness all those who would refuse to turn to Him, and all those who expect Him to run after them, instead of at last recognising that after all, it is a question of their own personal salvation and that they are the ones to see to it that they are not condemned.

There is no such thing as an all-forgiving weak God, forgiving everything and even allowing sinners to go unpunished. That must not be! We must wake up and realise that the picture hitherto painted of Jesus as weak and yielding are false and nothing but the desires of those who are weak in themselves, and who would rather avoid making any efforts towards their own salvation to represent Him as such.

He also advised His disciples to keep their eyes open, to be keenly observant. To be ready to defend themselves but never harm anyone on that account. They must not act like fools or simpletons but to always be keenly on their guards. They will be attacked, there will be enemies who would be rid of them. They are on hostile ground and the darkness would always find those who are willing to be used as tools against the messengers of the Light. They must be strong also in the earthly sense so as not to make it easy for their detractors to attack them, and if they are attacked make it difficult for their enemies to succeed.

The difficult road for believers

Matthew 10:17-20 **But beware of men: for they will deliver you up to the councils, and they will scourge you in their synagogues; (18) And ye shall be brought before governors and kings for my sake, for a testimony against them and the Gentiles. (19) But when they deliver you up, take no thought how or what ye shall speak: for it shall be given you in that same hour what ye shall speak. (20) For it is not ye that speak, but the Spirit of your Father which speaketh in you.**

In the same vein, there are many people who are always willing to oppose the Light, and the religious representatives are no exception. These are people who have devised earthly intellectual ordinances for people to follow and if someone comes to oppose what they have built up, even if this person speaks the truth, they would use whatever means they have at their disposal to be rid of such a one. In this way, they act as tools of Lucifer, whose goal and mission is to oppose the Will of God. These human beings willingly offer themselves up to be used by this fallen Archangel in his fight against our salvation in God's Message.

There are also other human beings, who have from the outset made a spiritual decision never to be for the Light. They would have nothing to do with anything spiritual, and would bitterly oppose those who have made a decision for the Light. The numbers of these people are quite considerable and they often occupy positions of power.

So under such conditions, it is inevitable that those who follow the Light would be persecuted, tortured and even killed. Jesus advised His disciples not to worry about what to say because the answer to the questions that these people will pose can only come from the Wisdom of God. The cunning of these people's intellects would make it difficult for an ordinary human being to answer them in such a way as to escape from their traps. The disciples are advised to keep their spirits open to receive answers and solutions to every problem that may be posed.

Matthew 10:21-23 **And the brother shall deliver up the brother to death, and the father the child: and the children shall rise up against their parents, and cause them to be put to death. (22) And ye shall be hated of all men for my name's sake: but he that endureth to the end shall be saved. (23) But when they persecute you in this city, flee ye into another: for verily I say unto you, Ye shall not have gone over the cities of Israel, till the Son of man be come.**

The true Word of Jesus, contrary to popular belief will cause a deep division among mankind. It will divide mankind into two opposing camps. Family relationships have nothing to do with it. It is now a question of how one stands spiritually. There will be those who will be for Jesus, and those who would be bitterly opposed to His Word. It is meant to be so. People are meant to judge themselves through the Word of God. The Word of God is the Judge for mankind. Exactly as one reacts to this true Word, either accepting or rejecting it, we judge ourselves.

Just because of this very fact, those who are unable to adhere or accept this Word would have a boundless hatred for those who use this Word with vigour. They may be family members, friends and the like. What matters before God are human spirits, nothing more. The boundless hatred they have can be taken so far as to want to kill those who have accepted the Word if they find no other way to help themselves in terms of discouraging them.

Just because they see something in these people which they can never possess, their feeling of inferiority and their acute awareness of it turns into rage and anger. He further advised His disciples not to face the hatred head on. They were to preserve their lives and continue their appointed tasks elsewhere. They would not have completed their tasks before the Son of Man comes. They would not have finished spreading the Word of the Lord before the necessary extension of knowledge to be brought by the Son of Man commences.

We will touch upon the issue of the Son of Man presently but here what Jesus was saying is that His true Word would not have taken root among all races by the end of time. Jesus was only trying to indicate that the time of the Son of Man was not too far off, and in fact that His Coming was to be expected in the not too distant future. Meanwhile, we are meant to work in the sense that He has given us. We must be firm in our faiths and be steadfast to the very end.

Reassurance for believers

Matthew 10:24-25 **The disciple is not above his master, nor the servant above his lord. (25) It is enough for the disciple that he be as his master, and the servant as his lord. If they have called the master of the house Beelzebub, how much more shall they call them of his household?**

If they had already labelled Jesus as belonging to the Devil, then it must be obvious that His followers and disciples are not in for a better treatment. They will be branded and hated in the same way. The disciples must be made aware of this and be inwardly prepared for the hardships ahead. They woudl be ostracised and persecuted because people would believe that they had a right to. After all they belonged to the devil. Away with them!

In the way of most human beings, it is much easier to attack and persecute and even kill once they have justified to themselves the sub-humanity of others. If their master was of the devil, they too, who are his children must also be, and in that case in their thinking they are justified in putting them in prison. This was a warning to His disciples to be aware of the very difficult road ahead and not to let it take them too much by surprise.

Matthew 10:26-27 **"So have no fear of them; for nothing is covered that will not be revealed, or hidden that will not be known. (27) What I tell you in the dark, utter in the light; and what you hear whispered, proclaim upon the housetops."**

The effect of the Power of the Light is to expose human beings in such a way that their true nature become known. All that clings to an individual in the way of faults and weaknesses, even if the individual or others are not aware of it will come to light once exposed to the Power of God. These characteristics are strengthened and must manifest in an active form. An individual who harbours a murderous tendency within his soul and has so far not committed this crime because in one way or the other the earthy circumstances have favoured him will be placed in situations where indeed he will show his true colours. These faults had been hidden in the past but are now for all to see. This is the effect of this Power.

This is the effect that the Word of Jesus has. Those who had hitherto considered themselves to be friends and whom perhaps are trusted implicitly will because of one's allegiance to the Word reveal how they truly stand towards us and indeed in regard to the Word of Jesus. If they are true friends, then they will wish us well, but if on the contrary they have never really loved us, their hatred against us will be intensified. It will be impossible for them to hide their true feelings anymore, or indeed to hide their faults and weaknesses.

This effect actually applies to everyone and it will first have its effect on those who are followers of Jesus' Message so that these learn to know themselves and purify themselves in time. Here naturally, one is referring to followers of the true Word of Jesus and not the distorted concepts that are to be found in many organizations today.

Matthew 10:28 **"And do not fear those who kill the body but cannot kill the soul; rather fear him who can destroy both soul and body in hell."**

The consequences of not adhering to the Laws of God are those of spiritual death. What this means is that one's personality is torn to pieces and one ceases to be. This is the most horrible thing that can befall a human spirit and should be avoided at all costs. It is better to continue to adjust to the Will of God than to allow ourselves to deviate from the path due to threats from our adversaries. The worst that these people can do is kill the physical body. They will never be able to touch the soul.

If, however, one allows oneself to be deviated from the right path, then we would have allowed ourselves to serve the darkness and will share in the fate of evil-doers, which is spiritual destruction. We should never allow a short span on earth to determine our entire existence, which goes far beyond this. We should never allow the threats of physical suffering or death push us into making decisions that must lead to the far greater suffering of eternal damnation. We should remember that Jesus did not deny His origin and His Teaching when He was threatened with the same. It is always the last trump card of the darkness, but we should never allow it to triumph. The consequences of giving in are far more disastrous and longer lasting.

Matthew 10:29-31 **"Are not two sparrows sold for a penny? And not one of them will fall to the ground without your Father's will. (30) But even the hairs of your head are all numbered. (31) Fear not, therefore; you are of more value than many sparrows."**
The values that God places on every human life is revealed here. Just as the lilies in the fields, no one will be allowed to harm us as long as we have faith in God. If God could care for apparently smaller things like lilies and sparrows, how much more then will He care for us human beings. It is our lack of faith that makes us doubt His Omnipotence. Our ignorance of the Laws in this Creation and how they really operate has further made matters worse.

Matthew 10:32-33 **"So every one who acknowledges me before men, I also will acknowledge before my Father who is in heaven; (33) but whoever denies me before men, I also will deny before my Father who is in heaven."**

In the face of all trials we should never deny God. Even at the threat of physical suffering, which is the ultimate weapon that can be used against us. As Jesus mentioned in the earlier verses, it is better to fear God Who is capable of destroying both body and spirit than to fear those who can only destroy the body. The sufferings will only be temporary and release comes with physical death. The suffering brought on by the process of spiritual disintegration, however, which is the fate of those who do not follow the Laws of God are far more severe and longer lasting, culminating in the loss of the personality.

To deny God is one of the gravest sins that we can commit. There is only an *either or* with God. We are either for Him or we are not. We deny Him through acting in ways that are not in accordance with His Will. Other people will want to see examples in us and expect us to act in ways that they have come to expect of children of God. To act contrary is to confuse these people and to deny God and His Will. We pay lip-service to God but we do not act in ways pleasing to Him. Refusing to acknowledge God in public is not the only way that we can deny Him. Not acting according to what is expected of children of God is, as mentioned above another way.

The Word of God as a two-edged Sword

Matthew 10:34-36 **"Do not think that I have come to bring peace on earth; I have not come to bring peace, but a sword. For I have come to set a man against his father, and a daughter against her mother, and a daughter-in-law against her mother-in-law; and a man's foes will be those of his own household."**
The Word of God is like a double-edged sword and as mentioned earlier, it will cause discord in many ranks because by its nature it confronts each individual with the reality about himself and the decision of his life. Is it going to be acceptance of the Word of God and the granting of eternal life? Or the rejection of it leading to unbelievable torments? Each individual's soul is faced with this decision, and depending on how the individual stands spiritually, he must decide one way or the other.

If he is inwardly evil, the odds are that he will decide to continue in his evil ways but if good, he will welcome the opportunity offered by the

Word of God to develop himself further. Earthly relationships do not come into it. As explained earlier, the real nature of each individual is what will be exposed by this process. For those who have decided for the Light, the reaction of others towards him will often be a lesson in human nature. More often than not attempts would be made to hinder him, and if their persuasive efforts do not work they would resort to stronger measures which could be anything from coercion to violence.

Matthew 10:37-39 **"He who loves father or mother more than me is not worthy of me; and he who loves son or daughter more than me is not worthy of me; and he who does not take his cross and follow me is not worthy of me. He who finds his life will lose it, and he who loses his life for my sake will find it."**

This is the Law of the First Commandment. These are the arms that must be cut off, the eyes that must be plucked out if they stand in the way of the realization of the Word of God. The Word of God is what should be most paramount in our lives. All else is transitory. Therefore, to place earthly relationships above God is to place these things before Life Itself. These are then the gods we now worship. They now replace the real God, Who is the Creator and Sustainer of our lives.

The cross that Jesus is referring to here is not the cross of Suffering of the Christian Church but the true Cross of Truth. Thus, he who does not take the Cross of Truth offered to him in the Word is not worthy of It. Jesus offered each one of us a Cross of Truth, which is His Word. We are meant to accept It by taking It up and acting accordingly. If we fail to do this, then we are not worthy of the Kingdom of Heaven. The cross that the Christians have adopted as a symbol is not the true Cross of Truth. It was simply the form that the Romans used in those days to execute people.

The Cross of Truth is not unknown to those who are open and alert. It is the *equal armed* Cross and has been known since antiquity, even before the advent of Christianity. This Cross is the visible form of Truth and where this Cross is found, there Truth is to be found. Jesus, through His Word has offered every one of us a symbolic form of Truth. We must take it up, in other words, accept it and live accordingly. In fact, Jesus Christ is inseparably linked to this true Cross. He embodies It and personifies It. He who therefore follows Jesus, follows the Truth. But the Word of Jesus, which He embodies is this Truth. It is not just a question of one's personal opinion in declaring to oneself that 'I am a follower of Jesus'. No, we must be seen by the Light to be acting according to what the Cross demands, according to what the Truth demands, according to the Word of Jesus. This Cross, this Truth embodies the Will of God and it is the adherence to this that will guarantee an entrance into the Kingdom of Heaven. So it is "Those who *do* the Will of My Father not those who say Lord, Lord".

Mathew 10:40-42 **He that receiveth you receiveth me, and he that receiveth me receiveth him that sent me. (41) He that receiveth a prophet in the name of a prophet shall receive a prophet's reward; and he that receiveth a righteous man in the name of a righteous man shall receive a righteous man's reward. (42) And whosoever shall give to drink unto one of these little ones a cup of cold water only in the name of a disciple, verily I say unto you, he shall in no wise lose his reward.**

In contrast to the picture that contemporary preachers would like to paint of Jesus, He has revealed Himself to be strong and unyielding. He was strict and proud. He has warned us against casting our pearls before swine and has also told His disciples to dust their feet from under them if their words are not accepted in any town. It is difficult to see where this picture of an all-forgiving Jesus so bandied about by these preachers comes from. Even the tone of His speech reveals a steadfast and an unwavering attitude that does not fail to impress. There is no sign at all of any weakness in the tone of His speech. It is strict, just and fair. He who would have it otherwise only tries to reveal his own weakness thereby in his inability to make the effort to bring forth the good volition, which is the only way forward for everyone.

Reassuring John's disciples about the genuineness of His Mission

Matthew 11:2-6 **Now when John had heard in the prison the works of Christ, he sent two of his disciples, (3) And said unto him, Art thou**

he that should come, or do we look for another? (4) Jesus answered and said unto them, Go and shew John again those things which ye do hear and see: (5) The blind receive their sight, and the lame walk, the lepers are cleansed, and the deaf hear, the dead are raised up, and the poor have the gospel preached to them. (6) And blessed is he, whosoever shall not be offended in me.

The works of Jesus are the proof of His origin and His genuine Mission. By their works ye shall know them. This He tried to convey to the disciples of John. Jesus did not look outwardly different from other human beings. The only proof of His origin and genuineness are the force of His Words and the miracles which He performed. The simple Truth which emanated from Him had never before been revealed and it is only One with connection to God who could teach in the way that He did, and perform the miracles that He performed.

His miracles could only be performed by One with a direct connection to God and as mentioned earlier, these were meant to help seekers and make it easier for them to believe in Him, therefore making the road to salvation a little easier for these people. John knew that He was the Messiah but he wanted his own disciples to gain conviction for themselves. Jesus helped them in this direction by saying that His works spoke for themselves. *These works that I perform are the proof of my origin and my connection with God. The words that proceed from my mouth in their power also give testimony to my direct connection to the Light.* That is the good news. The news that liberated people from their spiritual bondage. The news that showed people the way one more time. The news liberated them from the bondage of rigid religious practices. The people were exulted and for the first time in their lives could breath freely because the dogmatic restrictions had been lifted off their shoulders.

About John the Baptist

Matthew 11:7-11 **As they went away, Jesus began to speak to the crowds concerning John: "What did you go out into the wilderness to behold? A reed shaken by the wind? (8) Why then did you go out? To see a man clothed in soft raiment? Behold, those who wear soft raiment are in kings' houses. (9) Why then did you go out? To see a**

prophet? Yes, I tell you, and more than a prophet. (10) This is he of whom it is written, 'Behold, I send my messenger before thy face, who shall prepare thy way before thee.' (11) Truly, I say to you, among those born of women there has risen no one greater than John the Baptist; yet he who is least in the kingdom of heaven is greater than he.

Jesus here confirmed the status of John as His Forerunner. It is usual for Divine Envoys to have Forerunners, who prepare the way for them in terms of loosening the soil of the souls of the people for the receipt of the Message of the Divine Messenger. They are meant in advance to tell the people about God and His Messenger so that they would more easily recognize the Envoy when He comes. John was on a pure spiritual mission and he had no time for anything superfluous. He took only what he needed for his earthly existence, as anything more would distract him and make the fulfillment of his mission more difficult.

Among those born of women refers to us, earthmen; human beings. Jesus again here confirms something hitherto unknown about John. He was not an ordinary human being. His origin goes beyond that realm from which human beings have their origin. So, among those *normally* born of women, which refers to earthmen, none is greater than John. That is indeed literally true if John's spiritual origin goes beyond those of earthmen.

Arrogant and disgruntled generation

Matthew 11:16-19 **"But to what shall I compare this generation? It is like children sitting in the market places and calling to their playmates, (17) 'We piped to you, and you did not dance; we wailed, and you did not mourn.' (18) For John came neither eating nor drinking, and they say, 'He has a demon'; (19) the Son of man came eating and drinking, and they say, 'Behold, a glutton and a drunkard, a friend of tax collectors and sinners!' Yet wisdom is justified by her deeds."**

Those who will never accept the Word will never accept It. They will always have excuses to reject It. It is of no use to be more accommodating towards these people. Jesus considered them childish. Even if they were given the clearest proof of the existence of God and of the truth of His Word, they still would not believe. They would always have one thing or the other to say. John came to them strictly living his life and denying himself like all prophets of old in Israel had done and they still thought that he was possessed. Jesus came and lived a normal life and they said that it was too normal because He mixed with sinners and so on and so forth. If He did some other thing in order to make Himself more appealing to them, they would still criticize in one way or the other. All this in order to continue to foster that spiritual indolence which prevents personal exertions. They would never want to exert themselves and if in the Judgment, they are cast out, they would still never accept that this was a justifiable retribution for their spiritual indolence. They would think of themselves as victims instead of sinners. Corrupt to the core, rotten fruit who are a danger to those around them. It would never indeed be possible to save such people and it is better if they are left alone to their designs.

Jesus, however, was not unduly concerned about these people. The response that He was receiving among others justified His Mission and the way that He was going about it. His Work was bearing fruit and the people were beginning to change their ways.

Upbraiding the cities

Matthew 11:20-24 **Then began he to upbraid the cities wherein most of his mighty works were done, because they repented not: (21) Woe unto thee, Chorazin! woe unto thee, Bethsaida! for if the mighty works, which were done in you, had been done in Tyre and Sidon, they would have repented long ago in sackcloth and ashes. (22) But I say unto you, It shall be more tolerable for Tyre and Sidon at the day of judgment, than for you. (23) And thou, Capernaum, which art exalted unto heaven, shalt be brought down to hell: for if the mighty works, which have been done in thee, had been done in Sodom, it would have remained until this day. (24) But I say unto you, That it shall be more tolerable for the land of Sodom in the day of judgment, than for thee.**

Again the strictness and severity which are characteristic of Jesus. He was not grieving and lamenting here. He was not perhaps feeling sorry for Himself here. He was chastising these people and telling them about the just consequences of not listening to His words. The miracles and the mighty works which were meant even further to help them, to make it easier for them to believe in Him and change for the better did not help. What then will change these people? Probably nothing. Even the greatest works and power did not induce them to change. These works did not penetrate into their souls.

With these words, He passed judgment on those who would not listen to the only Word that would prevent them from destruction under the just Laws of God. There was probably nothing anymore that could be done for the inhabitants of these cities. If these mighty works of miracles were not enough to awaken them from their spiritual lethargy, then nothing would. Those who had been chosen by God had rejected Him and Jesus was certain that if the works that He had accomplished in these Jewish cities had been accomplished in non-Jewish ones, the inhabitants would have since changed for the better. From then on, the Word was now to be allowed to spread among all nations. The Israelites had lost their spiritual supremacy and abandoned. With this realization, Jesus had now to let His Word be spread and the mantle of leadership be taken over by some other people.

He concluded by saying that the fates of the inhabitants of these Jewish cities and the cities themselves would be so unbearably grievous at the time of reckoning. A fate worse than that of Sodom and Gomorrah could hardly be imagined and could hardly be more terrible. It is tantamount to a complete spiritual destruction of those who had rejected the only Word that could save them. The inhabitants of the cities of Sodom and Gomorrah perhaps would still have a second chance to reconsider and change for the better but those who so brazenly rejected the Son of God, in spite of the great works He accomplished amongst them were to be given no further opportunities.

To whom much is given, much is not only expected, but demanded and this is the case with those who had been chosen as hearers of the Word of Jesus at that time in Israel. The peoples of Sodom and Gomorrah had no opportunity to witness such great works, nor did they have the privilege of the Word of God brought to them. Now, if such had had to suffer such a fate as they did, then it is not difficult to imagine the fate awaiting those of Israel. The rejection of the Word of God is one of the worst crimes that could be committed and to make matters worse, the murder of the Son of God. It is difficult to believe that people expect mercy from God when He had already so many times made His Word available to mankind, only to be persecuted every single time. There indeed must come a time when His forbearance will be over. Jesus said that not a dot shall be unaccounted for, and the longer it takes for mankind's trespasses against the Laws of God to accumulate, the more terrible the effects will be.

Simplicity and Humility

Matthew 11:25-30 **At that time Jesus answered and said, I thank thee, O Father, Lord of heaven and earth, because thou hast hid these things from the wise and prudent, and hast revealed them unto babes. (26) Even so, Father: for so it seemed good in thy sight. (27) All things are delivered unto me of my Father: and no man knoweth the Son, but the Father; neither knoweth any man the Father, save the Son, and he to whomsoever the Son will reveal him. (28) Come unto me, all ye that labour and are heavy laden, and I will give you rest. (29) Take my yoke upon you, and learn of me; for I am meek and lowly in heart: and ye shall find rest unto your souls. (30) For my yoke is easy, and my burden is light.**

The understanding of Christ's Words requires the use of the intuitive perception. It requires that the hearer exercise his intuition, which is tantamount to saying that he must listen with an open spirit. It is impossible to understand Christ's Words with the intellect and this is the reason that the men of intellect, the scribes and lawyers really could not grasp His Words. Those who still retained within themselves some degree of spiritual activity strangely enough were the simple people. These were the people who understood Jesus and it was from their ranks that the disciples came.

In fact, it is only the simple at heart who will always understand the Word of God because this Word in Itself is simple. The Word of God does not require that we first go to university in order for us to understand

Him. God speaks to our spirits and it is the quality of our spirits which determine how well we understand Him. The intellect has absolutely nothing to do with this. It would be a contradiction to expect God, Who stands above the earthly conception of time and space to communicate with His creatures through an implement with no mobility or life of its own. An implement which is unable to reach beyond these earthly limits.

The simpler we are, the more our understanding for God's Word increases. This simplicity is brought about because the confusion caused by intellectual pondering is eliminated. Intellectual sagacity is not a sign of greatness. It may be important for earthly matters, but when it comes to questions that really matter, then, it must indeed take a back seat. The greatest human beings have been those who have used their intuitions and have received great things from the Creative Power that surrounds us. They are able to make great discoveries not through the intellect as have been widely believed but by the exercise of the intuition, and the humility which is associated with it.

In fact, the intellectual sophistry of the would-be great ones would never allow God to reveal Himself to them. They always doubt and will never be able to receive in all naturalness and simplicity. It is for this reason that they are now cut off from the greatest revelation of all time. The Word of God through Jesus.

Jesus went further to say that it was indeed the Will of God that it be so. The Will of God are the Laws of Creation and the Laws in their activities which are never arbitrary determines the place given to the intellect only as an earthly tool and adjunct to the spirit. God did not have to deliberately prevent any of the scholars in the understanding of His Words. They prevented themselves from this through themselves.

Through their own wrong activities, they so distorted themselves that they placed their own intellects above their intuitions. In so doing, they prevented themselves through their own hands from understanding the Word of God. God is just, and whatever happens to a man is a result or a consequence of his own wrongdoing. If these people are incapable of understanding Christ's words, then it is their fault and theirs alone in having so distorted themselves that they have rendered themselves incapable of doing so.

The Laws then takes effect naturally in them. Through their own activities, their spiritual aspects wither and degenerate because they failed to use it. It is a natural law that a part which one fails to use withers, whereas those parts that are kept in constant use become stronger and stronger. These people, having for centuries ignored their spiritual parts and paid attention only to their intellectual parts have had to watch as others who had not been so guilty found it easier to understand Christ's words. It was simply their own fault that they allowed this spiritual part to become so weakened as to be no longer of much use. They have therefore, through their own wrong activity been bypassed by God. God has bypassed them as He could no longer communicate with them. They are now spiritually blind and deaf.

It suffices to note here that most of us would have noticed differences amongst human beings and for good reason. There are those who have a strong conscience and intuition and there are those with not so strong an intuition. There are those who are spiritual and there are those who are not. There are those who find it easy to understand spiritual things and there are those who do not find it so easy.

There are of course reasons for this and are often the consequences of the ways that we have chosen through our free wills to develop ourselves. It is a shame that those who are spiritual are now been ridiculed more and more by the not so spiritual. The spiritual are afraid of being ridiculed and more often than not do not like to make it known that they are spiritual. It is unfortunate that the great majority of mankind choose to ridicule the best human beings that are left, and these mockers would very soon have to be the smallest on this earth.

Those with a substantial spiritual part should take heart. The time is now at hand. The time for the victory of the spirit. They do not have to hide anymore. It is time for them to show their hands. To raise their heads high and look the other man in the eye. It is those who have so distorted themselves that they do not concern themselves anymore with the great questions of this Creation that should be ashamed of themselves. They do not ask about God, yet they would take of His bounties on this earth. They would enjoy the benefits that life on earth bestows without asking about Who made all these possible. They are the ones who very soon will have to hang their heads in shame. Being spiritually bankrupt, it would be impossible for them to raise themselves for full activity when the time comes. A little digression is in order here..

There are two parts to the brain: a spiritual part, which is the cerebellum (back brain) and an intellectual one called the cerebrum (frontal brain). The back brain, through the solar plexus communicates with the spirit. It receives from the spirit and transmits what it receives to the frontal brain for further processing. Many of us would by now have seen a brain, whether on television or in biology classes at school. What will strike some of us is the huge size of the frontal brain as compared to the other parts of the brain. It has been explained by biologists that the greater intellect of mankind was the reason for the development of the massive frontal brain. That the *need* for a greater intellect for man led to this. The back brain on the other hand, is so small in comparison, even though it looks very similar to the frontal brain in appearance.

The spiritually receptive part of the brain is much smaller than the intellectual part of the brain. That is the general story with mankind. All the brains that are examined have this characteristic. Is it then surprising to see that mankind of today is an intellectual one? All have developed the brain in the same way. The spiritual part of their brain is very small. Are we then surprised that there is no spiritual activity as far as this mankind is concerned? The tool that he was meant to use for spiritual activity lies within him small, degenerate and shriveled. This is a natural consequence of millennia of one-sided overuse of the intellectual brain by the whole of mankind. Through the law of adaptation, that part which was more often exerted became bigger and consequently stronger. Whereas that part, which was ignored never got to develop at all. This condition eliminated spiritual activity but strengthened intellectual activity.

The man of today therefore, is an intellectual man not a spiritual one. Both parts of the brain should have been developed absolutely equally for joint activity; the back brain receiving from the spirit and the intellect carrying out the instructions from the spirit here on earth. This distortion, however, became the normal condition of the physical bodies of earthmen since all human beings took part in this decision to follow the intellect. This condition of the earthly brain therefore, became hereditary, passing this characteristic from one generation to the other. This is the hereditary sin which followed the Fall of Man, which fall was the momentous decision to follow the dictates of the intellect rather than the spirit.

The back brain is more or less active in various people and it is more active in some than others. Those in whom it is more active are better able to understand spiritual concepts and are the ones with the quality of "deep inner feeling". These are also the people with the inner mobility to understand the Word of God. These human beings are very few indeed and are even getting fewer as materialism becomes more and more popular. The pursuit of only earthly ends without any thought for what comes after this.

Those who have stayed behind, however, and have retained their spiritual parts and have kept their back brains active are the simple and the babes that Jesus referred to here. They will receive the greatest gifts and witness the greatest miracles, as they have retained their connection with God. All over the centuries, these are the people who have been persecuted, murdered and marginalized by those who are of the intellect. History proves this.

Humankind, from time immemorial has divided itself into two. Those who belong to God through the quality of the possession of the intuitive perception, and those who do not. The latter have always used force against the former. They have killed, tortured and persecuted them. This is the proof that these people do not belong to God. Those who belong to God would never use these horrible means against others. Those who belong to God would never kill or torture other human beings.

It does not matter under what guise they do all these. Whether they are members of a Church, or even heads of these Churches. "By their actions ye shall know them". The very fact that they used and are still using means which have been censured by Jesus proves that indeed they do not belong to Him. The earthly authorities have often been on the side of these people as these authorities themselves were formulated through the earthly intellect. Do not then expect real justice from any earthly organization. Real Justice is to be expected only from God through His Laws. There would have been justice on earth if these Laws had been harmonised with the Divine Laws but they are not.

The laws were written by the intellect and have been used over thousands of years against those who hold a contrary opinion and who choose to live their lives differently. The narrowness of the intellect would rather have everyone live uniform lives, sanctioned by men who do not know the first thing about real life. We must therefore look about us more keenly in order to recognize who the enemy really is. We should look within ourselves and recognize that it is not our neighbours who are to blame for anything. It is the individual himself who must change first. If we change our own intellectual outlook and begin to live a spiritual life, then perhaps we may be able also to induce the same change in our neighbour. We are all uniformly bound. Until this is done, until we recognize that change starts with us, with each individual, there can be no question of any hope for mankind.

To continue with the next verse, Jesus said that all things had been given to Him by the Father. Jesus was the Son of God. He was an Envoy of God. Since He was an Envoy, He had been given all authority of a Regent. When a regent sends an envoy on a mission, he grants this envoy full powers of negotiation on his behalf. The same is true here. Jesus had been granted all Powers and all Authority by God as the representative of God. If we wanted to see God, we have to go through Jesus. If we wanted to communicate with God, we had to go through Him. He had full authority in this Creation to act on behalf of God. There is nothing that would not yield to Jesus in the whole of Creation; there is nothing that would not be brought into line with His Name. There is nothing that Jesus would not be able to accomplish.

With the greatest love in His heart, He asked those who would listen to come to Him for succour and relief. To come to Him so as to lighten their spiritual burden through the Teachings that He expounded. He asked them to learn from Him and realize that it is not that difficult to know God as long as they trust Him and are willing to adjust themselves. They should throw off all earthly learnedness and the wanting to know better. They should throw off all intellectual pondering and learn to be simple human beings. The burden that the people carried with themselves were husks which they had learned in their religious schools and which hitherto had been deemed necessary for an entrance into the Kingdom of God.

Jesus promised to make their burdens light by telling them to shake off these preconceived ideas which weighed like heavy pressure upon them.

The Pharisees, through their strict religious rule put a very heavy yoke on the people indeed, and many of them were made to believe that they had to adhere to so many of these rules before they could enter the Kingdom of Heaven. These rules were often mundane earthly externals which had nothing to do with real spiritual ascent. This realization was what Jesus wanted to bring to the people.

Jesus reveals His true identity

Matthew 12:1-14 **At that time Jesus went on the sabbath day through the corn; and his disciples were an hungred, and began to pluck the ears of corn, and to eat. (2) But when the Pharisees saw it, they said unto him, Behold, thy disciples do that which is not lawful to do upon the sabbath day. (3) But he said unto them, Have ye not read what David did, when he was an hungred, and they that were with him; (4) How he entered into the house of God, and did eat the shewbread, which was not lawful for him to eat, neither for them which were with him, but only for the priests? (5) Or have ye not read in the law, how that on the sabbath days the priests in the temple profane the sabbath, and are blameless? (6) But I say unto you, That in this place is one greater than the temple. (7) But if ye had known what this meaneth, I will have mercy, and not sacrifice, ye would not have condemned the guiltless. (8) For the Son of man is Lord even of the sabbath day. (9) And when he was departed thence, he went into their synagogue: (10) And, behold, there was a man which had his hand withered. And they asked him, saying, Is it lawful to heal on the sabbath days? that they might accuse him. (11) And he said unto them, What man shall there be among you, that shall have one sheep, and if it fall into a pit on the sabbath day, will he not lay hold on it, and lift it out? (12) How much then is a man better than a sheep? Wherefore it is lawful to do well on the sabbath days. (13) Then saith he to the man, Stretch forth thine hand. And he stretched it forth; and it was restored whole, like as the other. (14) Then the Pharisees went out, and held a council against him, how they might destroy him.**

It is often affirmed in places that Jesus was poor and probably unlettered. Nothing could be further from the truth. One coming out of God only needs to take what is necessary for His earthly life and Mission, nothing more. The quotes here proves that not only was He well-informed and educated, He was very articulate in the way He rebuffed His adversaries, using the law that these people thought they knew best against them.

"Something greater than the Temple is here". How many of us have thought about the significance of this statement. With this statement, He revealed His identity. While the scribes would quibble about mundane things; the Son of God Himself was here amongst them. What is the Sabbath or a Temple when a Part of the Creator Himself was in their midst? In any case, it would have required spiritual insight to understand these words and of course these people possessed nothing of the sort.

They were perched men of intellect whose radiation out of their spirits had been completely choked off through excessive intellectual activity. They would rather pay attention to unimportant details of the Sabbath and the Temple than listen to the Word of God with their spirits. In the way of all intellectuals, the attention and obsessive clinging to details obstructs the broader view of life. The free comprehensive view which they lacked. They were so small in mind that in the presence of greatness, all they saw was the Sabbath. The Lord Who instituted the Sabbath, which they thought they understood stood in their midst, but they were so blind that they could not see Him. Even the greatest tribulation is still not enough to awaken people who had so gone under that they could only turn their gaze downwards, squatting about dejected on the ground.

They would go so far as to prevent Him from performing an act of mercy to another human being because it was on the Sabbath. If indeed God had instituted and decreed that we should never do anything at all on the Sabbath, then it would have been alright. But there was no such decree. This decree of not undertaking any activity whatsoever on the Sabbath was man-made. It was written by man and had not originated from God. They would use what they had thought out and what they had devised with their own brains against the Son of God, passing off such laws as coming from Him.

At this stage, as far as they were concerned, He had broken the ultimate law. He had to go. He had to be destroyed. They had their excuse, because He was meant to have broken one of their sacred laws. They now would seek counsel and begin to plot ways to destroy Him. They would from now on look for opportunities to entrap, and at the first opportunity kill Him.

Matthew 12:22-32 **Then was brought unto him one possessed with a devil, blind, and dumb: and he healed him, insomuch that the blind and dumb both spake and saw. (23) And all the people were amazed, and said, Is not this the son of David? (24) But when the Pharisees heard it, they said, This fellow doth not cast out devils, but by Beelzebub the prince of the devils. (25) And Jesus knew their thoughts, and said unto them, Every kingdom divided against itself is brought to desolation; and every city or house divided against itself shall not stand: (26) And if Satan cast out Satan, he is divided against himself; how shall then his kingdom stand? (27) And if I by Beelzebub cast out devils, by whom do your children cast them out? therefore they shall be your judges. (28) But if I cast out devils by the Spirit of God, then the kingdom of God is come unto you. (29) Or else how can one enter into a strong man's house, and spoil his goods, except he first bind the strong man? and then he will spoil his house. (30) He that is not with me is against me; and he that gathereth not with me scattereth abroad. (31) Wherefore I say unto you, All manner of sin and blasphemy shall be forgiven unto men: but the blasphemy against the Holy Ghost shall not be forgiven unto men. (32) And whosoever speaketh a word against the Son of man, it shall be forgiven him: but whosoever speaketh against the Holy Ghost, it shall not be forgiven him, neither in this world, neither in the world to come.**

In spite of all the mighty Works by Jesus and the casting out of demons, His enemies still had something to say against Him. They would never be satisfied. And Jesus knew exactly how to answer them. It would be impossible for Satan to cast out Satan. What would he achieve by trying to do so. What would he achieve by working against himself. Jesus here alluded to the fact that He first had to conquer Lucifer before He could carry out His work. He alluded to the strong man who first had to be bound before his house could be robbed. Meaning that in the final analysis, Lucifer would have to be rendered powerless before his servants and his effects could be defeated.

If Jesus was using the Power of God in His activity and His detractors had indeed intended to mislead the others into believing that He was not, then they would have to take responsibility for such an untruth. Not only would they have to pay for the blasphemous offence of denying the Power of God, they would also have to account for every soul that they tried to mislead. Then He went on to say that sins against Him personally could be forgiven but never those against the Holy Spirit.

The Holy Spirit activates the Laws of this Creation and if these Laws are contravened, then it is a sin against the Holy Spirit. Sins against individuals can be forgiven by those individuals, even those personally against the Son of God. The Son of God could forgive because it is a personal sin against Him. A sin, however, which acts generally contrary to the Laws of God would have to carry the full retribution against the perpetrators. An intentional trying to mislead the people into not taking the Word of God seriously, and attacking this Word falls under this category of sins against the Holy Spirit. God through His Laws had allowed Jesus to come for the sake of an extension of knowledge for mankind through the Teaching of these Laws. Knowledge of these Laws would allow us to change our ways and attain to salvation. Anyone who fights against this God-given activity which had been brought about through the Will of God as revealed in the Holy Spirit sins against this Holy Spirit and would have to bear the consequences, unconditionally.

No individual will be able to forgive him his sins until he has passed through the mills of the Laws of God and has come to realize what he had done and atoned for these sins. There can be no subterfuge. He has obstructed the Will of God and would have to face the retribution, which is the fate of those who do this. He warned that those who are not with Him are against Him. There can be no in-between with the Laws of God. It is either or. There can be no sitting on the fence with His Word. It is either we accept it, and as such we are counted as belonging to Him, or we reject it and are counted as belonging to Lucifer. It is said that even the lukewarm shall be spewed out. That is how it is with God. This is the reason for Jesus saying that he who is not with Him is against Him and he who does not gather with Him scatters. The Laws of God make it impossible to sit on the fence, indifferent. Indifference is tantamount to a rejection, a negation. It is simply impossible. One is categorized automatically, either as belonging or not. One indeed may see oneself as neutral but our opinions of ourselves do not count as far as the Laws of God are concerned. It is how the Light sees us that counts.

The origin and consequences of thoughts

Matthew 12:33-37 **Either make the tree good, and his fruit good; or else make the tree corrupt, and his fruit corrupt: for the tree is known by his fruit. (34) O generation of vipers, how can ye, being evil, speak good things? for out of the abundance of the heart the mouth speaketh. (35) A good man out of the good treasure of the heart bringeth forth good things: and an evil man out of the evil treasure bringeth forth evil things. (36) But I say unto you, That every idle word that men shall speak, they shall give account thereof in the day of judgment. (37) For by thy words thou shalt be justified, and by thy words thou shalt be condemned.**

Nothing is more clear in the way Jesus explains one of the cornerstones of the Divine Will: the Law of Reciprocal Action. The Law of Sowing and Reaping. Also the nature of men is made abundantly clear. A man who is good, pure in heart can only produce thoughts which are in accordance with his nature, and vice versa. The good man through his nature can only speak good words, produce good thoughts and also only do good deeds. It is simply the lawful consequences that everyone knows about. It simply cannot be otherwise.

Every word that we utter, every thought that we produce and every action that we perform are our responsibility. These are our works and we must bear the consequences for these works. There is no indication here of His carrying the sins of anyone on His shoulders. The Laws are there from all eternity, why should Jesus Who had said that He had not come to overthrow the Laws of God go against them? The Laws have always since the beginning of Creation taken care of reward and punishment for all mankind. Why should they suddenly change with the coming of Jesus? These Laws are inflexible, eternal and perfect. They would not be deemed so if they changed their natures all the time. Jesus, being out of God also was perfect and would not go against the Laws that He was part of.

Some will say that if we believe in Jesus then that is when He can carry our sins on His shoulders. Well, no. If we believe in Jesus and we truly follow His Word, then we will become better human beings and will produce better thoughts, better words and better deeds. These good works will cling to us and gradually nullify our previous evil works. That way, our previous sins will be forgiven because through the Laws of God our good works now counteract our previous evil works. There is no carrying of sins on anyone's shoulders. We have to do all the work ourselves.

This is the effect of Christ's words. This is the reason He spent so much time trying to exhort us to change for the better. Changing for the better leads to the forgiveness of sins only in the way mentioned above. Christ knew this and this explains His emphasis on righteousness and good works. Of course, belief in Jesus is a first step but we must do what He asks of us and this is the reason He said that "Not all those who say Lord, Lord but those who *do* the Will of God will enter the Kingdom of Heaven."

His Words are meant to induce a change for the better in us. This change then leads us to produce good works, which work backwards to nullify the old. We pay back our debts in this way. There is no other way out. If we do not do this, then we bear a double guilt of firstly, ignoring the Word from the Light, which was meant to help us and secondly, we not only fail to eliminate the old evil, we even add to it.

We are all judged by our works. The spiritual standing of every human being is determined by his works, which are the forms of his thoughts, words and deeds. If our works are good, we rise higher but if evil, we descend lower. The Judge sees our works because they are attached to us and through the Laws, He allows the consequences of our works to return to us in retribution, no matter how small. Everything is accounted for and recorded, nothing is lost in this Creation. This is why Jesus said that not a word, not a jot will escape being accounted for.

Through our activities, we will be judged. If our works have been predominantly evil, then we go to places which correspond to our natures and vice versa. Another Law comes into effect here: the Law of Spiritual Gravity. Our works are either heavier or lighter depending on their nature. If they are dark and evil, then, as a natural consequence, they are heavier but if they are good, they are lighter. These works are attached to our spirit bodies and they make them lighter or heavier as mentioned above. Those whose works have been predominantly evil will have heavy spiritual bodies and those who have been good will have light spiritual bodies.

The consequence of this is that those with light spiritual bodies will be able to *rise* in the Beyond to places corresponding to their weights through the activity of this Law of Spiritual Gravity, whereas those whose works have been predominantly evil will *sink* to regions which also correspond to their weights. This process is entirely natural and automatic. In the places where they find themselves, they will meet human spirits of like nature, and also the forms which they have produced through the exercise of their free wills. So we are judged and segregated through our works.

Matthew 12:38-42 **Then some of the scribes and Pharisees said to him, "Teacher, we wish to see a sign from you." (39) But he answered them, "An evil and adulterous generation seeks for a sign; but no sign shall be given to it except the sign of the prophet Jonah. (40) For as Jonah was three days and three nights in the belly of the whale, so will the Son of man be three days and three nights in the heart of the earth. (41) The men of Nin'eveh will arise at the judgment with this generation and condemn it; for they repented at the preaching of Jonah, and behold, something greater than Jonah is here. (42) The queen of the South will arise at the judgment with this generation and condemn it; for she came from the ends of the earth to hear the wisdom of Solomon, and behold, something greater than Solomon is here.**

In spite of all the signs that Jesus had wrought, these people still asked for signs. The Son of God was amongst them and had performed signs never before seen, yet they asked for more signs. If He complied, they would ask for still more. Tribes which had lesser prophets incarnate amongst them listened to these prophets and repented, but the Israelites, who had the ultimate asked for more signs. Here, we are not talking of some obscure prophet or perhaps an earthly king. Here, it was a question of a gift of God to an ungrateful generation. Jesus had already with this statement passed judgment on those who were present at that time and who refused to heed His Word.

Matthew 12:43-45 **"When the unclean spirit has gone out of a man, he passes through waterless places seeking rest, but he finds none. (44) Then he says, 'I will return to my house from which I came.' And when he comes he finds it empty, swept, and put in order. (45) Then he goes and brings with him seven other spirits more evil than himself, and they enter and dwell there; and the last state of that man becomes worse than the first. So shall it be also with this evil generation."**

The fate of those who hear the Word and do not use it is explained here. Those who hear the Word and do nothing with It are ten times worse than those who have never heard It. The Power in the Word which has been given to those who receive It must be put to use to make them change for the better. If not used, then this Power Itself will turn against them and destroy them. It would help push them back into their former faults and in a much more serious way. This is what is meant by this parable.

The man in question heard the Word, was happy, got rid of his former faults, but with time he failed to continue to exert himself. When his former faults returned, he allowed these faults room to come in and backslided. His former faults grew stronger in him because they were now able to attract similar forms to themselves. He would now be forced to make far greater efforts to free himself than he initially did and he runs the risk of further sliding downwards and the faults may even prove too strong for him to overcome. The reason he got worse was that the Power of God that he rejected will now work against him, instead of in his favour. It will become a curse to him instead of a blessing. It is just as any talent that is not well-used becomes the downfall of those who fail to use them properly.

Since that generation had rejected the Word of Jesus, the Power in this Word will now be a curse to them. It would now act against them and help push them into the abyss. The darkness will seize them, since the Light will no longer raise Its Hand to help anymore. They had rejected the help that the Light had offered. Their fall will be swift and decisive. Let this be a warning to all of us.

Jesus' brothers and sisters

Matthew 12:46-50 **While he yet talked to the people, behold, his mother and his brethren stood without, desiring to speak with him..... (48) But he answered and said unto him that told him, Who is my mother? and who are my brethren? (49) And he stretched forth his hand toward his disciples, and said, Behold my mother and my brethren! (50) For whosoever shall do the will of my Father which is in heaven, the same is my brother, and sister, and mother.**

Only those who would listen to Jesus and had committed themselves to the living of His Word proved themselves as belonging to God and as belonging to Jesus. These became His spiritual children, his spiritual brothers and sisters. Earthly kinship holds no grounds here. It is only temporary. It is only those who share the same spiritual values and homogeneity that are truly brothers and sisters. These are brethren in the real sense of the word. Of what use is it to have an earthly brother who does not share the same spiritual values with you and on the contrary works in the opposite direction? Earthly religion is not what is meant here, nor the superficial way we tend to judge other human beings. It is only God who decides who a brethren is, not human beings. It is only He who sees the spirit. It is only the quality of the spirit that matters, and through the inflexible workings of His Laws He may bring us together to work to achieve some great task in His Name.

Here, is not the question of a membership of the some church or even holding the same political views. It is nothing earthly, and as mentioned above, human beings are not to be the judge of this. Those who failed to accept the Word of Jesus obviously could not have any claims of kinship on Him. His mother did not initially accept Him and as such at that time could not have any claims on Him. The yardstick for laying claims on

Jesus depended solely on how we stand in regard to His Word. As He explained, it is only those who *do* the Will of God who can have this claim of kinship on Him.

The consequences of spiritual lassitude

Matthew 13:11-12 **He answered and said unto them, Because it is given unto you to know the mysteries of the kingdom of heaven, but to them it is not given. (12) For whosoever hath, to him shall be given, and he shall have more abundance: but whosoever hath not, from him shall be taken away even that he hath.**

This is one of the least understood sayings of Jesus. Through Abd-ru-shin, however, in his book "In the Light of Truth: The Grail Message", we understand that he who is given a particular talent but fails to use it runs the risk of losing it. It will devolve to other people. The stronger always attracts whatever is similar to itself and as such those who are weak, and those who refuse to will in the correct manner will lose whatever abilities they have to those who use these abilities, and it could even be so bad that the weak will at a particular point not be able to generate thoughts of their own, and consequently became servile to the stronger. All that man has to do is will in the right manner and he will be protected from this Law of Creation and will then have nothing to fear.

The tares and the good seeds

Matthew 13:24-30 **Another parable put he forth unto them, saying, The kingdom of heaven is likened unto a man which sowed good seed in his field: (25) But while men slept, his enemy came and sowed tares among the wheat, and went his way. (26) But when the blade was sprung up, and brought forth fruit, then appeared the tares also. (27) So the servants of the householder came and said unto him, Sir, didst not thou sow good seed in thy field? from whence then hath it tares? (28) He said unto them, An enemy hath done this. The servants said unto him, Wilt thou then that we go and gather them up? (29) But he said, Nay; lest while ye gather up the tares, ye root up also the wheat with them. (30) Let both grow together until the harvest: and in the time of harvest I will say to the reapers, Gather ye**

together first the tares, and bind them in bundles to burn them: but gather the wheat into my barn.

God is the One Who sows the good seeds. These good seeds are the human beings who act according to His Will. The Devil, Satan, Lucifer is one who sows the bad seeds or the tares, which refers to human spirits who have decided through their own free will to serve him. They are human beings like us, and at the end of time just like us, will have to face the Judgment. This answers the questions of why God did not just eliminate Lucifer and all those human beings who serve him.

There is a cycle in Creation which has as its beginning the creation and the entering into the World of Matter of human spirits. The end of this cycle is the time when some part of this Creation would have come to the end of its allotted time. In other words, there is a beginning and an end to all materially created globes. A time comes at the end of their life cycles when these globes have to undergo disintegration, followed by a reforming through different combinations. This is the final judgment for these globes. Human beings who live on these globes too will go through this final judgment. Human beings are allowed to make a choice as to how they develop themselves through the use of their free wills. The time allotted to us in our cycles is sufficient for the completion of our development and the full development of our abilities.

All human beings are allowed to use their free wills to make a decision as to the direction of their destinies. Those who in the meantime have become bad are not destroyed immediately but are allowed just like those who are good to remain until the end of the cycle, when all shall render account. At the end, however, through the inflexible Will of God, a separation takes place between the sheep and the goats. Between the weed and the grain. Through the effect of the Judgment, all human beings are to become conscious of the effect of Lucifer's activities and as a result learn a lasting lesson never to allow such a thing to happen again. All the weed, which here refers to those who have been rejected are destroyed. This is the final Judgment at the end time, which is accompanied by spiritual death, the loss of the personality of those rejected.

Our works are like seeds which had to be allowed to go through the full cycle of germination, ripening, growth, the bearing of fruit and decay.

The same goes for the works of Lucifer. Anything in Creation has to go through this same cycle so that at the time of harvest it will reveal itself for what it is. Evil works will reveal their fruit, and good works likewise will reveal what they are made of. The evil fruit will be destroyed at the end of time while the good will be preserved. Anything at all, once introduced into Creation must follow its cycle to the very end. Lucifer therefore, when he introduced his principles into Creation could not just be eliminated arbitrarily just like that. His principles, like everything else in Creation had to follow this selfsame cycle of development whereby at the time of harvest they will show themselves to all mankind for what they really are. The effects and consequences of these principles on mankind in our adhering to them will be shown for all to see.

The fruits of these principles will reveal themselves just like what happens when seeds are planted. It is the same Law of Creation that controls these happenings. For once, mankind will see on themselves what effects these principles have had on them. How they had been held from the right path for millennia on end, and how these principles had always been directed away from the true Will of God and how they had fought to prevent our redemption through the Word of God. Nothing will escape us as we realize with horror that that which we had held to be great was nothing more than a tool, with no life of its own and that this tool was fashioned from nothing but dust, and that it had held sway over the eternal spirit due to our voluntary submission to it.

The grain of mustard seed

Matthew 13:31-32 **Another parable he put before them, saying, "The kingdom of heaven is like a grain of mustard seed which a man took and sowed in his field; (32) it is the smallest of all seeds, but when it has grown it is the greatest of shrubs and becomes a tree, so that the birds of the air come and make nests in its branches."**
Christ here referred to the gradual growth that will characterize the spread of the Word of God. At the beginning, it was always going to be difficult because of the prevailing darkness, but in spite of all the darkness and the opposition to the Word of God, this Word must still be spread and must take root on earth. In spite of all the fight against It, It will grow and final-

ly the Kingdom of God will come to be established. Only a very few people initially will accept the Word, but unstoppable, It will become so strong through the support of the Power of God that finally all human beings will come to acknowledge It and come to nest in Its fold.

All fighting will be of no avail and all opposition will prove to be as nothing. It will crush all opposition in Its path. Like an unstoppable juggernaut, It will force Its way into the consciousness of mankind. All those who would accept It will be allowed to enjoy of this Kingdom, but all those who dare to oppose It will be crushed so that those at last who accept It might work in peace without the detraction brought about by those who oppose the Light.

Matthew 13:33 He told them another parable. "The kingdom of heaven is like leaven which a woman took and hid in three measures of flour, till it was all leavened."

Jesus compared the Kingdom of God to small yeast hidden in a large measure of flour. The yeast gradually worked its way through the whole flour. Here, He described the gradual taking root of the Word in the souls of people. As many people thought about the Word of Jesus within themselves, It grew stronger and stronger within them, and the darkness surrounding them had to give way.

As this phenomenon occurred with individuals, so with the populace in general. As the Word of God spread among the people, the darkness surrounding them had to loosen its grip. This way, the Light penetrated the darkness more and more. Gradually, the entire land would be suffused by this Light until there would be nothing left of the darkness. This is how it will be. It could not be completed at that time because Jesus' Mission was violently cut short. The darkness, seeing itself losing ground roused all its supporters in its violent struggle against the Mission of Jesus, and goaded them to commit such deeds as could hardly be imagined against the Son of God.

The Word of God will gradually take hold of the entire earth and all the human beings in it. We all must open ourselves at last to this Word to allow It to penetrate into our spirits and by so doing disperse the darkness within us. Working this way, in every human being, the darkness will be forced to retreat and the establishment of the Kingdom of God on earth draws nearer. The darkness will then be forced to lose ground on the entire earth as rays upon rays of Light penetrate the darkness of the souls of mankind. Just as in the yeast parable, the yeast of the Word of God will gradually take over the whole bread of mankind.

The decision, however, rests with us. It depends entirely on us if we want the Word of God to succeed on earth, or if we want to darkness to continue to dictate our destinies. If we all open ourselves to the rays of the Word of God, then it will be impossible for the darkness to have any foothold here. We could decide to either open our spirits to God and His Word, or to continue to give in to the darkness. The fate of the earth and all its inhabitants rests on our decision to either allow the Light to flow through, opening our spirits to It or allow the darkness to flow through in the same manner. Through opening ourselves to the inflow of spiritual power, we allow God to establish His Kingdom here now. If we fail to do this, we allow Lucifer instead to set his foot here and declare this place to be his kingdom, which he already has.

This is how it has been in the past. Now, it is different. Whether we like it or not, the Kingdom of God *must* now be established here. Hitherto, it had depended on mankind's will to determine the fate of this earth through the exercise of their free wills and the process described above. Mankind, however, never voluntarily chose the path leading to God. Over and over again, we chose the path leading to the darkness, making the road to destruction ever wider. In spite of all the prophets sent to mankind to induce them voluntarily to change, and finally with the Son of God, nothing happened. The ultimate crime was finally committed: the murder of the Word of God. With this deed, we set the seal to our fates. With this deed, there was to be no second chance for those who behaved in such a dastardly way. It is from then on retribution in the most terrible way for these people who would dare to imagine that they could treat the Word of God with such disdain and expect to get away with it.

Now our free wills in terms of its ability to decide whether the Light or the darkness controls the earth has henceforth been suspended. It has been of no use anyway. It has brought nothing but disaster to this part of Creation. It has brought suffering upon suffering on those other creatures that have had the misfortune of sharing this earth with us. Like the germinating mustard seed, unstoppable, but not dependent on anything but the Will of God for its sustenance, the Word and the Will of God must now be forcibly established here, and human beings demanded to adhere to It. Those who would not will be destroyed and removed from this earth. All those remaining will be forced to relentlessly adhere to this new Kingdom. The Millennium therefore, is not going to be as rosy as many of us have preferred to picture it. It will be a time of the strictest demand for the adherence to the Will of God so that at last peace is established. As the germinating mustard seed forcibly made its way to become a tree, so will be the establishment of the Kingdom of God.

Matthew 13:36-43 Then Jesus sent the multitude away, and went into the house: and his disciples came unto him, saying, Declare unto us the parable of the tares of the field. (37) He answered and said unto them, He that soweth the good seed is the Son of man; (38) The field is the world; the good seed are the children of the kingdom; but the tares are the children of the wicked one; (39) The enemy that sowed them is the devil; the harvest is the end of the world; and the reapers are the angels. (40) As therefore the tares are gathered and burned in the fire; so shall it be in the end of this world. (41) The Son of man shall send forth his angels, and they shall gather out of his kingdom all things that offend, and them which do iniquity; (42) And shall cast them into a furnace of fire: there shall be wailing and gnashing of teeth. (43) Then shall the righteous shine forth as the sun in the kingdom of their Father. Who hath ears to hear, let him hear.

This is self-explanatory and has been discussed above. Everything will be allowed to develop and go through its life cycle so that it will germinate, develop and show its fruits for all to see. At the end of time, which is comparable to the harvest time on earth, the bad fruits are destroyed and the good ones retained.

The Son of Man, Whom Jesus referred to here will be discussed more fully by Him later. The seeds are the human spirits who have been planted by this Son of Man and the field into which He planted the human spirits is the world. Jesus here painted a picture of the activity in Creation that no one until now has been able to fully grasp. This is the vast survey of the origin, the development and evolution of human spirits. With a few words, He described the entrance of the human spirit into this material world and how this entrance took place, and also alluded to the great cycle of development that each human spirit and indeed the material world is subject to. The cycle of development of the germination, ripening, growth and the harvest.

Human spirits have their origin in the spiritual part of Creation called Paradise. They originated as unconscious spirit seeds or germs. With the coming into being of the vast spiritual Creation, the human spirits could not come directly into consciousness under the great pressure of the Power of God in the Spiritual Realm, while within this same Realm were other spirits who could already come into consciousness. The urge to come into consciousness, however, resided in the human spirit and it was this urge which arose like a prayer to God to grant the possibility of coming into consciousness. It is only through coming into full consciousness that the human spirit could attain to its full value and contribute to the further development of Creation.

In Paradise, it was impossible for these human spirits to come into consciousness because the pressure existing therein was too great to permit the unfolding of their abilities. This pressure was due to the proximity of God. The urge within the human spirits, as mentioned earlier rose like a prayer to God, and He yielded and granted that these human spirit seeds also be allowed to develop and realize the potential which they carried within them.

Only in lower lying regions of Creation, where the pressure was not so great because of the greater distance of these regions from God could these spirit seeds be able to unfold, and perhaps over a long period of time develop their abilities to perfection. God allowed the formation of material creation (the world) into which these spirit seeds could descend. In this material creation laid the possibility for the unfolding of the human spirit because it was so far away from God that the pressure here allowed this unfolding. The pressure has slackened so greatly that it permitted the human beings to come into consciousness, something absolutely impossible in Paradise due to the enormous pressure therein.

With the formation of this material realm; the world, the road was open for the human spirits also to gradually come to self-consciousness through the development of the abilities that they carried within. There was therefore to be no further ado than for them to make their descent into this vast material field that had now been opened to them. The formation of this material field, of this material world had been carried out under the direction of the Holy Spirit. The Spirit of God allowed the formation of this realm. Under His Command also these seeds descended into this vast field. It was like the Hand of the Holy Spirit was sowing these seeds in the World of Matter, the material world. Under His Gaze and scrutiny, these seeds made their way from the Spiritual Realm, from which they could not unfold to the lower lying world or field that had been prepared for them. It was this great event in Creation that Jesus rendered in such a stupendous pictorial form. The very beginning of our journey and its very end is what Jesus so described.

Nothing takes place in Creation without the authority of the Holy Spirit. Such a stupendous event therefore, as the beginning of the cycle of development of mankind could not have occurred without His Permission or Sanction. It is this sanction that could be described as that He with His own Hand sowed these seeds. With our entrance into this world, it was like we had been buried in matter. Sowed into the ground. In the world, within the field, in matter, we were to gradually awaken to the recognition of ourselves. While in matter, we were to fully awaken the free will and use it for the development of our abilities. All the seeds that the Holy Spirit planted were good but with the passing of time, some of the good seeds became bad through the use of their free will to choose what is evil. Some human spirits at the very outset chose evil. Each one would follow his self-chosen path.

Each one had started on his journey, which was meant to develop his abilities, perfect his personality and return to Paradise his home at the completion of the development of these abilities. By this time he would have been strong enough spiritually to withstand the power of the pressure brought about by the proximity of God. During our sojourn in matter, however, we came across Lucifer's principles and some of us succumbed to his enticements. The abilities which we were meant to develop were never developed, but instead we acquired new abilities from Lucifer, which abilities were never part of the original make-up of human spirits.

The sower of the seeds was the Holy Spirit and the reaper will also have to be the Holy Spirit since the sower always reaps whatever he sows. Since He did not sow the evil spirit seeds, He will not accept these as His, but will reject them as not belonging to Him. Why should He reap a harvest that is not His? He planted only the good and if some had returned as bad then it is the fault of these human spirit seeds who had not seen to it that they remained good. It is the duty of these spirit seeds, through the gift of the free will to make certain the goodness of their hearts. The Angels are His messengers who will help in the preparation and the execution of the Judgment.

Matthew 13:44-46 **Again, the kingdom of heaven is like unto treasure hid in a field; the which when a man hath found, he hideth, and for joy thereof goeth and selleth all that he hath, and buyeth that field. (45) Again, the kingdom of heaven is like unto a merchant man, seeking goodly pearls: (46) Who, when he had found one pearl of great price, went and sold all that he had, and bought it.**
Any human being who finds the Word of God and knows the value of It leaves all the old behind. He leaves all that may hinder him and pursues only that which he knows will profit him, forever. He who loves God and has discovered Him will give up everything else and pursue that which He has commanded him to do.

This is not to say that we should live in material poverty but what Jesus was saying here is that if we have discovered God and His purpose for our lives, then we should then pursue this purpose with all our vigour, neither looking right nor left. We must make every sacrifice to make sure that we fulfill this purpose.

We must make every effort to guarantee that we do the Will of God because as has been mentioned earlier, our earthly lives and conditions are temporary but the attainment of the Kingdom of God is eternal. This decision will often involve renunciation of our old way of doing things. It is simply the renunciation of the materialistic way of life and the building anew of a spiritual one. The selling of everything in the parable indicates the discarding of all that is old associated with this man and his willingness to make a fresh start.

The same could be said of the merchant who discarded the old. The old value system and habits and his former ways of doing things he was ready to sacrifice for the new, which he found in the Word of God.

Matthew 13:47-52 **"Again, the kingdom of heaven is like a net which was thrown into the sea and gathered fish of every kind; (48) when it was full, men drew it ashore and sat down and sorted the good into vessels but threw away the bad. (49) So it will be at the close of the age. The angels will come out and separate the evil from the righteous, (50) and throw them into the furnace of fire; there men will weep and gnash their teeth. (51) "Have you understood all this?" They said to him, "Yes." (52) And he said to them, "Therefore every scribe who has been trained for the kingdom of heaven is like a householder who brings out of his treasure what is new and what is old."**

The same process of separation at the close of age is emphasized by Jesus. We should ask ourselves why these emphases. Jesus has already painted several pictures of the same event to His disciples and followers. It is obvious that this event is so important that He explained it over and over again using different modes of expression, painting different pictures of the same event.

With these explanations, He wished to emphasize how important it was that we understand the mechanism of Creation, and also the coming Judgment so that we do not have to be lost at the end time. The Judgment is the Last or Final Judgment and the consequences of being found wanting at this time was what made Jesus spend so much time explaining this event to us. The consequences are disastrous in the extreme. It is only through the understanding of the impending events in the Judgment that we can escape the consequences. Without understanding, it is impossible to free ourselves in time from the World of Matter and escape the terrible disintegration which must engulf the part of the world in which we live.

As explained earlier, we find ourselves in this material world because of our inability to come to full consciousness in the Spiritual realm. We needed to descend down here so that through the experiences that we acquire we might unfold our abilities, perfect our personalities and go back to Paradise. This is the great cycle of development of a human spirit. In the process of this cycle, through the activity of Lucifer, some human spirits do not follow this course outlined by the Divine Will. They follow an entirely different course set out by the fallen one, Lucifer. Therefore, in material creation good and evil human spirits live side by side. Hence the great picture of the weed and the seeds.

The field that we descended into was the finest part of material creation called the Fine Ethereal realm, the uppermost part of the World of Matter. It must suffice to explain here that Creation itself is divided into two large parts: the Spiritual realm, which has nothing material about it and represents the origin of all human spirits, and the Material part, which is further divided into:

1. The World of Ethereal Matter
2. The World of Gross Matter.

The former lies higher and it is lighter than the latter. Between Spiritual world and the Material world is that world where the animals and the nature beings have their origin: the Animistic world.

On descending into fine ethereal matter, the seeds then made their way gradually downwards through the medium ethereal and heavy ethereal realms until they reach the gross material world. Now this realm is subdivided like the Ethereal world into fine, medium and heavy. Each of this is a distinct layer. On passing through each of this layer, they acquired the covering of these layers as bodies or coverings, much like we acquired the bodies or coverings of the earth at incarnation.

Gradually, we make our way downwards. In doing this, we experience every one of these layers as we descend and pass through them. In experiencing each layer, we get to know them and our knowledge as a result increase. We become more and more aware of our environments and as such become more and more aware of ourselves and our abilities. This is the beginning of self-consciousness, which must gradually continue until we have fully achieved full self-consciousness through the experiencing of all the layers of Creation.

So we acquired the bodies of fine, medium and then finally with our incarnation on earth that of heavy gross matter. We also experience the earth and we awaken more. We return to the Ethereal realm or to areas in fine or medium gross matter depending on how we have lived on earth. There is a going back and forth between the ethereal, fine gross material or medium gross material and the earth in repeated incarnations until we have fully developed all our abilities. Each time we go through this mini-cycle we learn more, we atone for our guilts, we know that little more about Creation and we become more aware of our abilities.

It finally reaches that point where we would have known and learnt enough that an incarnation on earth becomes unnecessary; then a mini-cycle of reincarnation is completed. What is then left is our journey within the Ethereal realm. This is a vast realm where most of the maturing takes place. We gradually rise through this realm in the opposite way that we came; progressing from heavy ethereal, then medium ethereal, and then fine ethereal until we reach the Spiritual Realm again at the end of a long journey of self-awareness and discovery. This is then the true end of our cycles. These are the fortunate seeds that have followed a straight line and have not wasted too much time in reincarnation upon reincarnation on earth brought about by guilt, which they must atone for through these reincarnations.

Those who are not so fortunate, are caught up in the world of fine and medium gross matter and on earth. They have not been so pure as to be able to completely leave gross matter behind. They still cling to all their faults and weaknesses, which really are to be found only in these realms. Here they stay until the Judgment Day. The allotted time for the development of their abilities has not been well-spent. It has been frittered away. Among these of course are many good souls who have been prevented from seeking the Will of God through pressure from the evil ones and who only need a little guidance for a total change. Then, of course there are the evil ones.

This is the great picture as the Holy Spirit looks down on the field. Just before the final Judgment, these good ones who still need some guidance will be helped so that they can in a very short time complete their development. The Word will be offered once more to mankind so that these good ones will not be lost without any good reason, through no fault of their own but through the disturbance brought on by those who are heading for perdition. Those who make use of this new Word will be harvested into the basket by the Holy Spirit, while those who still reject It will finally prove themselves as being utterly depraved and will be destroyed.

Many of us did not take full advantage of the Word and Mission of Jesus, either through spiritual indolence or through the willful prevention of the spread of this true Word by the distortion of the intellect. In any case, this Word has not until now been understood by mankind because of the false interpretation given to It in the desire of those who had the opportunity. They used this Word for their own earthly ends and not for the salvation of mankind. Otherwise, it would have been easy to find the right interpretation of Christ's words if we had looked for it.

Because of all this and also because the Justice of God would never allow the minority of people who still longed for Him to perish with the undeserving ones, He would still allow His Message to be once more spread among all mankind. This is the completion of the Mission of Jesus which was so violently cut short and also the necessary extension of knowledge for all mankind which is so important at this time. It is the duty of all human spirits at this time to look out for this new Teaching. It will be impossible for us to complete our development without It. We should look for It lest we be weeded out with the evil ones.

The Teaching of Jesus was like a new treasure that enhanced the old Mosaic teachings. He who was well-grounded in the religion of the Jews would be in a unique position to understand Christ best. Not in the manner of the scribes and Pharisees, but in the examination of these laws with open spirits. He would welcome the Word of Christ and indeed would understand Him best. He would be best prepared spiritually to receive of this Word. His old treasures, which are what he had imbibed in his spirit through absorption in the Mosaic law would be revitalized by the new Word of Jesus. It would complement it and make many things which had not hitherto been clear understandable.

Rejection in His own Country

Matthew 13:53-58 **And it came to pass, that when Jesus had finished** these parables, he departed thence. **(54) And when he was come into his own country, he taught them in their synagogue, insomuch that they were astonished, and said, Whence hath this man this wisdom, and these mighty works? (55) Is not this the carpenter's son? is not his mother called Mary? and his brethren, James, and Joses, and Simon, and Judas? (56) And his sisters, are they not all with us? Whence then hath this man all these things? (57) And they were offended in him. But Jesus said unto them, A prophet is not without honour, save in his own country, and in his own house. (58) And he did not many mighty works there because of their unbelief.**

It is characteristic of those who worship the intellect first to regard the person and his personal appearance before they consider whether it is worth listening to his words. These people thought that they knew Jesus' family. How come one who came from a family that we all know be doing the works that He was doing?

It is not the personal appearance that matters, but what the person is saying or doing. All who would come to the earth are obliged to use a physical body, even the Son of God. This physical body will not be different from those of other human beings. Outwardly a man among men but His core will be different. His core is that of God's. That is what makes all the difference. All His Words and Works He drew from this Core.

All human beings are of spiritual nature but the difference between them is the degree to which they have refined this spirit. That will manifest in their behaviours and in the works that they do. The same applies to Jesus but in a different way because His core was not spirit but of God. As such the Works that He will accomplish will be very different from the most developed human being and the words that He will speak will be drawn from a Wisdom that human beings do not have access to. With the same strictness to which we have alluded, He did not perform many works in His home town, not out of vindictiveness, but more out of sadness for the hopeless condition and perched nature of some of the human beings.

Earthly tradition against the Laws of God

Matthew 15:1-9 Then came to Jesus scribes and Pharisees, which were of Jerusalem, saying, (2) Why do thy disciples transgress the tradition of the elders? for they wash not their hands when they eat bread. (3) But he answered and said unto them, Why do ye also transgress the commandment of God by your tradition? (4) For God commanded, saying, Honour thy father and mother: and, He that curseth father or mother, let him die the death. (5) But ye say, Whosoever shall say to his father or his mother, It is a gift, by whatsoever thou mightest be profited by me; (6) And honour not his father or his mother, he shall be free. Thus have ye made the commandment of God of none effect by your tradition. (7) Ye hypocrites, well did Esaias prophesy of you, saying, (8) This people draweth nigh unto me with their mouth, and honoureth me with their lips; but their heart is far from me. (9) But in vain they do worship me, teaching for doctrines the commandments of men.

Jesus confirmed here that the scribes and Pharisees teach the people of Israel doctrines which they have devised with their own brains. These people have devised traditions which are now meant to pass as the Word of God. It is quite possible that history has repeated itself in the development of many religions, whereby men interwove their own thoughts into the words of their Teachers and these words are now meant to pass as inviolable Truth.

In this, they seek to mislead people and indeed have misled many by bringing them under their influence when they should have set them free by telling them to serve God only with the activity of their own spirits. In this way, they thrust themselves between the upward gaze of the seeker and God. They wanted to be considered as intermediaries and interpreters of the Word when all they in reality wanted was to bind the people to themselves, whereby their power over them would be unquestioned.

The history of religion has been unfortunately the same, whereby the custodians of the words of the Teacher saw an advantage only for themselves and would not shrink from altering the teaching of the Teacher if this would win adherents to the faith and strengthen the earthly empire that they were trying to build up. Initially, they exploited spiritual indolence by promising an easy way into Heaven but as their earthly power increased they shed their masks and resorted to using force against those who would not accept their interpretations of the Word. They used the threats of torture and murder to maintain their hold on the people. In so doing, they showed that they really never served their master and had never intended to follow the word that he gave. No genuine spiritual teacher ever taught the means that they used against their adversaries. They were but serving only one master, Lucifer who would use any means in his subjugation of the whole of mankind.

Matthew 15:10-11 **And he called the people to him and said to them, "Hear and understand: (11) not what goes into the mouth defiles a man, but what comes out of the mouth, this defiles a man."**
What comes out of the mouth of a man are his words. If these are evil, then they are capable of defiling. They come from within him and they take on form as they leave him, which form corresponds to the nature of the words. Being evil, they are dark and heavy. And being dark, they are capable of soiling the ethereal cloak of the producer. This is the defilement that Jesus spoke about. These forms, being dark are also capable of soiling the ethereal cloak of those for whom they are intended. They attach to these persons and sully their cloaks in the same way as they sully the cloaks of their producers.

These forms are capable of attracting similar forms to themselves, thereby becoming stronger around the person for whom they are intended and in the end can poison the thoughts of these people. These are the processes of defilement that Jesus spoke about but which no one has been able to understand until now. Through the explanations given in the book "In the Light of Truth: The Grail Message" by Abd-ru-shin, we are now able to understand this process. As for words so also for thoughts and deeds. These, in the same manner take on forms corresponding to their natures. They act in a similar way and can poison in the same way.

Matthew 15:12-20 **Then came his disciples, and said unto him, Knowest thou that the Pharisees were offended, after they heard this saying? (13) But he answered and said, Every plant, which my heav-**

enly Father hath not planted, shall be rooted up. (14) Let them alone: they be blind leaders of the blind. And if the blind lead the blind, both shall fall into the ditch. (15) Then answered Peter and said unto him, Declare unto us this parable. (16) And Jesus said, Are ye also yet without understanding? (17) Do not ye yet understand, that whatsoever entereth in at the mouth goeth into the belly, and is cast out into the draught? (18) But those things which proceed out of the mouth come forth from the heart; and they defile the man. (19) For out of the heart proceed evil thoughts, murders, adulteries, fornications, thefts, false witness, blasphemies: (20) These are the things which defile a man: but to eat with unwashen hands defileth not a man.

The scribes and Pharisees do not possess any spiritual insight and they would propose to lead people spiritually. Obviously, this would be impossible for them. Lacking any spiritual insight, it would be impossible for them to show the people the true spiritual path that these are to take. Being spiritually blind they will not see the spiritual way that the people are to follow. It is obvious that they will give wrong explanations of the Will of God because they do not know this Will. They will lead the people onto the wrong paths, which will lead them to spiritual destruction. How could they even imagine themselves to be spiritual guides when they do not know this path themselves? They thought that they knew the path and this is the result of the restriction placed upon them by the intellect with the wanting to know better that accompanies this.

Slaves of the intellect always think that they know everything better because they are supposed to have *thought* things out. For them, they are standing at the highest level and it is inconceivable for them that there would be those who could stand above them. Of course, they are standing at the highest level. The highest level that the intellect is able to reach, which is at the boundary where gross matter abuts on the ethereal world. It is lowly and the lowest point in Creation.

The real happenings in this Creation are well beyond this because they happen at a spiritual level and it is only those who are capable of swinging themselves beyond this intellect who will have access to the knowledge that will forever be closed to the intellectuals. The disciples here, in spite of all the explanations still do not understand their Master. As we have seen many times, they sometimes ask Him to give them further explanations. They often caused Jesus great suffering in their lack of understanding of sometimes apparently simple matters.

Matthew 16:1-4 The Pharisees also with the Sadducees came, and tempting desired him that he would shew them a sign from heaven. (2) He answered and said unto them, When it is evening, ye say, It will be fair weather: for the sky is red. (3) And in the morning, It will be foul weather to day: for the sky is red and lowring. O ye hypocrites, ye can discern the face of the sky; but can ye not discern the signs of the times? (4) A wicked and adulterous generation seeketh after a sign; and there shall no sign be given unto it, but the sign of the prophet Jonas. And he left them, and departed.

The scribes and Pharisees can interpret mundane signs but have not been able to recognize the most important ones. All the signs and great works that Jesus had performed, they had remained blind to. They still wanted more signs. It is obvious that these people will never be satisfied, no matter what signs Jesus gave.

They have been asking for signs since the beginning of His Mission. They had witnessed miracles upon miracles but they still wanted Him to give them a performance. They wanted to be entertained by the Son of God so that they might believe Him. They who should be the ones serving God wanted God to serve them. They make demands on God. Arrogant and ungrateful servants, self-complacent and lazy. They would rather sit in their armchairs and demand that a Son of God give them a performance only to still ask for more signs.

Matthew 16:5-12 And when his disciples were come to the other side, they had forgotten to take bread. (6) Then Jesus said unto them, Take heed and beware of the leaven of the Pharisees and of the Sadducees. (7) And they reasoned among themselves, saying, It is because we have taken no bread. (8) Which when Jesus perceived, he said unto them, O ye of little faith, why reason ye among yourselves, because ye have brought no bread? (9) Do ye not yet under-

stand, neither remember the five loaves of the five thousand, and how many baskets ye took up? (10) Neither the seven loaves of the four thousand, and how many baskets ye took up? (11) How is it that ye do not understand that I spake it not to you concerning bread, that ye should beware of the leaven of the Pharisees and of the Sadducees? (12) Then understood they how that he bade them not beware of the leaven of bread, but of the doctrine of the Pharisees and of the Sadducees.

Beware of the yeast of the Pharisees that can spread slowly but surely amongst you! The doubts and questioning, which is characteristic of the men of intellect was already beginning to take hold among the disciples. They, in the midst of all this greatness could only think of bread. All that Jesus had taught them and accomplished in their midst they had forgotten. They had forgotten that all they had to do was concentrate on the great task ahead and that they will be provided for.

Again and again intellectual doubts crept up on them and concerns about what to eat and what to drink came to preoccupy them. They were beginning to yield to the intellect, and against this Jesus warned them. Unless we become childlike in our faith, it would be impossible to progress. We will only make things more difficult for ourselves. We even run the risk that if things are not going the way that we expected quickly enough, we might change our minds about continuing on the right path. These are intellectual thoughts that start in the mind and if allowed can take over completely, with all the attendant consequences. Against this Jesus warned His disciples. It is only through simplicity and the knowledge that God is the dispenser of all things that we can progress.

Jesus' real identity and Peter's declaration

Matthew 16:13-20 **Now when Jesus came into the district of Caesare'a Philip'pi, he asked his disciples, "Who do men say that the Son of man is?" (14) And they said, "Some say John the Baptist, others say Eli'jah, and others Jeremiah or one of the prophets." (15) He said to them, "But who do you say that I am?" (16) Simon Peter replied, "You are the Christ, the Son of the living God." (17) And Jesus answered him, "Blessed are you, Simon Bar-Jona! For flesh**

and blood has not revealed this to you, but my Father who is in heaven. (18) And I tell you, you are Peter, and on this rock I will build my church, and the powers of death shall not prevail against it. (19) I will give you the keys of the kingdom of heaven, and whatever you bind on earth shall be bound in heaven, and whatever you loose on earth shall be loosed in heaven." (20) Then he strictly charged the disciples to tell no one that he was the Christ.

This has been misinterpreted by many people and some hardly credulous practices have sprung up as a result of this misinterpretation. When Peter issued this declaration, it was issued through the conviction he had arrived at in his intuitive perception, and this is the reason Jesus said that flesh and blood had not revealed the answer to him. Meaning that it was not the intellect or the pondering therefrom which have allowed him to arrive at this conclusion. Spiritual insight was what gave him the answer to this.

Peter's simplicity of intuitive perception allowed him to receive the enlightenment as to the identity of the Son of God. Nothing else. Not the greatest intellect could have achieved this, and just this would have been an obstacle. Peter's refined intuition allowed him to achieve this. The rock that Jesus mentioned had nothing to do with Peter personally. The simplicity of intuitive perception which Peter demonstrated and which allowed him to recognize the Son of God is the rock that Jesus was talking about. It is on this kind of simple and refined intuitive faculty that the future is to be based. In fact, the future Kingdom of God would be impossible without it, or to put it differently, anyone without this simplicity of intuitive perception would not be able to experience the Kingdom of God.

It boils down to what Jesus had been saying all along. The pure intuition, the simplicity and the avoidance of intellectual sophistry is so powerful that there is nothing that we would not be able to achieve if we have it. Nothing will be closed to those who have kept their intuitions pure. The intuition, as has been mentioned is the instrument of the spirit. If this intuition is pure, then the human being concerned is directly connected to the Kingdom of Heaven in Paradise, to the purity that animates this highest Kingdom. He may still be on earth but through the quality of a pure intuition, this radiation that streams from it is able to reach all the way to the Spiritual realm. Therefore, such a one has the keys to the Kingdom of Heaven. He has access to it through the quality of his pure intuition.

Anyone with this quality will never have to suffer spiritual death, because he is always connected to his home Paradise, avoiding the disintegration in the World of Matter which brings disintegration of the spirit and spiritual death in its wake. He need not fear spiritual death or hell because the purity of his intuition allows him to avoid such dark regions. He need not fear physical death either, as this brings him release, and he is then free to go back home from whence he came.

Jesus always spoke in a comprehensive manner and it would never have been His intention to make the human being Peter into what has become the general and accepted belief of so many people. Jesus, Who is the Son of God could see things in a wider perspective and spoke also in such a manner. *The simplicity and the purity of intuitive perception shown by Peter will be the rock on which Jesus will now build His Kingdom.* We could also say this in another way that only those who possess this quality will be allowed to see this Kingdom. It is not open to people who do not possess this childlike quality. This childlike quality is the key to the Kingdom of Heaven. This quality is the weapon against going to hell and suffering spiritual death.

Matthew 16:21-23 **From that time Jesus began to show his disciples that he must go to Jerusalem and suffer many things from the elders and chief priests and scribes, and be killed, and on the third day be raised. (22) And Peter took him and began to rebuke him, saying, "God forbid, Lord! This shall never happen to you." (23) But he turned and said to Peter, "Get behind me, Satan! You are a hindrance to me; for you are not on the side of God, but of men."**
It is doubtful whether Jesus would have issued this statement. He would never have called one of His disciples by this name. Jesus was never known for sharp temper, and it is inconceivable that He could be angry in this way but we will explore this later.

Matthew 16:24-28 **Then Jesus told his disciples, "If any man would come after me, let him deny himself and take up his cross and follow me. (25) For whoever would save his life will lose it, and whoever loses his life for my sake will find it. (26) For what will it profit a** man, if he gains the whole world and forfeits his life? Or what shall a man give in return for his life? **(27)** For the Son of man is to come with his angels in the glory of his Father, and then he will repay every man for what he has done. **(28)** Truly, I say to you, there are some standing here who will not taste death before they see the Son of man coming in his kingdom."

In the same vein as before, Jesus tells His disciples of the struggle ahead. He hinted that the struggle might involve the possibility of their losing their lives. Then, He gave the assurance that losing their earthly lives is nothing compared to losing their spiritual lives. As He said before, it is better to fear He Who can destroy both body and spirit than those who can only destroy the body. Of what use will it be to value one's earthly life more than the spiritual one, which is the real life. The loss of the spiritual life is accompanied by torments that are unimaginable and ultimately involves the erasure from the Book of Life, tantamount to the loss of all personal conscious existence.

Even if we gained all that is material, if we controlled all the material wealth on this earth, it would only be temporary and we would have to leave it behind one day. There is no question of an eternal life on earth.

He referred again to the Son of Man and that this Son of Man is to come to repay every man his debts. We would have noticed that Jesus always mentioned the Son of Man in connection with the end time and the Judgment. He also, as we saw earlier, mentioned the Son of Man in connection with planting of spiritual seeds. The time has not yet come to discuss the Son of Man. It will be reserved for a later time when Jesus spoke more fully about Him.

The fate of prophets and Jesus' prediction of His own death

Matthew 17:10-13 **And the disciples asked him, "Then why do the scribes say that first Eli'jah must come?" (11) He replied, "Eli'jah does come, and he is to restore all things; (12) but I tell you that Eli'jah has already come, and they did not know him, but did to him whatever they pleased. So also the Son of man will suffer at their hands." (13) Then the disciples understood that he was speaking to them of John the Baptist.**

Just like the prophets before him in Israel, John the Baptist did not fare any better. He was thought to have a demon just because he was strict in his attire and meals. Jesus Himself was not to fare better either. He knew this and began to prepare His disciples for His imminent departure. He was to be torn so violently from them and He wanted to prepare then inwardly to expect this. He started talking more often about His impending death so that it would not be a surprise to the disciples when it happens.

This takes us to the issue whether Jesus knew beforehand about His death and if He knew why did He not do something about it? Why did God not do something and save His Son from all this? These are legitimate questions and many believers have often racked their brains about this.

Yes, God knew about it and God sees everything. Jesus knew about it as He was descended from God. It did not mean, however, that God sanctioned it. As mentioned earlier, the sufferings and the death of Jesus was already predicted centuries before the event. The prophet Isaiah used the whole of chapter 53 to describe this event and how Jesus was to fare among mankind. Prophecies are given as a warning to people so that those concerned would change for the better and prevent the fulfillment of such visions or prophecies. The same was the case here. At the time that the prophecy was revealed, the spiritual conditions of the inhabitants of Israel was so dark that they had become servants of the darkness, instead of what they ought to be: servants of the Light. They had sunk so low that they now served the darkness and could easily be used by this darkness against some messenger from the Light.

It was already the case in Israel that prophets had been stoned to death or tortured. Given this dark spiritual state, in which all were in opposition to the Light, it was then not surprising that a Messenger out of God would be furiously opposed by these same people and ultimately do away with Him. The darkness had enough followers in the household of Israel that it could call this household its own. He could call on his troops in opposition to anyone who would oppose his reign over this people.

The prophecy therefore, which concerned Jesus was revealed to Isaiah, one of their prophets, detailing the events that would surround Jesus when

His time comes. Prophecies are not given without a purpose. They are not given for informational purposes only. They are given to be acted upon. Those that these prophecies concerned should have seen this prophecy as a great indictment of their spiritual state and should have changed their ways as a result.

It was ignored, however, and by the time Jesus came, Lucifer's minions had increased even more. They had increased greatly in number and were now to be found in positions of prominence in the society, including the clergy. How ironic? Since the people of Israel did not use the time before the coming of Jesus to change spiritually, the die was cast and Jesus knew that what had been feared some centuries earlier, and against which a warning had been given was now a distinct possibility.

The reason why He still came in spite of the dangers goes to show the desperate spiritual plight of the human beings who were still good and longed for God. In the midst of all the darkness, there were still a minority who, in spite of the persecutions of those who do not long for the Light still sought God and His Kingdom. These people would have had to go down into perdition with the others under the actions of the Divine Wrath. They would have had to go down in spite of their pure volition if no way was shown to them about how to adjust their lives to God.

The prophets of old had tried but failed in this. They were always persecuted and in fact their words were no longer strong enough to awaken mankind from the sleep of death which had gripped many a soul. The darkness surrounding man was so great that it would have been impossible for any earthly prophet to make any impact. Someone stronger was needed. Someone so powerful that He could burst asunder the dark night of the soul. It was God Himself, through His undimmed Word Who offered this possibility. The darkness surrounding the spirits was that desperate and perdition would have followed irretrievably. But good human beings would have been lost in the process. This the Justice of God would never permit. So, for the sake of this few, who were still longing for God, Jesus still came down with His Word. This is the reason He came and this is the sacrifice that He gave. To now assert the contrary and still cling to contemporary opinions only reveals that many of us have given ourselves up as lost.

Only the Love of God is capable of accomplishing such a deed. Instead of acknowledging these facts and thanking God for His inexpressible Love and Mercy, many will hold forth to their taught beliefs. Even the most terrible tribulation will still not be enough to awaken these people. So in spite of all the dangers, He still came. It was now left to the people of Israel to use their free wills to either accept or reject Him. They will have to account for the use of their free will in this manner, however.

God placed His Laws in Creation. Jesus will fulfill His Mission in spite of all earthly dangers. In incarnating, He placed Himself under all the Laws of His Father. These Laws are also operative on this earth. If the people of Israel decided to reject Him and even plot to kill Him, so be it! God does not intervene to change the wills of men. He will never interfere with the decisions of men. Men have free will but they must bear all the consequences resulting from its use.

God will not suddenly change the wills of the people of Israel, or perhaps bring Jesus from the cross. That would be an arbitrary act. There was no question of Jesus coming down from the Cross unless He had physical help. That is the Law of Creation, and God will never act contrary to His Own Laws. He is Perfect and perfection means immutability. No change! The physical laws state that it would be impossible to come down from a cross in a crucifixion unless there is physical help available to the crucified person. Jesus also had to obey this law since it was one of the Laws in Creation of which He is a Part.

If the people of Israel had taken that prophecy to heart and changed for the better, then their religion would have developed in such a way that people with spiritual insight would have been the ones in the clergy and not the intellectuals which happened to have been the case. Those with spiritual insight would immediately have recognized Jesus as the prophesied Messiah, and Jesus' Life and Mission would have had a different outcome. Indeed, many people recognized Him as the Messiah but not among the generality of the ruling classes who held both political and religious power.

Why did He not flee some will ask? Why did He not tell the priests what they wanted to hear? Make peace and be done with it! Let it be said that a confrontation was inevitable. To have fled would have defeated the purposes of His Mission. Firstly, He was sent to accomplish His Mission among the people of Israel because still, in spite of their stiff-necked nature, they still bore the greatest possibility for the understanding of His Words. Secondly, He had achieved so much in the souls of the people that to flee would have undermined the purpose of it all. The people would have begun to doubt Him and that would have completely undermined the Work of Redemption.

Also, when the confrontation came and He was asked about His Origin, to have denied this would have been disastrous. Everything He had worked for and all the beliefs of His followers rested on this very fact. It was then not surprising that that was what the darkness wanted to use most against Him. When He refused to deny His Origin and even reaffirmed it, the high priest tore his clothes and declared a verdict of death.

He could have saved Himself by denying His Origin, but this would have been going against His own teaching where He said that we should never fear those who could only destroy the body but Him Who could destroy both body and spirit. It was the last trump card played by the darkness hoping that Jesus, at the threat of physical suffering and death would deny His Origin. This would have completely destroyed His Work and the seeds of Salvation that He had already planted in the souls of the believers would have been eaten away.

He, however, vanquished the darkness completely. He was prepared to die for what He believed in and laid down His Life so that His Message might be preserved for posterity. His Teaching would have disappeared completely, and He would have been a footnote in history if He had fled or denied His Origin. He died so that the way to Salvation might be open to us through His Word. He died so that we might continue to have His Word, and if we act accordingly Salvation will be ours. His Word will be the germinating mustard seed or the yeast in the large body of dough, which, if acted upon would spread within us, and force the darkness to loosen its grip on us. This is what He died for. In the hope that mankind might adhere to His Word.

What then do we have today? Have mankind adhered to His Word? Only a very few people used the Message of Jesus for the salvation of their own souls. The vast majority, including the leaders simply followed in the example of Israel. They formed a religion out of the Word of Jesus.

Simplicity, Childlikeness and Humility

Matthew 18:1-6 **At the same time came the disciples unto Jesus, saying, Who is the greatest in the kingdom of heaven? (2) And Jesus called a little child unto him, and set him in the midst of them, (3) And said, Verily I say unto you, Except ye be converted, and become as little children, ye shall not enter into the kingdom of heaven. (4) Whosoever therefore shall humble himself as this little child, the same is greatest in the kingdom of heaven. (5) And whoso shall receive one such little child in my name receiveth me. (6) But whoso shall offend one of these little ones which believe in me, it were better for him that a millstone were hanged about his neck, and that he were drowned in the depth of the sea.**

The person who is childlike is the greatest in the Kingdom of Heaven. It is the quality of childlikeness and not the child itself that Jesus was referring to. This quality of childlikeness is the representation of purity for mankind. A human being who is childlike in the real sense of the word has attained to purity. This purity links him to the Luminous Heights. The more childlike we are, the purer we are. The purer we are, the higher we rise and as such the greater and more spiritually powerful. The quality of purity is therefore the most important because it links us in the most direct way to the Purity of God from Whom we receive the greatest power.

We should therefore as human beings pursue this purity which is the most important. The purer we are, the purer our intuitions. This has the effect of keeping us linked with Paradise, which is our home. Occasionally, we feel the consciousness of being protected by the Power of God just like the perfect human spirits in Paradise continuously feel this protective Power. Again Jesus was speaking comprehensively and symbolically and as such could not be referring to a specific child. He was saying that we should be like them in their simple unassuming nature. This is, however, difficult for the man of today because of his intellectual sagacity. Yet he can achieve nothing for his spirit without this childlikeness.

The lack of understanding here has led many to believe that all children are innocent. There is not the case. Certainly we know of children who are definitely not innocent. How do we account for this discrepancy? This once more proves that Jesus was not speaking specifically about children, or a particular child, but was, as usual, speaking in a broad way about the quality of childlikeness.

Children are nothing but human spirits who have reincarnated, either as a result of their own fault, or forced to do so because of one karmaic burden or the other. It may also be because they need to complete their development. No child is innocent in the way that we like to ascribe innocence. Children often come with very heavy karma, which as maturity sets in they have to start making efforts to cast off. We should already have arrived at this conclusion with our experiences.

Unconditional and limitless forgiveness

Matthew 18:21-22 Then Peter came up and said to him, "Lord, how often shall my brother sin against me, and I forgive him? As many as seven times?" (22) Jesus said to him, "I do not say to you seven times, but seventy times seven….."

We have been commanded to always forgive those who sin against us. It is a Commandment and we must obey it. The consequence of not obeying it is that we are retarded in our spiritual development in the way already discussed. Also in our relationship with God, the measure of mercy we use against our fellow human beings will also be the measure used against us. The level of leniency we give is what we will receive from the Lord.

There is to be no limit to the number of times we forgive our fellow men. We are to be patient and forgiving always. That way, we do not carry any baggage with us in our hearts when we have to cross into the Beyond. We cross freely with nothing that will hinder our free movement towards the Light.

Matthew 19:3-9 The Pharisees also came unto him, tempting him, and saying unto him, Is it lawful for a man to put away his wife for every cause? (4) And he answered and said unto them, Have ye not

read, that he which made them at the beginning made them male and female, (5) And said, For this cause shall a man leave father and mother, and shall cleave to his wife: and they twain shall be one flesh? (6) Wherefore they are no more twain, but one flesh. What therefore God hath joined together, let not man put asunder. (7) They say unto him, Why did Moses then command to give a writing of divorcement, and to put her away? (8) He saith unto them, Moses because of the hardness of your hearts suffered you to put away your wives: but from the beginning it was not so. (9) And I say unto you, Whosoever shall put away his wife, except it be for fornication, and shall marry another, committeth adultery: and whoso marrieth her which is put away doth commit adultery.

What God has joined together let not man put asunder here refers to marriages *made in heaven*. If two people bring complementary qualities with them, and they find each other, and have decided to marry, such a union is made in Heaven because of the complementary qualities of these two people. They are meant for each other and the permanence of their relationship is guaranteed through the complementary qualities that they possess. Their marriage will bring blessings into Creation.

If then an outsider, whether the parents or someone else tries to break up this relationship, they are going against this Commandment by Jesus. They are breaking up a relationship which will bring happiness and blessing in Creation, and are therefore contravening what God had already joined together through His Laws.

It will never be the wish for such people to separate because their union is permanent due to their complementary qualities. Those who break up such a union must bear heavy responsibility for preventing a union that would have brought immense blessing to Creation. It will be very difficult indeed to free themselves from this guilt.

The advice to the rich young man

Matthew 19:16-21 **And, behold, one came and said unto him, Good Master, what good thing shall I do, that I may have eternal life? (17) And he said unto him, Why callest thou me good? there is none good but one, that is, God: but if thou wilt enter into life, keep the com-**

mandments. **(18) He saith unto him, Which? Jesus said, Thou shalt do no murder, Thou shalt not commit adultery, Thou shalt not steal, Thou shalt not bear false witness, (19) Honour thy father and thy mother: and, Thou shalt love thy neighbour as thyself. (20) The young man saith unto him, All these things have I kept from my youth up: what lack I yet? (21) Jesus said unto him, If thou wilt be perfect, go and sell that thou hast, and give to the poor, and thou shalt have treasure in heaven: and come and follow me.**

The advise to the rich young man has been misunderstood. Many have taken up this advice without any modification whatsoever and consequently have brought tremendous suffering upon themselves. The advice given to the rich young man was for him personally. Firstly, Jesus told him to obey all the Commandments, he replied that he had obeyed all the Commandments, yet he felt that there was still something lacking, something that he had to do if he wanted to attain to the Kingdom of Heaven. This young man, after examining his own soul was troubled enough to ask Jesus persistently about what he had to do. Jesus looked at him and knew exactly what the weaknesses of this young man were. He gave him advice as to what he needed to do to address his peculiar condition.

He was to give up all his wealth, because these had become an obstacle to him personally. They had become a hindrance. He had become so spiritually indolent as not to be able to rouse himself to do anything about his spiritual salvation. If then, this was the case with this young man, then the best advice that Jesus could give was to get rid of what had become an obstacle to him, which was his wealth. After all, nothing is more important than the attainment of the Kingdom of Heaven. This young man, and perhaps those like him are the only ones to follow this advice. If one is able to control one's wealth and use it in such a way that it brings blessings to mankind, then by all means they should be used that way. Why give away wealth when it can be used to good purpose in capable hands?

Matthew 19:22-26 **But when the young man heard that saying, he went away sorrowful: for he had great possessions. (23) Then said Jesus unto his disciples, Verily I say unto you, That a rich man shall**

hardly enter into the kingdom of heaven. (24) And again I say unto you, It is easier for a camel to go through the eye of a needle, than for a rich man to enter into the kingdom of God. (25) When his disciples heard it, they were exceedingly amazed, saying, Who then can be saved? (26) But Jesus beheld them, and said unto them, With men this is impossible; but with God all things are possible.

The eye of the needle does not literally mean an eye of a needle. Once more mankind has misunderstood one of Christ's great sayings. It was a picture meant to show how difficult it would be for those who are not able to control their wealth like this young man to attain to the Kingdom of Heaven. They are so taken up with their wealth that it is this that they worship. It would indeed be very hard for them to bring forth the volition necessary for progress towards the Luminous Heights.

It is the same with all those who are like this young man. The problem is their inability to arouse the will for something better. There are those of course who are able to rouse themselves for spiritual activity, and it would be unjust to ask these to give up their wealth when it could be put to good use in their capable hands.

Eternal life: The same reward for all

Matthew 20:1-16 **"For the kingdom of heaven is like a householder who went out early in the morning to hire laborers for his vineyard. (2) After agreeing with the laborers for a denarius a day, he sent them into his vineyard….."**

The reward for all human beings who make it back to Paradise is the attainment to eternal life. The reward is the same whether for those who were the first to attain to it or for those who are the last to get there. They all attain the same status of eternal life. As mentioned earlier, there are those who completed their cycles of development much quicker and are already in Paradise, even though they set out at about the same time as we did. They took a straight course and did not waste any time at all. They have already achieved the status of eternal existence.

When finally we complete our cycles and find our way into Paradise, we will also achieve the same status. Exactly the same. Those who got there first will not be more than us just because they got there first. The status is exactly the same, the goal is exactly the same. This is what this parable meant to indicate. Everyone receives the same wages, no matter for how long he or she has been working. That is the promise made to every human spirit when it left Paradise at the beginning of its cycle of development. There is nothing unjust about it. It is not a race or a competition as to who gets to Paradise first. The only requirement is that we make certain we get there through harmonising our lives with the Laws of God.

Matthew 20:20-23 **Then the mother of the sons of Zebedee came up to him, with her sons, and kneeling before him she asked him for something. (21) And he said to her, "What do you want?" She said to him, "Command that these two sons of mine may sit, one at your right hand and one at your left, in your kingdom." (22) But Jesus answered, "You do not know what you are asking. Are you able to drink the cup that I am to drink?" They said to him, "We are able." (23) He said to them, "You will drink my cup, but to sit at my right hand and at my left is not mine to grant, but it is for those for whom it has been prepared by my Father."**

Zebedee's sons are human spirits and have asked that they sit by the side of Jesus in His Kingdom. Jesus is a Part out of God, and as such His origin is completely different from those of human beings. Human beings can never be Divine. Even in their highest maturity, they will always be of the spirit. A species can never go beyond its origin. Here Zebedee's sons, being ignorant of the Laws of God asked that they be made Divine. They asked that they also share in the Nature of the Creator, which is impossible for them.

This is the reason that Jesus asked them if they could drink from His cup. He did not refer to a physical cup, nor the cup of suffering as has been interpreted. He asked them whether they would be able to bear the Power of Radiation, which those who are able to live in the proximity of God must be able to bear. Zebedee's sons, being human spirits would not be able to bear this Radiation and as such it would be impossible for them to sit beside Jesus in His Divine Kingdom.

It is those who at the very outset have been created Divine who can share in Jesus' Divine Kingdom. This is why He said that it was not for Him to grant but for those for whom it had been prepared. These are the Beings Who have been created at the outset as Divine by God. Through this, they already earn the right to sit by Jesus through the nature of their being. No human being can be made into a Divine Being. He has his origin in a specific realm, the Spiritual and it is impossible to add the nature of the Divine to his nature. This is the reason Jesus answered the mother that she did not know what she was asking. She was asking the impossible.

Matthew 20:24-28 **And when the ten heard it, they were moved with indignation against the two brethren. (25) But Jesus called them unto him, and said, Ye know that the princes of the Gentiles exercise dominion over them, and they that are great exercise authority upon them. (26) But it shall not be so among you: but whosoever will be great among you, let him be your minister; (27) And whosoever will be chief among you, let him be your servant: (28) Even as the Son of man came not to be ministered unto, but to minister, and to give his life a ransom for many.**

Jesus here exhorted His disciples to be humble. Never ask to be great. Their purpose was to serve and never to seek to be masters. They were to follow His examples, whereby He served with His entire Being. He served God and in the process also helped human beings. It is only in serving God that we become great. In serving, we put our abilities to use, which become stronger and stronger. We also as a consequence obey the Law of necessary movement in this Creation. Also in serving, we practice what to the human being is absolutely vital: *humility*. Without this, he can never achieve anything for his spirit.

Of what use is it to sit in an armchair and indolently expect to lord it over others. In demanding that others serve us, something unsound and unnatural is created, whereby we will have to resort to force to ensure that this demand is kept, if those that we demand to serve us refuse to do so. This is actually the bane of mankind of today. The reasons for some of the ills in society is this demand that others serve us while we sun ourselves in glorified indolence. There is bound to be a one-sidedness and resentment which must breed conflict. If everyone wished to serve, then there would be that voluntary exchange of services, whereby peace and harmony would reign. There would be no slaves and masters and therefore no need to resort to force to compel the wills of others. The wish of many, however, never to lift a hand in service through the domination of the intellect has led to this unnatural aberration.

They would rather be served than to serve and they insist on maintaining this position, and in fact, could only maintain this position through the use of violence. It is an unnatural position and this is the reason that it demands the use of force for it to survive.

The importance of real, genuine faith

Matthew 21:18-22 **Now in the morning as he returned into the city, he hungered. (19) And when he saw a fig tree in the way, he came to it, and found nothing thereon, but leaves only, and said unto it, Let no fruit grow on thee henceforward for ever. And presently the fig tree withered away. (20) And when the disciples saw it, they marvelled, saying, How soon is the fig tree withered away! (21) Jesus answered and said unto them, Verily I say unto you, If ye have faith, and doubt not, ye shall not only do this which is done to the fig tree, but also if ye shall say unto this mountain, Be thou removed, and be thou cast into the sea; it shall be done. (22) And all things, whatsoever ye shall ask in prayer, believing, ye shall receive.**

Faith can move mountains! Through an ardent longing and belief in God, a connection is made with His Power. It is the access to this spiritual power that allows believers to achieve what to intellectuals are impossible. Jesus did not mean the movement of physical mountains, but the achievement of such great things that indeed must be considered miraculous. The disciples demonstrated this after they had received the Power from the Holy Spirit and were able to accomplish deeds which confounded their critics.

It is the openness to this Power, and the ability of believers to allow this Power to pass through them that achieves this effect. The Power simply flows through those who have opened themselves properly for It and takes effect according to Its nature. The human being is able to guide the direction of flow of this spiritual power through his will. This, however, requires that we be pure of heart. It is only purity of the intuitive perception which allows a connection to this pure power. It will never flow to a human being whose inner being does not already offer an anchorage through the nature of his pure intuition.

It is only granted to the simple and the pure in heart as Jesus has made known through His declaration on Peter. It is such a rock of simplicity and faith that allows a connection to the spiritual power which flows from On High. Here, of course, we must avoid the expression Divine Power. It is impossible for quite natural reasons for Divine Power to flow through human beings. Human beings have a spiritual nature and it is a gradation of this Divine Power which flows through us. This is spiritual power. It is, however, still so powerful that it can achieve the miraculous, as demonstrated through the works of the disciples.

Jesus here talks about the importance of prayer. With prayer, the human spirit is able to unfold itself before its Creator and can often gain connection with His Power through this. But it is not the conventional type of prayer that can achieve this. We are too used to offering mundane prayers. We say prayers by the hundred which prevents the participation of our intuitions in this process. Without the intuition, a prayer is but an empty sound. As Abd-ru-shin explains in his book "In the Light of Truth: The Grail Message", for prayers to be so effective as to rise to the Feet of the Creator, it really must be that which has been pushed all the way there through the purity of the intuition.

Words may indicate a direction but they can weaken the power of prayers, especially if we have to think too much about the words, even if these are formed prayers memorized and recited. When Jesus said that we will receive whatever we ask for in prayer if we have faith, He meant that through our faiths, we do not even have to ask for anything anymore. Our prayers, if we have faith will be prayers of gratitude to the Creator for the wonderful Creation and for being allowed to participate in its further development.

To have faith means to live aright. To have faith means that the individual has so absorbed the knowledge of the Laws of God that it has become second nature to him. Such a one in his thoughts, words or deeds is pleasing to God because he serves God through the activity of his spirit. The goods works carried out by him through the retroactive effect of the Laws of God will automatically bring rich blessings upon him. He does not have to specially ask for anything. The Laws of God returns to him the rich harvests of his rightful activity. He knows this through his faith in God, and he knows that he will be protected and cared for. He does not have to specially ask for this or for that. His works are his prayers.

Matthew 21:28-32 **But what think ye? A certain man had two sons; and he came to the first, and said, Son, go work to day in my vineyard. (29) He answered and said, I will not: but afterward he repented, and went. (30) And he came to the second, and said likewise. And he answered and said, I go, sir: and went not. (31) Whether of them twain did the will of his father? They say unto him, The first. Jesus saith unto them, Verily I say unto you, That the publicans and the harlots go into the kingdom of God before you. (32) For John came unto you in the way of righteousness, and ye believed him not: but the publicans and the harlots believed him: and ye, when ye had seen it, repented not afterward, that ye might believe him.**

The pretence towards God of the religious leaders of Israel has been exposed by Jesus here. They pretend that they serve Him. They accepted their charge and agreed that they would serve God, but they do not, as shown through their attitude to His Son. Others, however, who are regarded as sinners accepted the charge of God. In spite of their status as great religious representatives, they will now run the risk of being rejected by God because of their hostile attitude. Their cunning and the hardness of their hearts was exposed by Jesus. They accepted that they would do the bidding of God, but their hearts were set on disobeying Him. They never had any plans on carrying out God's charge. They only had their own ends at heart.

Parable about the fate of prophets and His own death

Matthew 21:33-44 **Hear another parable: There was a certain householder, which planted a vineyard, and hedged it round about, and digged a winepress in it, and built a tower, and let it out to husband-**

**men, and went into a far country: (34) And when the time of the
fruit drew near, he sent his servants to the husbandmen, that they
might receive the fruits of it. (35) And the husbandmen took his servants, and beat one, and killed another, and stoned another. (36)
Again, he sent other servants more than the first: and they did unto
them likewise. (37) But last of all he sent unto them his son, saying,
They will reverence my son. (38) But when the husbandmen saw the
son, they said among themselves, This is the heir; come, let us kill
him, and let us seize on his inheritance. (39) And they caught him,
and cast him out of the vineyard, and slew him. (40) When the lord
therefore of the vineyard cometh, what will he do unto those husbandmen? (41) They say unto him, He will miserably destroy those
wicked men, and will let out his vineyard unto other husbandmen,
which shall render him the fruits in their seasons. (42) Jesus saith
unto them, Did ye never read in the scriptures, The stone which the
builders rejected, the same is become the head of the corner: this is
the Lord's doing, and it is marvellous in our eyes? (43) Therefore
say I unto you, The kingdom of God shall be taken from you, and
given to a nation bringing forth the fruits thereof. (44) And whosoever shall fall on this stone shall be broken: but on whomsoever it
shall fall, it will grind him to powder.**

The parable of the wicked husbandmen is one of the most poignant in the
Bible. Here, Jesus Christ painted the picture of His earthly Life and
Activity and the fate to befall the perpetrators for what was to befall Him.
He painted the whole picture of the history of mankind with their penchant
for killing the prophets sent to them.

The vineyard is the World of Matter. The husbandmen are human beings
and the householder is the Lord. His servants are the prophets and the son
is Jesus, the Son of God. It is one of the most moving parables, and it
depicted the picture of God letting out the World of Matter for human spirits to use for their development, and this is exactly what it is. We are nothing but guests in material creation. It has temporarily been let to us for use
for the development of our abilities. God sent in prophets to teach us of His
Laws, but instead of listening to these prophets, we tortured and killed, and
ultimately when God sent His Own Son, we did exactly the same.

The fate of mankind is already obvious through this deed in that those who perpetrated this dastardly crime would be destroyed and the Kingdom of God given to those who are now prepared to serve Him in truth. It is difficult to see the role for a propitiatory sacrifice in all this. It was clearly not in the will of the vineyard owner to have his son killed. He sent his son in the expectation that perhaps, through the moral authority that this son has, he might be able to persuade these people to pay their rents. In the same way, through the moral authority of Jesus as the Son of God, we were expected to receive Him and obey Him. But as the case with the vineyard owner's son we killed the Son of God.

In the same way that the inheritance that was to be that of the workers in the vineyard was taken away from them because of their wicked act, the inheritance that was to be Israel's as first amongst nations has been taken away through this dastardly crime against the Love of God. With this crime, the calling of the people of Israel was revoked and given to other peoples. The opinions of men are of no consequence in this matter. What men think of themselves has nothing to do with what God thinks of them. These are completely different issues.

For a long time now these have been two different worlds in which mankind have, through their arrogance tried to create a world that is totally divorced from reality and the spiritual. Mankind, for a long time has been living in a dream. The reality of how things really stand will soon be made known to them. He who would set himself against this Word of God and His Will would be crushed to pieces. He who would dare to set himself against the Power of God will be destroyed.

Matthew 21:45-46 **And when the chief priests and Pharisees had heard his parables, they perceived that he spake of them. (46) But when they sought to lay hands on him, they feared the multitude, because they took him for a prophet.**

Enraged, the clerics would like to do nothing better than to arrest Jesus right then and there and have Him executed. His accusation of them was becoming unbearable and the feeling of powerlessness that this engenders can only fan their hatred the more. They planned and schemed His destruction. He was too troublesome. He now even had the people on His side and it would not be long before they would no longer feel the need to follow the traditions of their fathers of which they were self-appointed custodians.

The abandonment of the called people of Israel and the giving away of the Kingdom to others

Matthew 22:1-14 **And Jesus answered and spake unto them again by parables, and said, (2) The kingdom of heaven is like unto a certain king, which made a marriage for his son, (3) And sent forth his servants to call them that were bidden to the wedding: and they would not come. (4) Again, he sent forth other servants, saying, Tell them which are bidden, Behold, I have prepared my dinner: my oxen and my fatlings are killed, and all things are ready: come unto the marriage. (5) But they made light of it, and went their ways, one to his farm, another to his merchandise: (6) And the remnant took his servants, and entreated them spitefully, and slew them. (7) But when the king heard thereof, he was wroth: and he sent forth his armies, and destroyed those murderers, and burned up their city. (8) Then saith he to his servants, The wedding is ready, but they which were bidden were not worthy. (9) Go ye therefore into the highways, and as many as ye shall find, bid to the marriage. (10) So those servants went out into the highways, and gathered together all as many as they found, both bad and good: and the wedding was furnished with guests. (11) And when the king came in to see the guests, he saw there a man which had not on a wedding garment: (12) And he saith unto him, Friend, how camest thou in hither not having a wedding garment? And he was speechless. (13) Then said the king to the servants, Bind him hand and foot, and take him away, and cast him into outer darkness; there shall be weeping and gnashing of teeth. (14) For many are called, but few are chosen.**

A sad picture because it showed that the called ones, the chosen ones are the very ones who would choose to follow their own desires and ignore the Word of the Creator. Those who had been given all the talents that they needed to grasp His Word would be the very ones to ignore this Word. There is nothing more tragic in its manifestations. Of what use then was all the preparations, all the talents and gifts bestowed on these people if they were not going to use them.

In spite of the many attempts by God to help us by sending teachers, we never changed, but as usual persecuted these teachers. In this case, those who were invited were the called people of Israel who rejected, persecuted the prophets and servants of the Lord. In the end their cities was ravaged and destroyed as a consequence, and the Word of God was given to other peoples (the people in the highway in this parable).

Again the fate to befall those who dared to act in this way was revealed. It is inconceivable to expect that God after the murder of His Son would not mete out justice to those who were responsible. He will mete out the most severe justice against these people who dared not only to ignore His Word but went so far as to allow themselves to be used as tools for the execution of His Son.

As indicated by this parable, these people will be destroyed and others, who hitherto had been deemed unworthy will be given the Kingdom. The emphasis of Jesus on this very event through the telling of many parables about it shows the importance of this. There is to be no loving forgiveness for the wicked. They will receive exactly what they have sown. The fact that Jesus used different words to essentially paint the same picture showed His attempt to impress this on His disciples.

Many called ones were given the opportunity to work, but few made themselves available for duty when the time came. Many had in the meantime forgotten their duties, or got involved in so many earthly material pursuits that they could not rouse the inner spiritual strength necessary for the fulfillment of their promised duties. The few that were chosen were those who had preserved themselves and were able to hear the call when it came. They were the ones who presented themselves for duty.

The phrase "many are called few are chosen" does not mean that God arbitrarily chooses, but that the choosing here is done by human beings themselves through their ability to hear the call of the Lord and answer it. After all, they gave the promise that they would fulfill their duties when the time comes. It was therefore their duty to listen for this call. Those who answered to their duties were therefore the ones who through the inflexible Laws of God had chosen themselves as ready for duty. Nothing more. No injustice is possible here. Human beings receive exactly what they put into Creation in relation to the efforts that they are willing to put into their own development. It is therefore wrong to think that God would arbitrarily choose some human beings and ignore others even if these were ready to serve Him and had previously been called by Him.

The separation of the spiritual from the material

Matthew 22:15-22 **Then went the Pharisees, and took counsel how they might entangle him in his talk. (16) And they sent out unto him their disciples with the Herodians, saying, Master, we know that thou art true, and teachest the way of God in truth, neither carest thou for any man: for thou regardest not the person of men. (17) Tell us therefore, What thinkest thou? Is it lawful to give tribute unto Caesar, or not? (18) But Jesus perceived their wickedness, and said, Why tempt ye me, ye hypocrites? (19) Shew me the tribute money. And they brought unto him a penny. (20) And he saith unto them, Whose is this image and superscription? (21) They say unto him, Caesar's. Then saith he unto them, Render therefore unto Caesar the things which are Caesar's; and unto God the things that are God's. (22) When they had heard these words, they marvelled, and left him, and went their way.**

The die was cast and His enemies had finally made up their minds to destroy Him. They set about their plans. They wanted an opportunity. If only Jesus could speak out of turn? Then, they would have their excuse to arrest Him, and would be able to justify this to their people, and also to the Roman authorities. They set about to try and entrap Him in His words. Because Jewish religious law carried no weight with the Roman authorities, they tried to see whether He would say something against Roman law. Jesus would not oblige, however, and He rebuffed them.

Render unto God's what are God's. This is a clear separation of the spiritual from the material. If they would enjoy the protection which the Roman empire bestows, then they had the obligation to pay their taxes. At the same time, since they were creatures of God, they must also conduct their lives in such a way that was pleasing to Him. They could raise no argument against this Wisdom and left in shame.

No marriage in the hereafter

Matthew 22:23-33 **The same day came to him the Sadducees, which say that there is no resurrection, and asked him, (24) Saying, Master, Moses said, If a man die, having no children, his brother shall marry his wife, and raise up seed unto his brother. (25) Now there were with us seven brethren: and the first, when he had married a wife, deceased, and, having no issue, left his wife unto his brother: (26) Likewise the second also, and the third, unto the seventh. (27) And last of all the woman died also. (28) Therefore in the resurrection whose wife shall she be of the seven? for they all had her. (29) Jesus answered and said unto them, Ye do err, not knowing the scriptures, nor the power of God. (30) For in the resurrection they neither marry, nor are given in marriage, but are as the angels of God in heaven. (31) But as touching the resurrection of the dead, have ye not read that which was spoken unto you by God, saying, (32) I am the God of Abraham, and the God of Isaac, and the God of Jacob? God is not the God of the dead, but of the living. (33) And when the multitude heard this, they were astonished at his doctrine.**

Marriage in the way that we know it exists only on earth. In the Beyond, each stands in service in this Creation with his or her abilities. Those in the Beyond therefore, through homogeneity in the nature of their abilities come together for the achievement of particular tasks. The coming together of two people of opposite sex on earth also should since have had the same high goals. Procreation should have taken a second place. The perversion of the sexual instinct, however, made this impossible. In the Beyond, there is no procreation as this is only necessary on earth for the coming into being of the physical bodies of earthmen. Hence no need for marriage in the accepted sense. Each person stands for himself over there.

This just goes to show that these so-called religious leaders really had nothing further in their minds than the upholding of traditions that they had devised with their brains. They placed their earthly intellectual precepts above the Will of the Creator. In this way, these precepts were meant to pass as God's Law. At least they made the people believe this. When Jesus began to expose this hollow structure, however, showing the flimsy structure on which the authority of these religious leaders was based, there was no other alternative than for them to hate Him and plan for His elimination.

When people die, contrary to contemporary Christian teaching, there is no question of lying in there in suspended animation, and then waiting until the return of the Saviour. This teaching is so defective that anyone giving it the most basic thought would dismiss it as ridiculous. So we are meant to lie in suspended animation: where, no one seems to know; some say purgatory, wherever and whatever that is meant to be. Then, what happens to our physical bodies that would have decayed? Well, we get them back. But how? Through some magic wand all the physical bodies of all those who have died are given back? These are the good, remember. What about the evil? They go to hell. It is refreshing that at least they can envisage a kind of life after death for the evil, but none whatsoever for the good.

These have gone to sleep. They rest in peace. Nothing can be further from the truth! And this teaching, obviously from what we have been examining so far, was not taken from Jesus. Where then did this teaching come from? It is the same story all over again is it not? The introduction of precepts woven by the human mind into the pure Word of God, which are now meant to pass as inviolable Truth. They simply in this followed the examples of the scribes of Israel. Traditions with nothing to do with the real Teaching of Jesus have been interwoven into Christianity over the centuries and are now passed on as the Word of Jesus. This teaching is false. Jesus never said anything of the sort and this proof we have.

In His Teaching here He said that God was not a God of the dead but of the living. There is no resting in peace for anyone! Active life is what awaits every single human being, whether good or bad that passes into the Beyond through the process that we call death. Joyous activity for the good and suffering for the evil. No lying down in some suspended animation. No such thing! There is no giving back of any physical bodies. If these people are to come to the earth and they need physical bodies, then they would have to go through the same process that everyone else must go through, which process was laid down by God from the beginning of time. They must incarnate and become children again and follow the same cycle. No other way is available for the coming to earth of human beings. Comtemporary religious leaders would really have to show us where in the Word of Jesus we find things like the giving back of physical bodies and suspended animations and so much else.

Those who are good will continue to work on themselves in the Beyond until they are so perfect that they can return to Paradise, their home. Those who are evil have to go through such terrible experiences that may induce some of them to change for the better and rise in the Beyond. Those who do not change for the better remain in their dark realm, partaking of the sufferings and horror that they helped create through the nature of the activities.

At the end of time, those who have progressed so much in their adherence to the Laws of God will be permitted to see the new day, whereas the wicked will be swept away. Where are the dead in all these? Where is to be found the concept of suspended animation and the giving back of physical bodies in all these? What is stated here is the gist of Christ's Message. What He spent His lifetime teaching His disciples and what He hoped would be passed on to posterity. His Teachings obviously have not been properly explained and have not borne the fruits that they should have borne due to their lack of application by mankind.

The greatest Commandment

Matthew 22:34-40 **But when the Pharisees had heard that he had put the Sadducees to silence, they were gathered together. (35) Then one of them, which was a lawyer, asked him a question, tempting him, and saying, (36) Master, which is the great commandment in the law? (37) Jesus said unto him, Thou shalt love the Lord thy God with all thy heart, and with all thy soul, and with all thy mind. (38) This is the first and great commandment. (39) And the second is like unto it, Thou shalt love thy neighbour as thyself. (40) On these two commandments hang all the law and the prophets.**

With the same consistency that has marked His Teachings, Jesus reiterated that it is the First Commandment that is the most important because he who loves God will through the love that he has for his Creator always be willing to fulfill the other Commandments. If, however, he does not love his Creator, then he will not fulfill any of the Commandments. The fulfillment of any of the Commandments rests on the love that the creature has for his Creator. It is very much the same with earthly relationships between a father and a son. If the son loves his father, he is more than likely to obey him in all that his father asks of him.

Jesus went further and demands that we love our neighbours like ourselves. Not until now through the book "In the Light of Truth: The Grail Message" of Abd-ru-shin have we understood what this meant. What we do for our neighbours, we do in reality only for ourselves. If we think good thoughts towards our neighbours, then as has been explained earlier, these good thoughts are like seeds planted in a garden which will bring an abundance of harvest. We reap whatever we sow. If we sow good thoughts as regards our neighbours, then we reap back good rewards through the workings of the Laws of God. We will have what people have variously described as good fortune, good karma or good luck. If, however, we persist in showering our neighbours with unkind thoughts, then we reap these same evil in what has also been described as bad luck, evil fate, evil karma or evil fortune. Jesus meant this as a lifebelt for us so that in spite of everything, we would have something simple enough to cling to so that we do not have to become unnecessarily lost.

Matthew 22:41-46 **While the Pharisees were gathered together, Jesus asked them, (42) Saying, What think ye of Christ? whose son is he? They say unto him, The Son of David. (43) He saith unto them, How then doth David in spirit call him Lord, saying, (44) The LORD said unto my Lord, Sit thou on my right hand, till I make thine enemies thy footstool? (45) If David then call him Lord, how is he his son? (46) And no man was able to answer him a word, neither durst any man from that day forth ask him any more questions.**
This is self-explanatory, but in their blindness, the Pharisees did not see this. If Christ was the Son of God, then He would have to be Lord to David and indeed to all creatures. Since He was a Part of God, He shared the same Essence as God.

His physical body may have been descended from the line of David, but here it is a question of the real person and not the covering. This error unfortunately still persists today, whereby the prevailing conception is that the physical body is the man, but it will not be long before this enlightenment is spread among the whole of mankind. The Pharisees saw it the same way since just like today they lacked spiritual insight and the ability to see beyond the physical and material.

Denunciation against conceit, hypocrisy and spiritual arrogance

Matthew 23:1-12 Then spake Jesus to the multitude, and to his disciples, (2) Saying, The scribes and the Pharisees sit in Moses' seat: (3) All therefore whatsoever they bid you observe, that observe and do; but do not ye after their works: for they say, and do not. (4) For they bind heavy burdens and grievous to be borne, and lay them on men's shoulders; but they themselves will not move them with one of their fingers. (5) But all their works they do for to be seen of men: they make broad their phylacteries, and enlarge the borders of their garments, (6) And love the uppermost rooms at feasts, and the chief seats in the synagogues, (7) And greetings in the markets, and to be called of men, Rabbi, Rabbi. (8) But be not ye called Rabbi: for one is your Master, even Christ; and all ye are brethren. (9) And call no man your father upon the earth: for one is your Father, which is in heaven. (10) Neither be ye called masters: for one is your Master, even Christ. (11) But he that is greatest among you shall be your servant. (12) And whosoever shall exalt himself shall be abased; and he that shall humble himself shall be exalted.

The scribes and Pharisees have usurped Moses' seat and control the earthly religious power. Consequently, the disciples are advised to avoid conflict with them. They are to do whatever is asked of them but are not to follow their examples, because these leaders themselves do not practice what they preach. They institute laws that are meant to be followed by others. They are vain and all they do is done in order to earn the respect of the people. They love to appear important and want to be served instead of serving. The examples set by the scribes and Pharisees is that of vain self-glorification, conceit, craving for importance and spiritual arrogance. This example and this precedent, Jesus warned against. His disciples are not to be like these people. His disciples are to serve rather than be served. His disciples are to be humble and not set themselves apart from the generality of the people.

The example of the Pharisees and the scribes are the excrescences of the over-development of the intellect. It is only the intellect that craves for importance and honour. It is the intellect that clings to external values and appearance and wanting to set itself above others. Jesus' disciples are not to become slaves of the intellect. They are to use the spirit instead, with its quality of humility and love and mercy. In using their spirits in the fulfillment of the duties that Jesus bids them, they are not to confront the religious authorities. They are to work among the common people. They are not to destroy but build up. They are not to waste energy in confrontations but in useful activity among the populace.

If attacked, they are to bear everything calmly and turn their gazes only to the Lord. He has sent them among the people and it is among these that they are to accomplish their tasks. If they work truly among the people, then the Teaching of Jesus will take hold among the grassroots and work its way up. These leaders write laws that are very difficult indeed to adhere to, and these are the heavy burdens that Jesus refers to. These are nothing but masses of external laws which, as mentioned earlier have nothing to do with real ascent. Furthermore, for a mobile human spirit, they constitute a burden, a hindrance to free unfolding. These laws are rigid, but the mobile spirit will find it difficult to adjust itself to them, hence the inner conflict. For those who are totally spiritually dead and have nothing more in them but the intellect, it would be easy for these to adjust since these laws are written by and ultimately for the intellect. Those, however, who still have some degree of spiritual mobility will never be able to adjust to rigid laws of do's and don'ts.

He also warned His disciples against intentionally exalting themselves, as this is often followed by a downfall. The reason for this is that those who do this deny the gift given to them by God. In becoming arrogant, they make themselves and others believe that their abilities and talents and the works that they accomplish are the results of their own cleverness and greatness. This is not the case. They have been able to achieve these works because of the connection that they have to the Source of all

Knowledge. By so doing, they deny their God. No human being can accomplish anything without the Power of God. To state otherwise is to delude oneself. The justified result of such arrogance is that the individual loses his connection with the Light, and is therefore not able subsequently to accomplish such great deeds as before.

This is the downfall that Jesus warned against. To compound his problems because he is no longer able to receive, such a one will have to render account for the loss of the blessings that his deeds would have brought to humanity. He would have to account for the non use of his talents. The consequences therefore are grave and he may run the risk of spiritual perdition because he may not have enough time to redeem his guilt before the closing of the cycle. On the other hand, he who humbles himself will continue to be connected to the Light and grow stronger in his recognitions and even achieve greater works than before. As a result he will rise higher and higher in the spiritual sense.

Matthew 23:13-15 **But woe unto you, scribes and Pharisees, hypocrites! for ye shut up the kingdom of heaven against men: for ye neither go in yourselves, neither suffer ye them that are entering to go in. (14) Woe unto you, scribes and Pharisees, hypocrites! for ye devour widows' houses, and for a pretence make long prayer: therefore ye shall receive the greater damnation. (15) Woe unto you, scribes and Pharisees, hypocrites! for ye compass sea and land to make one proselyte, and when he is made, ye make him twofold more the child of hell than yourselves.**

The teachings of these teachers of the law, as has been mentioned before are nothing but intellectual ordinances that people are meant to adhere to. These ordinances have nothing to do with real spirituality. The sole practice of these ordinances on their own, without due regard to the real spiritual Laws will not guarantee an entrance into the Kingdom of Heaven. Through the institution of these practices, and the demand that the people do just this and nothing more, or the teaching that this is all that they had to do is tantamount to shutting the door to the Kingdom of Heaven against the people. Through this they have thrust their teachings, and indeed themselves between the people and the Kingdom of God.

By not giving the people what they really needed for the Kingdom of Heaven, and by indeed preventing them from listening to the Teachings of Jesus, they have effectively barred the peoples' way thereto. No other way leads into the Kingdom of God but the one that Jesus pointed out in the exercise of the volition of the spirit and the obeying of God's Will. In preventing the people from listening to Jesus, and in the non-presentation of a teaching which demands the obedience to the real Will of God, they have denied the people their inheritance, and indeed their rights through the nature of their spiritual origin to return back to Paradise their home.

It is the same today. In instituting ordinances and teachings which have never been sanctioned, and which are even contrary to what Jesus wanted, we, like the scribes and Pharisees have thrust ourselves between the people and God and His Kingdom. In failing to explain the true Will of God, and in failing to demand that the true way to God was the proper understanding of Jesus' Words and the adherence to the Will of God, we have proven ourselves to be doing just that which Jesus two thousands years ago spoke against and censured.

There is absolutely no difference today in the development of religions from what the scribes and Pharisees built up at that time, and the way in which they acted against the Will of God. The Christian Church, or organized religion in general, has, through instituting practices which have been shown to be contrary to God's Will, and in its failure to show people what they really must do if they really wanted to enter Heaven, shut the Kingdom of Heaven from the people. They failed to tell the people that it is the obedience to God's Will through the exercise of their volition to do good that matters and not the saying of prayers by the hundred. They have gone contrary to every single Word of Jesus. They did not even understand Him, and instead of openly admitting to this, force was used and His misunderstood Words and Teachings were replaced with explanations and practices which will never open the way to the Kingdom of God. History has repeated itself.

Every single word of Jesus puts a hole in this hollow structure and if only people would examine these Words themselves, they would be amazed that they had for centuries been led by the nose by those who had not the faintest idea of what Jesus was saying. But we are too busy dancing around the golden calf of materialism. It was never the intention of most of these people to enter the Kingdom of Heaven, even though ironically they are meant to be priests and custodians of that very Word meant to show us the way. The aim, for the majority, has always been earthly influence, wealth and fame just like Jesus pointed out in their love to be addressed as Rabbi on the streets. In the same way today, these people enjoy the prominence that their positions afford them. So they occupy this position and fail to use it for the purpose for which it was created, but for exactly the opposite. They bar the way. They would not go in themselves, but through their teachings they never allow others.

Matthew 23:16-22 **Woe unto you, ye blind guides, which say, Whosoever shall swear by the temple, it is nothing; but whosoever shall swear by the gold of the temple, he is a debtor! (17) Ye fools and blind: for whether is greater, the gold, or the temple that sanctifieth the gold? (18) And, Whosoever shall swear by the altar, it is nothing; but whosoever sweareth by the gift that is upon it, he is guilty. (19) Ye fools and blind: for whether is greater, the gift, or the altar that sanctifieth the gift? (20) Whoso therefore shall swear by the altar, sweareth by it, and by all things thereon. (21) And whoso shall swear by the temple, sweareth by it, and by him that dwelleth therein. (22) And he that shall swear by heaven, sweareth by the throne of God, and by him that sitteth thereon.**

No clearer words could be stated as to the difference between what man has introduced with his brain and the true Wisdom of God. The far-seeing and comprehensive view, which is characteristic of everything spiritual is revealed here. The narrow minded outlook of intellectuals is also demonstrated for all to see.

The intellect can only see things in a one-sided rigid manner. Its characteristics make it imperative that it sees only one aspect of a subject at a time. It lacks a free survey because being a product itself, it cannot do otherwise. But it is this very product which mankind now depends on for clarification on matters which obviously goes beyond its origin and ambit. Is it then surprising that it falls short?

It is the fault of mankind. We place demands on a tool that obviously lacks the ability to resolve or handle these demands. Is it surprising that finding itself confounded it will be forced to express itself using obscure terms and expressions? It is bound to come up with ridiculous conclusions, such as the verses quoted above. It is bound to press everything into obscure limits and narrow down to its level what are meant to be great things that go beyond it. It is all in its attempt to offer an explanation that it does this. No one can blame the intellect. It only offers explanations according to its nature.

It is those human beings who ask the intellect for enlightenment on matters that obviously go beyond it that are to blame. If they are misled, then it is their own fault, and they must bear the full consequences for their decisions. If they are misled in such a way that they are condemned to perdition, then they have only themselves to blame for this. After all, they also have within themselves the tool that was to bring them enlightenment. The tool which was made for this purpose. But they choose to ignore this tool. They cannot blame God for this because God did not create this distortion in the human brain. If we have distorted our bodies in such a way that we fail to hear the Voice of God, is the Latter then to blame for this?

Matthew 23:23-24 Woe unto you, scribes and Pharisees, hypocrites! for ye pay tithe of mint and anise and cummin, and have omitted the weightier matters of the law, judgment, mercy, and faith: these ought ye to have done, and not to leave the other undone. (24) Ye blind guides, which strain at a gnat, and swallow a camel.
The human aspects of religion. Love for our neighbours, forgiveness, tolerance, mercy and justice for our neighbours have been neglected and attention placed solely on externals that do not take anyone anywhere. The weightier matters of the law are these human aspects.

Matthew 23:25-28 Woe unto you, scribes and Pharisees, hypocrites! for ye make clean the outside of the cup and of the platter, but within they are full of extortion and excess. (26) Thou blind Pharisee, cleanse first that which is within the cup and platter, that the outside of them may be clean also. (27) Woe unto you, scribes and Pharisees, hypocrites! for ye are like unto whited sepulchres, which indeed appear beautiful outward, but are within full of dead men's bones,

**and of all uncleanness. (28) Even so ye also outwardly appear right-
eous unto men, but within ye are full of hypocrisy and iniquity.**

The teachers of the law ask the people to uphold external practices but do
not teach them to improve themselves as human beings. They do not
show them how to think, speak and act in ways which are pleasing to
God, which alone guarantees that their spiritual garments are bright and
clean. This corresponds to the *inside*. They would rather teach the people
of Israel to wash their hands before meals and bathe their physical bodies
several times a day than tell them that bathing the spiritual body is of
more importance through thinking good thoughts. They did not know
this, hence they are blind guides. They could know, however, but this they
elected to ignore and they would oppose Him Who was meant to bring
enlightenment.

Of what use is it to bathe the physical body a thousand times a day or
wash our hands hundreds of times if we are evil within. This evil soils the
spirit, which is the inside of the bowl that Jesus mentions. It is the condition of this *inside* that is relevant to how we are judged and not the temporary physical body. Even the most materialistic person understands
this. One can put on the brightest of clothes, but this has nothing to do
with the nature of the individual. This is what Jesus was trying to point
out here.

Matthew 23:29-39 **Woe unto you, scribes and Pharisees, hypocrites!
because ye build the tombs of the prophets, and garnish the sepulchres of the righteous, (30) And say, If we had been in the days of
our fathers, we would not have been partakers with them in the blood
of the prophets. (31) Wherefore ye be witnesses unto yourselves, that
ye are the children of them which killed the prophets. (32) Fill ye up
then the measure of your fathers. (33) Ye serpents, ye generation of
vipers, how can ye escape the damnation of hell? (34) Wherefore,
behold, I send unto you prophets, and wise men, and scribes: and
some of them ye shall kill and crucify; and some of them shall ye
scourge in your synagogues, and persecute them from city to city:
(35) That upon you may come all the righteous blood shed upon the
earth, from the blood of righteous Abel unto the blood of Zacharias**

son of Barachias, whom ye slew between the temple and the altar. (36) Verily I say unto you, All these things shall come upon this generation. (37) O Jerusalem, Jerusalem, thou that killest the prophets, and stonest them which are sent unto thee, how often would I have gathered thy children together, even as a hen gathereth her chickens under her wings, and ye would not! (38) Behold, your house is left unto you desolate. (39) For I say unto you, Ye shall not see me henceforth, till ye shall say, Blessed is he that cometh in the name of the Lord.

This is one of the reasons why it would be difficult to justify the teaching of a propitiatory sacrifice as an explanation for the death of Jesus. He has made His Will clear here that it is wrong. The history of mankind is replete with this tragedy, and this clearly shows that Jesus was not in favour of the persecutions which have been the fates of all those sent by God for the enlightenment of the peoples.

The question as to why this is always the case is not so far-fetched. Why is it that prophets and those sent by God to bring enlightenment always persecuted without exception? It is not as if it is written in the stars that they indeed must always go through this. The generality of mankind is to blame for this. The decision of mankind always to follow the darkness creates a condition whereby it would be difficult for those who have decided for the Light to unfold. The vast majority of the people, and those in authority through the dominion of the intellect have turned their backs on God. They serve the darkness and it is as such not surprising that these can easily be used by Lucifer to oppose those who strive for the Light. They would use whatever is in their power, even murder to ensure that the status quo is maintained, that the spiritual never gains any foothold on this earth. In so doing, they do not know that they are simply following a larger plan by Lucifer to ensure the continuation of his reign and the prevention of the establishment of the Will of God on earth.

Mankind, therefore is to blame for this ugly situation because we let ourselves be used as pawns of Lucifer in his violent struggle against the Will of God. He wants to avoid destruction and as such must fight with all his might to ensure that his principles reign on earth. The time would be up for him if mankind would choose to align their wills with that of God's. He would then be brought to justice for the confusion that he has been able to sow among mankind. He is, however, trying to avoid this justice by ensuring that there are still people who still revere him and his principles.

His fight therefore, against the Will of God and also for his own self-preservation are the reasons for this ugly recurrence of martyrdom amongst the prophets and followers of God. If mankind changes and decide for the Light, then this ugly happening will change and prophets will no longer be persecuted but welcomed by the majority of the people. We can see here that Jesus did not lament or grieve but threw out the gauntlet to these people. "Fill up the measures of your fathers". He summed up the terrible fate that is to befall these people, who have always acted in this Light-opposing way. There is to be no mercy or forgiveness for them. They will drink the cup of retribution and no help shall be extended to them in their sufferings.

Matthew 24:1-2 Jesus left the temple and was going away, when his disciples came to point out to him the buildings of the temple. (2) But he answered them, "You see all these, do you not? Truly, I say to you, there will not be left here one stone upon another, that will not be thrown down."

Jesus here predicted the destruction of the Temple of Jerusalem that was to occur about 150 years later.

Signs of the End Time

Matthew 24:3-8 And as he sat upon the mount of Olives, the disciples came unto him privately, saying, Tell us, when shall these things be? and what shall be the sign of thy coming, and of the end of the world? (4) And Jesus answered and said unto them, Take heed that no man deceive you. (5) For many shall come in my name, saying, I am Christ; and shall deceive many. (6) And ye shall hear of wars and rumours of wars: see that ye be not troubled: for all these things must come to pass, but the end is not yet. (7) For nation shall rise against nation, and kingdom against kingdom: and there shall be famines,

and pestilences, and earthquakes, in divers places. (8) All these are the beginning of sorrows.

The signs of the beginning of the Judgment of God. As explained in the book "In the Light of Truth: The Grail Message" by Abd-ru-shin, the Judgment is characterized by an immense influx of the Radiation of God into the entire Creation. This Radiation affects everything and brings movement into everything. That which had hitherto been dormant and inactive is brought to life. That which we have tried to hide from others or perhaps unaware of ourselves will become apparent. All faults and weaknesses will show themselves in the worst possible manner for all to see. This will lead to an unrestrained raging that will lead to great destruction. False prophets will arise to try to explain what they themselves do not understand to people. People will follow these prophets out of fear. These prophets will, however, not be able to offer the peace of mind that people desire. This is the proof that indeed they are nothing but false prophets. The people themselves will recognize them as such.

Natural disasters are due to the fact that over millennia we human beings, through our wrong volitions have led the development of the natural environment in the wrong direction. Through the influx of the Power of God, all that has been wrongly led will be torn apart and replaced by what should have been.

Matthew 24:9-14 **Then shall they deliver you up to be afflicted, and shall kill you: and ye shall be hated of all nations for my name's sake. (10) And then shall many be offended, and shall betray one another, and shall hate one another. (11) And many false prophets shall rise, and shall deceive many. (12) And because iniquity shall abound, the love of many shall wax cold. (13) But he that shall endure unto the end, the same shall be saved. (14) And this gospel of the kingdom shall be preached in all the world for a witness unto all nations; and then shall the end come.**

Because of the condition described above through the entrance in an unprecedented way of the Power of God into Creation, the faults and all the evil within human beings will manifest. Human beings, under this immense pressure will act out their wickedness. The effect on the environment and on other people is not difficult to imagine.

Obviously, Jesus was not referring to the teachings of the present day churches which have more or less been made earthly. He was talking about the teaching of His true Word. His Word, without the added interpretations of anyone. His Word restored to Its original form. His Word returned to Its original luster. It is this *new Word*, which is the same as Jesus' Word that will now be preached at the end time. We have already touched upon this earlier. The Word of Jesus in Its form will be revealed again in all Its vitality so that for the last time those who had been held back by the additions, which over the centuries had covered the true Word may save themselves. This new Word will be preached just before the end. There will therefore be very little time for us to make up our minds as to which direction to take. Hesitation is tantamount to a rejection. We should therefore be on the look out for this new Word.

The great Tribulation

Matthew 24:15-22 **When ye therefore shall see the abomination of desolation, spoken of by Daniel the prophet, stand in the holy place, (whoso readeth, let him understand:) (16) Then let them which be in Judaea flee into the mountains: (17) Let him which is on the housetop not come down to take any thing out of his house: (18) Neither let him which is in the field return back to take his clothes. (19) And woe unto them that are with child, and to them that give suck in those days! (20) But pray ye that your flight be not in the winter, neither on the sabbath day: (21) For then shall be great tribulation, such as was not since the beginning of the world to this time, no, nor ever shall be. (22) And except those days should be shortened, there should no flesh be saved: but for the elect's sake those days shall be shortened.**

The terrifying effect of the Judgment has here been described by Jesus. The catastrophic natural disasters and the sufferings are beyond words. It will be so terrible that if it should last for much longer every single human being and animal will die. However, those who have remained true to God will be allowed to see the new day. It is obvious here that only those who have adjusted their wills to that of God will survive, no one else. We should see to it that we are numbered among these.

The Coming of the Son of Man

Matthew 24:23-27 Then if any man shall say unto you, Lo, here is Christ, or there; believe it not. (24) For there shall arise false Christs, and false prophets, and shall shew great signs and wonders; insomuch that, if it were possible, they shall deceive the very elect. (25) Behold, I have told you before. (26) Wherefore if they shall say unto you, Behold, he is in the desert; go not forth: behold, he is in the secret chambers; believe it not. (27) For as the lightning cometh out of the east, and shineth even unto the west; so shall also the coming of the Son of man be.

We have been told to be on our guard against false teachings and false expectations. There will be those who for the sake of earthly gain will institute teachings designed to appeal to that greatest of man's faults: his spiritual indolence. Teachings designed to take the effort away from human beings. As before, they will exploit this weakness to paint a broad easy road to salvation for mankind. This is, however, contrary to what Jesus Himself has described. Jesus demanded spiritual activity from those who would inherit the Kingdom and this is the only way. But false Christs will appear who will try to pervert the Teachings of Jesus in telling people that there is another way. In doing this, they divert the peoples' attention away from looking for the last Word and Teaching which Christ promised.

Some of these false Christs will even be so powerful as to be able to perform some miracles and in so doing convince people. Of all these Jesus has warned us beforehand. We are meant to keep our spirits alert and if we do this, it would be impossible for us to be led astray. The Coming of the Son of Man shall be accompanied by a travail of a great tribulation. The effect of His Coming will make itself felt all over the world.

Matthew 24:29-35 Immediately after the tribulation of those days shall the sun be darkened, and the moon shall not give her light, and the stars shall fall from heaven, and the powers of the heavens shall be shaken: (30) And then shall appear the sign of the Son of man in heaven: and then shall all the tribes of the earth mourn, and they

shall see the Son of man coming in the clouds of heaven with power and great glory. (31) And he shall send his angels with a great sound of a trumpet, and they shall gather together his elect from the four winds, from one end of heaven to the other. (32) Now learn a parable of the fig tree; When his branch is yet tender, and putteth forth leaves, ye know that summer is nigh: (33) So likewise ye, when ye shall see all these things, know that it is near, even at the doors. (34) Verily I say unto you, This generation shall not pass, till all these things be fulfilled. (35) Heaven and earth shall pass away, but my words shall not pass away.

As has now become customary with Jesus, He again associated the Son of Man with the Judgment. The Son of Man then, Whom many have mistaken for Jesus is inseparably linked with the Judgment. Note here that Jesus spoke in the third person. He could easily have spoken in the first person, but He did not which indicates that He was not referring to Himself at all but to Another, otherwise why speak in the third person. From what we have seen so far, He was not accustomed to referring to Himself in the third person but only in those instances where He had been confused with the Son of Man.

"This generation shall not pass" does not mean that those people who lived in Israel at the time of Jesus will not taste earthly death before the time of Judgment as is impossible. With this Jesus was alluding to the fact that these people will reincarnate again to witness the Judgment. Those who persecuted Him and those who did not listen to His Word will have to incarnate on earth again at the time of Judgment to settle accounts. This is what He meant by 'this generation shall not pass'.

His Words are eternal. It is the Truth out of the Creator and as such It will for ever stand, even if all that has been created pass away. If the Creator were to limit His Radiation to Its unavoidable minimum then the end of all that has been created will be at hand. Only God will remain and in Him His Word.

The separation

Matthew 24:36-51 **But of that day and hour knoweth no man, no, not the angels of heaven, but my Father only. (37) But as the days of Noe**

were, so shall also the coming of the Son of man be. (38) For as in the days that were before the flood they were eating and drinking, marrying and giving in marriage, until the day that Noe entered into the ark, (39) And knew not until the flood came, and took them all away; so shall also the coming of the Son of man be. (40) Then shall two be in the field; the one shall be taken, and the other left. (41) Two women shall be grinding at the mill; the one shall be taken, and the other left. (42) Watch therefore: for ye know not what hour your Lord doth come. (43) But know this, that if the goodman of the house had known in what watch the thief would come, he would have watched, and would not have suffered his house to be broken up. (44) Therefore be ye also ready: for in such an hour as ye think not the Son of man cometh. (45) Who then is a faithful and wise servant, whom his lord hath made ruler over his household, to give them meat in due season? (46) Blessed is that servant, whom his lord when he cometh shall find so doing. (47) Verily I say unto you, That he shall make him ruler over all his goods. (48) But and if that evil servant shall say in his heart, My lord delayeth his coming; (49) And shall begin to smite his fellowservants, and to eat and drink with the drunken; (50) The lord of that servant shall come in a day when he looketh not for him, and in an hour that he is not aware of, (51) And shall cut him asunder, and appoint him his portion with the hypocrites: there shall be weeping and gnashing of teeth.

We are advised to keep our spirits alert lest we be caught off-guard by the sudden appearance of the Son of Man. As human beings, if we keep to all the Laws of the God, then we are ready when He comes. His Coming will find us in our places, keeping to His Will. If, however, we forget our tasks and in the meantime indulge in all kinds of wicked acts, obviously His Coming will surprise us. To keep watch is to keep our spirits alert. To keep our intuitions awake and alive. If we do, it would not be difficult for us to recognize the Coming of the Son of Man. If our intuitions are alert, it would be easy to keep to the Laws and as such keep ourselves pure. If we do this then, when the Son of Man comes, we will be chosen, whereas those who have not kept their intuitions alert will be rejected.

We will be like the faithful and wise servant who has administered the household of the Lord with care, kindness and mercy. Our reward will be great indeed, as we will inherit the Kingdom of Heaven.

Keep the lamps of the spirit burning

Matthew 25:1-13 **Then shall the kingdom of heaven be likened unto ten virgins, which took their lamps, and went forth to meet the bridegroom. (2) And five of them were wise, and five were foolish. (3) They that were foolish took their lamps, and took no oil with them: (4) But the wise took oil in their vessels with their lamps. (5) While the bridegroom tarried, they all slumbered and slept. (6) And at midnight there was a cry made, Behold, the bridegroom cometh; go ye out to meet him. (7) Then all those virgins arose, and trimmed their lamps. (8) And the foolish said unto the wise, Give us of your oil; for our lamps are gone out. (9) But the wise answered, saying, Not so; lest there be not enough for us and you: but go ye rather to them that sell, and buy for yourselves. (10) And while they went to buy, the bridegroom came; and they that were ready went in with him to the marriage: and the door was shut. (11) Afterward came also the other virgins, saying, Lord, Lord, open to us. (12) But he answered and said, Verily I say unto you, I know you not. (13) Watch therefore, for ye know neither the day nor the hour wherein the Son of man cometh.**

Those who fail to keep their lamps of the spirits alive, which is their intuitions have to face the fate that Jesus described here. Again, Jesus has used many pictures just like He did earlier in describing the Kingdom of Heaven with so many parables. It is to stress the importance of this event, which is the Last Judgment that He spent so much time on it so that His disciples would understand it. Those who fail in this way and have allowed their intuitions to become dull will not notice when the Son of Man comes. They will either be absent or asleep, whereas those whose lamps of their spirits are alive will recognize the Son of Man when He comes. Those who allowed their lamps to go out will not recognize the Son of Man because one needs the lamp of the intuition to be able to do so.

Without the intuition it becomes impossible to recognize Him. Men of the intellect therefore, who have no vibrations of the spirit run the risk of missing the most important event. It is this intellect which dulls all noble spiritual vibrations and will prevent the proper recognition, which depends solely on the proper vibration of the intuitive faculty. We have to watch out therefore to make certain that in the meantime while we await the Son of Man, we have not allowed our spirits to fall asleep. It is not the keenness of the intellect that matters. It is impossible to recognize the Word of the Son of Man with the intellect, just as it was impossible then for men of the intellect to recognize the Word of Jesus, Son of God. These are spiritual Words which do not speak to the intellect. They appeal to the spirit and it is only those who still have some degree of spiritual vibration left that will be able to recognize this new Word.

The foolish virgins allowed the lamps of their intuitions to go off, they therefore relied solely on the intellect. In doing this, they missed their opportunity when it came. We should watch out lest we face the same fate.

Do not bury your spiritual talents

Matthew 25:14-30 **For the kingdom of heaven is as a man travelling into a far country, who called his own servants, and delivered unto them his goods. (15) And unto one he gave five talents, to another two, and to another one; to every man according to his several ability; and straightway took his journey. (16) Then he that had received the five talents went and traded with the same, and made them other five talents. (17) And likewise he that had received two, he also gained other two. (18) But he that had received one went and digged in the earth, and hid his lord's money. (19) After a long time the lord of those servants cometh, and reckoneth with them. (20) And so he that had received five talents came and brought other five talents, saying, Lord, thou deliveredst unto me five talents: behold, I have gained beside them five talents more. (21) His lord said unto him, Well done, thou good and faithful servant: thou hast been faithful over a few things, I will make thee ruler over many things: enter thou into the joy of thy lord. (22) He also that had received two talents came and said, Lord, thou deliveredst unto me two talents: behold, I**

THE GOSPEL OF MATTHEW

have gained two other talents beside them. **(23)** His lord said unto him, Well done, good and faithful servant; thou hast been faithful over a few things, I will make thee ruler over many things: enter thou into the joy of thy lord. **(24)** Then he which had received the one talent came and said, Lord, I knew thee that thou art an hard man, reaping where thou hast not sown, and gathering where thou hast not strawed: **(25)** And I was afraid, and went and hid thy talent in the earth: lo, there thou hast that is thine. **(26)** His lord answered and said unto him, Thou wicked and slothful servant, thou knewest that I reap where I sowed not, and gather where I have not strawed: **(27)** Thou oughtest therefore to have put my money to the exchangers, and then at my coming I should have received mine own with usury. **(28)** Take therefore the talent from him, and give it unto him which hath ten talents. **(29)** For unto every one that hath shall be given, and he shall have abundance: but from him that hath not shall be taken away even that which he hath. **(30)** And cast ye the unprofitable servant into outer darkness: there shall be weeping and gnashing of teeth.

This is a picture of our relationship with our Creator. We have been given talents or abilities which we are meant to develop in this Creation. The development of our talents and their use is meant to bring many blessings to Creation. We are meant to use our talents to further Creation.

There are many who would develop their talents and use it for just this purpose but there are those who would not. Some will bury their talents and will acquire other abilities which are not part of the natural make-up of the human spirit. We are all given the same talents in an undeveloped form. The variation that we see among human beings is but the way each has chosen to develop. Through the use of their free will, human beings will always develop at different rates and this explains the variation in the level of spiritual development among mankind. Some indeed develop very quickly and have an abundance of spiritual talents. Others are much slower. As long as one continues to work in the right direction, even if slow, we will be accepted, because variation in the speed of spiritual development is always taken into account in Creation and provided for.

If, however, we choose not to develop out talents at all, then it will be taken from us and we will then cease to be. We will lose whatever personality we had developed up till then, and face up to the fate of the lazy virgins.

The Judgment by the Son of Man

Matthew 25:31-46 **When the Son of man shall come in his glory, and all the holy angels with him, then shall he sit upon the throne of his glory: (32) And before him shall be gathered all nations: and he shall separate them one from another, as a shepherd divideth his sheep from the goats: (33) And he shall set the sheep on his right hand, but the goats on the left. (34) Then shall the King say unto them on his right hand, Come, ye blessed of my Father, inherit the kingdom prepared for you from the foundation of the world: (35) For I was an hungred, and ye gave me meat: I was thirsty, and ye gave me drink: I was a stranger, and ye took me in: (36) Naked, and ye clothed me: I was sick, and ye visited me: I was in prison, and ye came unto me. (37) Then shall the righteous answer him, saying, Lord, when saw we thee an hungred, and fed thee? or thirsty, and gave thee drink? (38) When saw we thee a stranger, and took thee in? or naked, and clothed thee? (39) Or when saw we thee sick, or in prison, and came unto thee? (40) And the King shall answer and say unto them, Verily I say unto you, Inasmuch as ye have done it unto one of the least of these my brethren, ye have done it unto me. (41) Then shall he say also unto them on the left hand, Depart from me, ye cursed, into everlasting fire, prepared for the devil and his angels: (42) For I was an hungred, and ye gave me no meat: I was thirsty, and ye gave me no drink: (43) I was a stranger, and ye took me not in: naked, and ye clothed me not: sick, and in prison, and ye visited me not. (44) Then shall they also answer him, saying, Lord, when saw we thee an hungred, or athirst, or a stranger, or naked, or sick, or in prison, and did not minister unto thee? (45) Then shall he answer them, saying, Verily I say unto you, Inasmuch as ye did it not to one of the least of these, ye did it not to me. (46) And these shall go away into everlasting punishment: but the righteous into life eternal.**

Before the final end, there will be a preceding separation into sheep and goats. This means that all human beings will be divided up into two camps. Those who are for God and those who are not. This separation is automatic and mankind will separate themselves through the nature of their activities and behaviours. The Radiation of God mentioned earlier streams into Creation with an unprecedented force and affects human beings in such a way as to compel them to show their true colours.

Those with good spiritual seeds will be encouraged to continue to do so, whereas those who have evil within will be forced through this Power to continue to nourish this evil. Through this, it will be clear to the Light who is for It and who is not. This is an automatic spiritual separation that must precede the eventual destruction. Those who have now separated themselves through the nature of their evil behaviours will be hit by the blows of the Judgment and they will perish, whereas those who are good will be strengthened and preserved. Each one of us will therefore have to watch ourselves and make certain that we do not allow evil to gain a foothold and make us separate ourselves as the goats from the sheep.

4

Gospel of Luke

There are things that Jesus said which are unique only to Luke. It would also be appropriate to examine this Gospel and explore Jesus' Words therein and perhaps arrive at many a solution to some of our questions. There are many aspects which are similar to that of Matthew and which perhaps have already been covered, so we will limit ourselves to those aspects that have not previously been covered.

Luke 1:31 And behold, you will conceive in your womb and bear a son, and you shall call his name Jesus.
We must realise that only in Matthew do we find an attempt to fuse the

prophecy in Isaiah 7:14 "...Behold a virgin shall conceive and bear a son and shall call his name Immanuel..." with the one given here by the Angel Gabriel. At the time of Jesus there was a heightened expectation of the fulfilment of all the prophecies and this expectation must have led Matthew to try and fuse these prophecies without even realising that the names given were different. Isaiah prophesied Imanuel but the Angel Gabriel prophesied Jesus. These are very different prophecies. They require very different fulfilments and circumstances.

Luke 4:18-19 The Spirit of the Lord is upon me, because he hath anointed me to preach the gospel to the poor; he hath sent me to heal the brokenhearted, to preach deliverance to the captives, and recovering of sight to the blind, to set at liberty them that are bruised, (19) To preach the acceptable year of the Lord.

Jesus here, we must realise was not referring to earthly captivity and bondage as indeed most people and most Israelites at that time understood it. He was referring to spiritual bondage. The spiritual always came first with Jesus, as indeed we could glean from His attitude throughout His ministry.

If the people were spiritually free, then earthly freedom would come of its own accord. Most people, however, did not understand this, they saw only the earthly suffering and when they saw that Jesus was apparently not going to do anything about their earthly bondage, they refused to listen to Him. He did not fulfil their expectations of Messiah.

We must remember that these people of their own accord had built up a picture of the kind of Messiah they wanted. He had to correspond exactly to their wishes. The Will of God mattered not in this. They would stipulate conditions and demands on God for the Messiah that He was to send to His creatures. Human arrogance can indeed achieve much.

It was this non-fulfilment of the expectations of many people that led to the hostility and rejection that He experienced. Especially, as He showed so much Power in other directions (in His miracles and so on). They felt that He could use His Power to destroy the Roman legions and set them free, if He wanted to.

What, however, Jesus wanted to teach them was to show them how to look into themselves to discover their faults and reflect on how they came to be in the position of subjugation which they found themselves in. The path towards self-recognition was where Jesus was leading them. This would in the end allow them for all time to avoid sin and avoid the kind of wrongdoing that led them on to slavery and earthly oppression in the first place.

Luke 13:1-5 There were present at that season some that told him of the Galilaeans, whose blood Pilate had mingled with their sacrifices. (2) And Jesus answering said unto them, Suppose ye that these Galilaeans were sinners above all the Galilaeans, because they suffered such things? (3) I tell you, Nay: but, except ye repent, ye shall all likewise perish. (4) Or those eighteen, upon whom the tower in Siloam fell, and slew them, think ye that they were sinners above all men that dwelt in Jerusalem? (5) I tell you, Nay: but, except ye repent, ye shall all likewise perish.

God speaks to His creatures through events. These events are meant as a warning so that we might change our ways in time before the same terrible fate that we see others go through also overtakes us. Other human beings who are going through a terrible fate are not worse off than the rest of humanity, it is only that the time has come for them to receive back the consequences of the deeds that they had put into Creation.

There is always a cycle of the sowing, germinating, maturation, ripening and reaping of all the seeds in this Creation, whether these are the material earthly seeds of corn or rice, or the spiritual seeds of our thoughts and deeds. The same Laws of Creation guide these activities. When the cycle closes for every event, the perpetrators must indeed reap the consequences of their deeds. These consequences roll back and one cycle after another is closed in this way. It is therefore inevitable that one day the time will come for us to reap the consequences of our own deeds.

What therefore we see our neighbours go through will one day be the fate that we will have to bear if we do not learn to change in time. We are indeed meant to open our eyes and change ourselves in time for the better. We are meant to realise through the sufferings that our neighbours are going through that indeed the Laws of this Creation are not mocked. But of course, we dance away the opportunity. We allow ourselves to be comforted too easily. We fail to ask the great questions. As Jesus mentioned here, we are no better than those who suffer these horrible fates, and if we do not learn to change ourselves for the better in time, we will definitely reap the same fate, if not worse.

5

Gospel of John

We have just examined the Words of Jesus as recorded through the Gospels of Matthew and Luke. The Gospels of Saints Mark and Luke were more or less similar except in some minor details. The Gospel of John, however, is very different. It is sometimes felt to represent the developed theological concepts of the first century. It is certainly the most spiritual of the gospels. In examining the Gospel of John, certain concepts which had not been clear will become so and at the same time it will be easier for us to understand so many of what Jesus said and what He really meant. There are issues which are peculiar to John and are not to be found elsewhere.

John 1:1-5 In the beginning was the Word, and the Word was with God, and the Word was God. (2) The same was in the beginning with God. (3) All things were made by him; and without him was not any thing made that was made. (4) In him was life; and the life was the light of men. (5) And the light shineth in darkness; and the darkness comprehended it not.
This is self-explanatory. The Word of God is a part of His Essence. When Jesus brought His Teaching down to us, He brought down the Word of God. He brought down an Essence of the Creator and also the Power of God. God brought Himself to us. We, however, through the influence of the darkness failed to yield to the Word of God. We blindly reviled It and

rejected It. The Light of God in His Word shined when Jesus descended to this earth but the majority of mankind failed to understand Him. We did not want to understand Him because His Teaching was inconvenient to the happy, placid spiritual indolence that had come to characterize mankind.

Jesus demanded work and activity. That was too much for a mankind that had become used to expect to be served. Suddenly, we are meant to serve, and this unfamiliar position made us resentful. Why should we, who were so great serve our neighbours? Why should we love our neighbours? What do we gain from following a teaching that demanded that we give up our exalted positions? These were the questions asked by the intellects of men, and we just could not put up with a teaching as apparently rigorous as this.

In our uncomprehending way, we preferred earthly bliss which lasts for only a very short period to spiritual bliss which lasts for ever. We tried to make a bargain with the Love of God. What is in it for us? We asked. All the darkness had to do was induce us to overdevelop our intellects and no more. Lucifer could then leave mankind on its own, certain that it would always follow his dictates. And why not? The distortion in the human brain guarantees this. He had choked off the spirit. He did not have to especially exert himself very much. He could be certain that his will would always be carried out by those who had become his slaves: the majority of mankind.

John 1:6-9 **There was a man sent from God, whose name was John. (7) The same came for a witness, to bear witness of the Light, that all men through him might believe. (8) He was not that Light, but was sent to bear witness of that Light. (9) That was the true Light, which lighteth every man that cometh into the world.**

It is often the case that before Envoys of God incarnate, Forerunners are sent to the target population to prepare the way. Preparing the way means to remind the hearers of the prophecies and of the Coming of the Envoy. This Forerunner also revives the spiritual teachings of the people. By so doing, he refreshes the memories of the people of the knowledge of God. He concentrates minds and helps focus attention on the prophecies and the impending Coming. In this way, the people would already be on the lookout for the Envoy and it would be easy for them to recognize Him when He comes.

This was the role of John the Baptist. He aroused the people, reminded them of the prophecies, spoke to them about the impending coming of the Messiah and focused attention on this. He got the people thinking about spiritual matters and in this way softened the soil upon which Jesus was to work. It made it easier for Jesus because the people were already aroused spiritually, awaiting the Messiah. They were already open spiritually and it became easier for His Word to penetrate into their spirits.

John 1:10-13 **He was in the world, and the world was made by him, and the world knew him not. (11) He came unto his own, and his own received him not. (12) But as many as received him, to them gave he power to become the sons of God, even to them that believe on his name: (13) Which were born, not of blood, nor of the will of the flesh, nor of the will of man, but of God.**

Jesus, Who was a Part of the Creator came amongst His creatures but these creatures did not recognize their Maker. We rejected Him, and as a result rejected our God. Through thousands of years, men had lost that quality that would have allowed them to recognize God and His Word. Through the overdevelopment of the intellect, the spiritually receptive part of our brains had been neglected and cut off. Through this weakness, any vibrations from the outside never really reached the spirit. It was held in the intellectual brain and never penetrated through to the spiritually receptive brain for onward transmission to the spirit. Therefore, all the Words and miracles of Jesus did not go far into the souls of the majority of people whereby recognition of the Truth of His Word would have been effected.

The recognition of the Word of God and of His Messengers can never be effected through the intellect, because this being lifeless has no connection with the living Power that is God. It was therefore impossible for those who had subjected themselves utterly to the intellect to recognize God and accept Him. This is then the reason for the tragedy whereby creatures whom God had made failed to recognize Him and accept Him. These creatures had made themselves incapable of recognizing their God through their inner condition described above. No one else was to blame for this.

Those who accepted Him however, and adhered to this Word were made into children of God. They became adopted as children because they did things that were pleasing to God. This indeed is the prerequisite to this adoption. No parent would adopt an unworthy child, or a child who is deceitful, who only pays lip-service to the will of its parents. The child must be seen to be truly adapting itself to their will before they can adopt him. This is also true of our relation with God. We must be seen to be truly adapting ourselves to the Will of God before being adopted. It is not just a question of saying that we believe. It is more than lip-service. We must act, and this is why Jesus said it is not 'those who say Lord, Lord but those who do the Will of my Father'.

John 1:14 And the Word was made flesh, and dwelt among us, (and we beheld his glory, the glory as of the only begotten of the Father,) full of grace and truth.

The expression "the Word was made flesh" refers to the Incarnation of Jesus. This incarnation does not correspond to the way we have pictured it. In fact, mankind has not pictured anything at all. There is no clear explanation from anyone as to how the Incarnation came about, or as to what actually happened. According to the book "In the Light of Truth: The Grail Message" by Abd-ru-shin, an Immaculate Conception is a conception in purest love, in contrast to a conception in sinful lust.

When a couple comes together in the purest love for each other, then the conception that takes place is an immaculate physical conception. They have not come together through wild lust for each other but through the greatest love. This is, however, so rare amongst human beings that a special emphasis had to be placed on it. The radiation that comes from such a union is pure and so is the physical body that develops from such a union.

Now, quite aside from an immaculate physical conception, there is also an immaculate spiritual conception. An *Immaculate Spiritual Conception* is that which involves the direct entrance of a Part out of God into a developing physical body. The strength and purity of this Light connection being directly out of God makes this an Immaculate Spiritual Conception. An immaculate physical conception forms the basis for an Immaculate Spiritual Conception. Once the physical body was developing in such circumstances, it was easy for a direct Radiation out of God to reach down and enter the developing physical vessel in Mary.

This is why the events of the Annunciation were so important. Without this event, a gap would have formed which would have made it impossible to piece the events surrounding the birth of Jesus together. As explained earlier, the Annunciation brought about a spiritual upheaval in Mary. It helped to purify her intuitive perceptions and remove all thoughts of a base nature. She therefore bore purity within herself as a result of this event.

This condition of her soul made an immaculate physical conception possible. Her intuition was pure and her coming together with a man was not accompanied by any base thoughts. It could not be, because all she was occupied with was the expectation of a Divine Grace.

With an immaculate physical conception guaranteed, an Immaculate Spiritual Conception could then take place. This involved the direct Radiation connection from God all the way to the developing physical body in the womb of Mary, as mentioned earlier. This was then the entrance of a Part of God, a core of Divinity that is God's into the developing physical vessel. This was then the *Incarnation of Jesus*. This is the process of the Word of God, which is a Part of God *becoming* Flesh. It took on a physical body and appeared on earth as Jesus Christ.

John 1:15-18 **John bare witness of him, and cried, saying, This was he of whom I spake, He that cometh after me is preferred before me: for he was before me. (16) And of his fulness have all we received, and grace for grace. (17) For the law was given by Moses, but grace and truth came by Jesus Christ. (18) No man hath seen God at any time; the only begotten Son, which is in the bosom of the Father, he hath declared him.**

No human being is capable of seeing God. The nature of the human spirit has not within it the possibility to see the Creator. Only Two can see the Creator: the Holy Spirit and the Jesus, the Son of God. It is simply a question of the difference in species. It is natural and just. Now, since no human being is capable of beholding God, He can reveal Himself to us through the form in which He shows Himself to us through His Envoys. Those who have seen Jesus also naturally have seen the form of God and not perhaps God Himself, but the form of God in the Way He shows Himself to us and reveals Himself. The same is true for all creatures, even those in the Divine Realm. God can only be perceived in the Form in which He reveals Himself and not perhaps in His true Nature. That is only possible for Two, as mentioned above.

For those in the Divine Realm to see God, He still has to put on the cloak of Divine Essence for this to be possible. Likewise, for us to be able to see the Creator on earth, He has to, as in the case with Jesus, reveal Himself by putting on a cloak of material substance. The interpretation of the Greek text is very doubtful and one only has to look at the preceding line to know that the follow-on to that would be **"No man hath seen God at any time; the only begotten Son, which is in the bosom of the Father, He has revealed Himself through him or through the Son'.** This means that God Whom no man can see has revealed Himself to us on earth through His Son, Jesus.

John 1:29 **The next day he saw Jesus coming toward him, and said, "Behold, the Lamb of God, who takes away the sin of the world!"**
This statement is not meant to be taken as proof that Jesus' sole Mission was to die and as a result take the world's sins on His shoulders, as has been attempted from the beginning of Christianity. This is not the case. Jesus was the Word Incarnate. If the sins of the world were to be taken away, it was through adherence to this Word. We do not need to change John's sentence, only the prevailing interpretations.

Yes, the sin of the world would be taken away as soon as we adhered to the Word that Jesus represented. Not sooner. If we adhere to this Word as has been explained, the retroactive effects of our good actions will counteract our evil ones and we will be free. Mark us here that some interpretations of this verse use the expression "bears the sin of the world". This could be taken to mean something entirely different. If it is said that He bears the sin of the world, then indeed it could be taken to mean that He actually *bears the marks* of the sins of the world on Him. The sins of our guilt. Through our guilt, He was murdered and symbolically, He bears the wounds and the marks of this terrible crime. The sin of murder is what He bears on Himself. No matter how we interpret this, it does not absolve us from any responsibility. We, in any case will have to account for this dreadful crime wrought upon the Word of God.

John 2:13-16 And the Jews' passover was at hand, and Jesus went up to Jerusalem, (14) And found in the temple those that sold oxen and sheep and doves, and the changers of money sitting: (15) And when he had made a scourge of small cords, he drove them all out of the temple, and the sheep, and the oxen; and poured out the changers' money, and overthrew the tables; (16) And said unto them that sold doves, Take these things hence; make not my Father's house an house of merchandise.

Those who understand spiritual things know exactly the value of a Temple of God. Even more so One descended from God. These people had turned the Temple into a rowdy place where the urge for profit and greed reigned. The Temple of God is for the purest worship of the Almighty. To now turn it into a marketplace obviously would have galled such a One as Jesus, or anyone for that matter who understood the real purpose of a place of Worship.

Some scholars have argued that they were selling things necessary for worship, and that it was legitimate practice but the people who say these things have branded themselves to be incapable of giving any opinion on this matter. They call themselves scholars and as such examine the Word of God with the intellect, which will never be able to understand God. By this very fact alone, their opinions are not called for on these matters and it would be better if they kept quiet and not voice opinions on matters which they do not understand. The reaction of Jesus to this is proof that ever again these intellectuals are wrong.

John 3:1-8 There was a man of the Pharisees, named Nicodemus, a ruler of the Jews: (2) The same came to Jesus by night, and said unto him, Rabbi, we know that thou art a teacher come from God: for no

man can do these miracles that thou doest, except God be with him. (3) Jesus answered and said unto him, Verily, verily, I say unto thee, Except a man be born again, he cannot see the kingdom of God.

Being born again is entirely different from the prevailing conceptions of it. It is not just a question of declaring one's beliefs in Jesus and the entrance of the Holy Spirit into the individual. Being born of the spirit has nothing to do with the Holy Spirit. Nor was Jesus referring to the flesh.

It has everything to do with becoming a completely different human being through a change in behaviours and attitudes. If through the hearing of the Word of God, the individual absorbs this Word in such a way that it works changes in him, and he makes a decision to change his ways for the better and changes his way of thinking, his words and deeds; if now, after having heard the Word of Jesus, begins to think in a better way, begins to act in a better way and his attitude to his neighbours change, then, that is the complete transformation that Jesus was talking about. It is such a change in behaviour that He was referring to. Such a change is from within. Such a change is from the spirit of the individual. Volitions come from the spirit and if now all his volitions are now better as a result of his contact with the Word of God, then that person has been born again in the spirit. This has nothing to do with the Holy Spirit entering the individual.

The Word of God has touched his spirit and has made him to make a decision to change his volition for the better. He now becomes, instead of his former evil self, a good human spirit. Before the contact with the Word of God perhaps he was doing evil, he was an evil person, an evil spirit because he was harming his neighbours with his volitions, his deeds. Now with the contact with the Word, he decided to change himself. Through his desire to make good, he has now transformed himself from an evil spirit to a good one. His spirit has been reborn, renewed. This has nothing to do with the physical. The physical body is lifeless and is incapable of bringing forth such forms of volition that determine the fates of human spirits.

Therefore, it is the personal effort of the individual through making use of the Word of God that makes people reborn. The Holy Spirit does not enter into individuals. This is impossible for quite natural reasons.

The Holy Spirit is the third Personality in the Holy Trinity. It is an Individual, a Part of God. Being a Part of God, it is impossible for Him to enter into people. The human spirit will not be able to bear the approach of the Holy Spirit. The Holy Spirit, as mentioned before is not an amorphous energy and will not enter into human beings.

To be born again in spirit therefore is a condition of having worked on ourselves to purify our intuitive perceptions. It is a question of purifying and making our spirits pure. Our spirit cloaks which were probably very dark and heavy, we make clean and bright through the exercise of pure volition in the direction that Christ pointed, with loving our neighbours as ourselves and much else that He taught us.

John 3:9-15 Nicodemus answered and said unto him, How can these things be? (10) Jesus answered and said unto him, Art thou a master of Israel, and knowest not these things? (11) Verily, verily, I say unto thee, We speak that we do know, and testify that we have seen; and ye receive not our witness. (12) If I have told you earthly things, and ye believe not, how shall ye believe, if I tell you of heavenly things? (13) And no man hath ascended up to heaven, but he that came down from heaven, even the Son of man which is in heaven. (14) And as Moses lifted up the serpent in the wilderness, even so must the Son of man be lifted up: (15) That whosoever believeth in him should not perish, but have eternal life.

The interesting thing about this quotation is about the **"Son of Man Who is in Heaven"**. It has already been noted that Jesus' disciples had a lot of problems understanding their Master and that most of the contradictions that we have today resulted from this lack of understanding. An example is the above. Jesus, until this very day is still regarded as the Son of Man, but there are many verses that see Him referring to this Son of Man in the third Person, or as another person entirely. In verse 13 here he said **"even the Son of Man Who is in Heaven"** which can be taken to mean that He is not the Son of Man but that this Son of Man is in Heaven. He could not possibly be referring to Himself as He was clearly on earth when He made this statement. Then, we have the follow-on to that in verse 14 when He was quoted as saying that "even so the Son of Man be lifted up" which apparently referred to Himself.

These are the misrepresentations and confusions that made many people assume, perhaps with some degree of justification that the Son of God might perhaps also be the Son of Man, even though the Names are clearly different. This interchangeable use of the Son of Man and the Son of God has therefore caused great confusion. These are not the same persons as Jesus could not have been so illogical as to address Himself by the two Names. The fact that Jesus said that He had not come to judge and the fact that the Son of Man had been identified by Him as the Judge is one of the proofs that we can advance in support of two different Personalities.

John 3:16-18 For God so loved the world, that he gave his only begotten Son, that whosoever believeth in him should not perish, but have everlasting life. (17) For God sent not his Son into the world to condemn the world; but that the world through him might be saved. (18) He that believeth on him is not condemned: but he that believeth not is condemned already, because he hath not believed in the name of the only begotten Son of God.

Here Jesus confirmed that He had not come to judge the world. He had not brought the Judgment, and as we have seen in His Words, the Judgment is reserved for another that He has referred to as the Son of Man. He has come to bring the Word of God so that all those who accept It might be saved. Those who believe in Jesus and seek to adjust their lives to the Word that He represents will be saved from Judgment and be given life everlasting. Those who do not believe in Jesus will not be given a second opportunity to reconsider and these, when the Son of Man comes will face Judgment and destruction. The word 'Condemn' here should be taken to mean judge. Jesus only came to save the world. This He came to do through His Word.

The love that God has for the world is so overwhelming that He could send His Son to prevent the destruction of unworthy human beings. That is the sacrifice and the Love that we should ever be grateful for, and the only way to show our gratitude is by adjusting ourselves to His Word as He demanded.

John 3:19-21 And this is the judgment, that the light has come into the

world, and men loved darkness rather than light, because their deeds were evil. (20) For every one who does evil hates the light, and does not come to the light, lest his deeds should be exposed.

As explained earlier, here Jesus described the process of the Judgment in clear terms. The unprecedented surge of Light into the entire Creation through the arrival of the Son of Man puts everything in motion in this Creation, even that which would wish to hide. That which would wish to hide of course, are the works of the darkness. These works will not be able to hide anymore. All the evil lurking within human beings will be activated so that they may act in accordance with their nature and be exposed for all to see. It is of no avail for those who wish to hide, the Light will reach them and they will be forced to act in ways that correspond to their inner being. If they had previously been protected through their comfortable earthly circumstances, these will be taken away so as to allow them to show themselves.

Those who are good have nothing to fear. Nothing but good will come from them as they do not harbour any evil within themselves. The good that they harbour within will also be exposed for all to see, and for them to be shown to be children of God through their activities.

John 4:20-26 Our fathers worshipped in this mountain; and ye say, that in Jerusalem is the place where men ought to worship. (21) Jesus saith unto her, Woman, believe me, the hour cometh, when ye shall neither in this mountain, nor yet at Jerusalem, worship the Father. (22) Ye worship ye know not what: we know what we worship: for salvation is of the Jews. (23) But the hour cometh, and now is, when the true worshippers shall worship the Father in spirit and in truth: for the Father seeketh such to worship him. (24) God is a Spirit: and they that worship him must worship him in spirit and in truth. (25) The woman saith unto him, I know that Messias cometh, which is called Christ: when he is come, he will tell us all things. (26) Jesus saith unto her, I that speak unto thee am he.

Jesus here spoke of the establishment of the Kingdom of God on earth, when human beings who have accepted the Lord would worship Him in the proper way. During this time, which is not far off, the knowledge of the

Will of God would have so advanced that the people would know exactly what is needed for the true worship of the Almighty. It is only through knowledge of the Laws of God as explained by Jesus, or by One like Him that this would happen.

These would then be the true worshippers of God because they would have come to learn to know all the Laws of God and as a result adjusted themselves in happiness to His Will. It will be worship through the intuitive perception and through the opening of their spirits to the Power of God.

God is obviously not a Spirit but His Power is Spirit. He Himself is far above this, but His Holy Spirit, which is responsible for the coming into being of the entire Creation demands that we worship Him with our inner being. If we are able to worship God in spirit, then it does not matter where we find ourselves. As long as we are able to open ourselves to Him in humble supplication, then we worship. For those who truly worship God, time and place do not count. We will worship God with the activity of our spirits. It is through the deed that henceforth we shall worship the Creator.

Through our activities in thoughts, words and deeds, we shall show the Creator that we have absorbed His Word and that we are happy to adjust to all His Laws. That is true worship. It is not the saying of prayers by the hundred. If through our intuitive perceptions we honour our neighbours, and we do not do anything that will harm them, then, we honour the Creator and these good works are the testimony to Him that we love Him and His Laws and we voluntarily adjust ourselves to them. That is the true worship in truth and spirit. Through our everyday activities is how we should now worship and not just once a week on the Sabbath. Through how we adjust ourselves every single minute of the day is how we worship God in truth, and this is why Jesus said that neither on this mountain nor in Jerusalem. It is in our everyday lives wherever we are.

John 4:32-38 **But he said unto them, I have meat to eat that ye know not of. (33) Therefore said the disciples one to another, Hath any man brought him ought to eat? (34) Jesus saith unto them, My meat is to do the will of him that sent me, and to finish his work. (35) Say not ye, There are yet four months, and then cometh harvest? behold, I say unto you, Lift up your eyes, and look on the fields; for they are**

white already to harvest. (36) And he that reapeth receiveth wages, and gathereth fruit unto life eternal: that both he that soweth and he that reapeth may rejoice together. (37) And herein is that saying true, One soweth, and another reapeth. (38) I sent you to reap that whereon ye bestowed no labour: other men laboured, and ye are entered into their labours.

Obviously here Jesus referred to spiritual food which brings much happiness and is capable of sustaining Him. His sustenance is the happiness that He gets when people change and accept His Word. He went on to say that His sustenance is to do the Will of God Who sent Him. If He can do that then He is happy and filled. He is sustained. That for Him is the elixir of life.

He then asked His disciples to look around them at the people. They were ripe for spiritual help. They were ready to hear of the Word, and all that the disciples had to do was speak with them. Others had laboured, which meant the prophets of old who preceded them had done all the work, including John the Baptist in preparing this people for spiritual salvation. The easy part was what the disciples had to do, which was speak to them about the Kingdom of God. They would listen and accept. The experiences over millennia, and the work of prophets had brought these people to a point in their spiritual development where it would be easy to make them understand more about the Kingdom of God.

The seeds had already been sown by others in the spirits of these people. These seeds had blossomed, it had ripened and it was now ready for harvest. Others had done the hard work He told them and was now sending them out to reap what others had sown. To complete what others had started.

The healing at the pool:

John 5:13-14 And he that was healed wist not who it was: for Jesus had conveyed himself away, a multitude being in that place. (14) Afterward Jesus findeth him in the temple, and said unto him, Behold, thou art made whole: sin no more, lest a worse thing come unto thee.

Contrary to conventional concepts, diseases occur solely as a result of our not following the Will of God. Jesus proves this with this statement. Hereditary diseases or whatever diseases that we suffer occur as a result of something that we had put into Creation and are now paying for with this disease. This man that Jesus spoke to was crippled because of some heavy karma which resulted in him being paralysed, and Jesus having healed him advised him not to repeat the same mistake which might even lead to something worse happening to him. This goes to prove that his condition was brought on by himself through some guilt or the other.

This man had received grace from the Son of God and he was now to conduct himself in such a way as to prove himself worthy of this grace. If he backslided and reverted to his former evil ways, then he would have proven himself unworthy of this grace and will not be helped in future if something else happened to him. He will attract a greater guilt upon himself for not adhering to the Word of God, Who had given him such grace. The onus is on this man to adjust himself strictly to the Word of God. The same applies today as it did then. Those of us who had been helped by God out of some distress would do well to keep our promises to Him. If we fail to do this, then we will fall even deeper and the help of God will not be extended to us anymore.

It is time to realize that whatever happens to us can only be as a result of our faults and our not adhering to the Laws of God. It is not some genetic mishap. We are attracted to parents through the Law of Reciprocal Action, who carry these diseases within themselves. There can be no injustice in Creation. Through having these conditions, we are perhaps forced to ponder the reason for it and change for the better.

John 5:16-18 **And therefore the Jews persecuted Jesus, and sought to slay him, because he had done these things on the sabbath. (17) But Jesus answered them, My Father worketh hitherto, and I work. (18) Therefore the Jews sought the more to kill him, because he not only had broken the sabbath, but said also that God was his Father, making himself equal with God.**

There is no standstill in Creation. It is unnatural to set apart one day in which we all decide to do good, which we call the Sabbath. We must uphold the Laws of God and worship Him every minute of the day through our activities. But of course this principle was not understood by the Pharisees at that time and even today it is still not understood. They would have the Son of God adhere to their earthly mundane laws that they had devised with their brains.

John 5:19-21 **Then answered Jesus and said unto them, Verily, verily, I say unto you, The Son can do nothing of himself, but what he seeth the Father do: for what things soever he doeth, these also doeth the Son likewise. (20) For the Father loveth the Son, and sheweth him all things that himself doeth: and he will shew him greater works than these, that ye may marvel. (21) For as the Father raiseth up the dead, and quickeneth them; even so the Son quickeneth whom he will.**

Continuing from the verses previously, the Pharisees were angry that Jesus equated Himself with God. He tried to explain to them that God is in Him as He worked. The mystery of this union was not understood until now. Through the explanation given in the book "In the Light of Truth: The Grail Message" by Abd-ru-shin, it is now possible to do so. With the incarnation of Jesus, God severed a small Part of Himself, Which Part nevertheless remained connected with Him. It is this connection with God that made it possible for God to work through Jesus. The nature of this Divine Mystery which was the focus of many ecumenical councils was not resolved until now.

John 5:22-23 **For the Father judgeth no man, but hath committed all judgment unto the Son: (23) That all men should honour the Son, even as they honour the Father. He that honoureth not the Son honoureth not the Father which hath sent him.**

Since Jesus and the Son of Man possessed the same Core as God, then those who obey the Son have already obeyed the Father and vice versa. Here Jesus again re-iterated that the Judgment has been committed to the Son. Although He did not specify which Son but from what He had been saying all along, the Son is to be assumed to be the Son of Man.

John 5:24-27 **Verily, verily, I say unto you, He that heareth my word,** and believeth on him that sent me, hath everlasting life, and shall not come into condemnation; but is passed from death unto life. (25) Verily, verily, I say unto you, The hour is coming, and now is, when the dead shall hear the voice of the Son of God: and they that hear shall live. (26) For as the Father hath life in himself; so hath he given to the Son to have life in himself; (27) And hath given him authority to execute judgment also, because he is the Son of man.

Again the confirmation that the Son of Man executes the Judgment. He says here that the dead will hear the Voice of the Son of God. Here of course He did not mean the physically dead as we might like to interpret this. As always Jesus spoke in a comprehensive spiritual way and was referring to all that is spiritually dead among mankind. Those whose spiritual qualities were asleep. His Word was capable of awakening these qualities and bringing them to life.

If we listened to the Word that came from Jesus, we would change for the better and overcome the evil that we have within. This evil then will not be able to harm us because we will be free from it through adjusting to the Will of God. Otherwise, this evil will grow stronger through the effect of the Rays of God and can drive us to perdition. We must be able to deal with all the evil that we still have within us on time.

The Voice of the Son of Man shall reverberate through the lands and will awaken even the deadest (spiritually dead) souls and all the hitherto inactive evil in man to activity. Exactly as each one reacts to this Word he will be judged. If the individual heeds the Voice of the Son of Man, then he shall be allowed to see the new day, but if he rejects the Voice of the Son of Man, he shall face Judgment, which the Son of Man has been authorized by God to dispense.

John 5:28-30 **Marvel not at this: for the hour is coming, in the which all that are in the graves shall hear his voice, (29) And shall come forth; they that have done good, unto the resurrection of life; and they that have done evil, unto the resurrection of damnation. (30) I can of mine own self do nothing: as I hear, I judge: and my judgment is just; because I seek not mine own will, but the will of the Father which hath sent me.**

It is the same process as described above whereby all that is dead in creation, that is, all the hitherto inert spiritual qualities of man will be roused to show themselves through becoming active. Through this activity, it would be revealed to the Light. If it is a good activity it will survive but if not, it will be destroyed along with all the human beings who attach themselves to it.

All human faults and weaknesses will be struck by this Power of the Light and also all good qualities. All these will reveal to which side they belong: the darkness or the Light through their activities. The human beings who carry these qualities within themselves will be forced to act in the way these qualities demand. If evil they will force their possessors to act in that way and vice versa. As the evil reveals itself in its activities, it is destroyed by the Light along with the human beings who are custodians of this evil. We should therefore be on the look out for the faults that we possess and make all the efforts now to overcome them and not allow them to become too powerful. These faults will be struck down and we have to make certain that we do not get struck down with them.

John 5:31-40 **If I bear witness of myself, my witness is not true. (32) There is another that beareth witness of me; and I know that the witness which he witnesseth of me is true. (33) Ye sent unto John, and he bare witness unto the truth. (34) But I receive not testimony from man: but these things I say, that ye might be saved. (35) He was a burning and a shining light: and ye were willing for a season to rejoice in his light. (36) But I have greater witness than that of John: for the works which the Father hath given me to finish, the same works that I do, bear witness of me, that the Father hath sent me. (37) And the Father himself, which hath sent me, hath borne witness of me. Ye have neither heard his voice at any time, nor seen his shape. (38) And ye have not his word abiding in you: for whom he hath sent, him ye believe not. (39) Search the scriptures; for in them ye think ye have eternal life: and they are they which testify of me. (40) And ye will not come to me, that ye might have life.**

The Works that Jesus accomplished is the proof of His connection with the Creator. God, by allowing Him to accomplish such works testifies in

His favour. He testifies to the fact that Jesus was from Him. Because of this fact, His descent from God was not in question. Just because of this fact alone, the Pharisees and scribes should have believed Him and gone to Him for the redemption of their spirits.

They would rather search and read the Scriptures, expecting to discover therein a way to eternal Life, whereas the road was standing right amongst them. The same is true today whereby instead of looking around for the Truth that must be obvious, we close ourselves blindly to the new. The Pharisees should have accepted the new that came with Jesus but they did not, just because it was new. They would rather stick to the old and search therein. They felt that the new Teaching that Jesus brought was different to what they were used to. They thereby out of fear closed themselves to It.

It is the same today. Many of us would close ourselves to the new Teaching that Jesus has promised out of the same fear that it is not familiar, we would rummage and search the Scriptures intending to discover therein the way to eternal Life when all we have to do is be on the alert so as not to miss this new Teaching, and as such not miss the Bridegroom when He comes.

John 5:41-47 I receive not honour from men. (42) But I know you, that ye have not the love of God in you. (43) I am come in my Father's name, and ye receive me not: if another shall come in his own name, him ye will receive. (44) How can ye believe, which receive honour one of another, and seek not the honour that cometh from God only? (45) Do not think that I will accuse you to the Father: there is one that accuseth you, even Moses, in whom ye trust. (46) For had ye believed Moses, ye would have believed me: for he wrote of me. (47) But if ye believe not his writings, how shall ye believe my words?

The Pharisees and scribes and in fact, the generality of the people would prefer to be deceived and led astray by human beings who know how to tell them what they want to hear. These deceivers cunningly set out teachings adjusted to the weaknesses of their hearers. This actually happened many times in Israel when many would-be leaders declared themselves to be the Messiah and led the Israelites to senseless revolts against the Romans. These frequently led to massacres of the Jews.

The people would rather accept such people who would promise them earthly kingdoms and comfort than One Who promised them an eternal spiritual freedom from which was also to arise eventually the earthly freedom that they craved.

John 6:25-27 **When they found him on the other side of the sea, they said to him, "Rabbi, when did you come here?" (26) Jesus answered them, "Truly, truly, I say to you, you seek me, not because you saw signs, but because you ate your fill of the loaves. (27) Do not labor for the food which perishes, but for the food which endures to eternal life, which the Son of man will give to you; for on him has God the Father set his seal."**

Jesus speaks of the Son of Man in the third person, which indeed He frequently did. This goes to show that this Son of Man is not Jesus. He said that the Son of Man shall give the meat of life. The Son of Man, the Holy Spirit will give us the eternal meat, if we obey Him. The eternal meat is the Word and Power of God that nourishes the spirit. This is the manna for the spirit. Its elixir of life. He went on to say also in the third person that God had placed the seal of approval on the Son of Man. The seal of approval as His Son and to act as His Envoy in all matters in Creation.

John 6:30-32 **They said therefore unto him, What sign shewest thou then, that we may see, and believe thee? what dost thou work? (31) Our fathers did eat manna in the desert; as it is written, He gave them bread from heaven to eat. (32) Then Jesus said unto them, Verily, verily, I say unto you, Moses gave you not that bread from heaven; but my Father giveth you the true bread from heaven.**

The true bread of the Creator is His Word. His Word came down from Heaven in the form of Jesus. If we accept Him, we would have eaten from the true bread of eternal life that feeds our spirits. The Word is like food to our spirits. Without It, we would soon vegetate and this is literally true. The real food of the spirit is the Word of God. The spirit absorbs of the Radiation that comes from the Word of God for its sustenance. The lack of this emasculates the spirit just as the lack of physical food in time emasculates the physical body and makes it weak. This actually happens. The more of the Word of God that we are able to absorb into our spirits, the stronger we become because the closer we are drawn to Him.

John 6:34-40 **Then said they unto him, Lord, evermore give us this bread. (35) And Jesus said unto them, I am the bread of life: he that cometh to me shall never hunger; and he that believeth on me shall never thirst. (36) But I said unto you, That ye also have seen me, and believe not. (37) All that the Father giveth me shall come to me; and him that cometh to me I will in no wise cast out. (38) For I came down from heaven, not to do mine own will, but the will of him that sent me. (39) And this is the Father's will which hath sent me, that of all which he hath given me I should lose nothing, but should raise it up again at the last day. (40) And this is the will of him that sent me, that every one which seeth the Son, and believeth on him, may have everlasting life: and I will raise him up at the last day.**

He who has spiritual knowledge knows all things, he bathes in this knowledge, he absorbs this knowledge and without thinking has the answers to all questions. He will never thirst anymore for knowledge because his thirst has been quenched by the knowledge that he already possesses. Jesus was not referring to physical hunger and thirst. He was referring to spiritual hunger and thirst. The person with spiritual knowledge is continually been replenished so much so that his spiritual body will never become weak again due to lack of spiritual food or water. His spiritual body bathes in the Truth. He is constantly absorbing from the Truth and as such need never go hungry or thirsty. As long as he remains true to the Light, he will never want for anything. He will be strong because he is connected to the Light.

John 6:43-46 **Jesus therefore answered and said unto them, Murmur not among yourselves. (44) No man can come to me, except the Father which hath sent me draw him: and I will raise him up at the last day. (45) It is written in the prophets, And they shall be all taught of God. Every man therefore that hath heard, and hath**

**learned of the Father, cometh unto me. (46) Not that any man hath
seen the Father, save he which is of God, he hath seen the Father.**

This is to prove to the Pharisees that He was not talking about any physical bread. He was speaking about food for the spirit. Food to prevent the
spirit from weakening and eventually dying. It is only One from God
Who is capable of giving such food in the form of the Word.

Since Jesus was the Word incarnate in Flesh, then this Word is His
Flesh. Those who absorb of His Word have also eaten of His Flesh. The
words may sound sharp but that is the reality here. Those who absorb the
Word of God into themselves in its entirety have eaten of the Flesh of
Jesus and have drank Hid Blood.

The manna from Heaven that the Israelites' forefathers ate was meant
to sustain them physically. They died physically, but the bread that Jesus
was referring to was food for the spirit.

John 6:52-58 **The Jews therefore strove among themselves, saying,
How can this man give us his flesh to eat? (53) Then Jesus said unto
them, Verily, verily, I say unto you, Except ye eat the flesh of the Son
of man, and drink his blood, ye have no life in you. (54) Whoso
eateth my flesh, and drinketh my blood, hath eternal life; and I will
raise him up at the last day. (55) For my flesh is meat indeed, and
my blood is drink indeed. (56) He that eateth my flesh, and drinketh
my blood, dwelleth in me, and I in him. (57) As the living Father
hath sent me, and I live by the Father: so he that eateth me, even he
shall live by me. (58) This is that bread which came down from heav-
en: not as your fathers did eat manna, and are dead: he that eateth of
this bread shall live for ever.**
The Word is the Flesh of both the Son of God and the Son of Man. Those
who absorb of their Word have absorbed Them. He has eaten their Flesh
and drank their Blood. The Word becomes Flesh on earth through the
incarnation of these Two, as mentioned earlier. Those who absorb the
Word are eating of the Flesh and drinking the Blood of either the Son of
Man or of the Son of God.

John 7:33-34 Jesus then said, "I shall be with you a little longer, and then I go to him who sent me; (34) you will seek me and you will not find me; where I am you cannot come."

Jesus was going back into the Father in the Divine Realm which is closed to human spirits. Human spirits can only return to the Spiritual realm which is their origin but never beyond that, and this is the reason for Jesus saying that He was going to a place that we cannot follow Him into.

John 7:50-52 Nicodemus, who had gone to him before, and who was one of them, said to them, (51) "Does our law judge a man without first giving him a hearing and learning what he does?" (52) They replied, "Are you from Galilee too? Search and you will see that no prophet is to rise from Galilee."

This was one of the big controversies in the reluctance of the Pharisees to believe in Jesus. Being men of the letter of the law, they had read that the Messiah was to born in Bethlehem of Judea. Now this Jesus was from Nazareth. How could He then be the Messiah? It was not Jesus' place to tell them or convince them. Wherever He was born did not matter as long as He had His connection to God and He was able to work amongst the people. It was the duty of the Pharisees to find out more about Jesus. Their spiritual indolence, however, prevented this. Their salvation depended on this and they should have made greater efforts to investigate Jesus. They would have discovered that in fact He was born in Bethlehem. Whether that would have convinced them is open to question in view of their constant request for signs from Jesus.

John 8:31-32 Jesus then said to the Jews who had believed in him, "If you continue in my word, you are truly my disciples, (32) and you will know the truth, and the truth will make you free."

The question of freedom here has nothing to do with the earthly freedom that the Jews were expecting of their Messiah. Jesus was speaking about spiritual freedom. Freedom from having to commit sins. The individual who is truly free is he who is free spiritually from the entanglements that sins are bound to weave. As have been discussed, a transgression against the Will of God, whether in the form of evil thoughts, words or deeds leads to the formation of threads of fate attached to the producers of such works. These threads bind the individual and eventually control the free will of that individual because they attach this or that propensity to him so that he continues to behave in the fashion that these thought-forms desire.

Through this process, he has actually lost his free will. He is no longer free to decide in which direction his volitions are to go. These volitions go in the directions desired by the propensity only. In addition, he, through his evil actions has bound himself to those that he has harmed and will have to live through the consequences of every single wrong deed before he is free from these threads. These threads are like chains that fetter him down and prevent his ascent to better regions.

Those who know the Truth through their acceptance of the Word of God know exactly what they have to do to free themselves from these fetters. They have the knowledge that they must stop thinking, speaking and acting in an evil manner. This knowledge allows them to apply their volitions in a better direction, which leads them to form good works which in time counteract the evil that they had previously done. This counteractive effect eventually dissipates their previous evil and they become free, provided that they do not add more evil to the previous ones.

The Truth that Jesus brought is this knowledge that will set people free. Truth is knowledge and also the Way and since Jesus embodied this Truth, He could claim that He was the Way to the Father. The Truth that He represented and embodied is the Way to God and freedom from sin.

John 8:33-41 They answered him, We be Abraham's seed, and were never in bondage to any man: how sayest thou, Ye shall be made free? (34) Jesus answered them, Verily, verily, I say unto you, Whosoever committeth sin is the servant of sin. (35) And the servant abideth not in the house for ever: but the Son abideth ever. (36) If the Son therefore shall make you free, ye shall be free indeed. (37) I know that ye are Abraham's seed; but ye seek to kill me, because my word hath no place in you. (38) I speak that which I have seen with my Father: and ye do that which ye have seen with your father. (39) They answered and said unto him, Abraham is our father. Jesus saith unto

them, **If ye were Abraham's children, ye would do the works of Abraham. (40) But now ye seek to kill me, a man that hath told you the truth, which I have heard of God: this did not Abraham. (41) Ye do the deeds of your father. Then said they to him, We be not born of fornication; we have one Father, even God.**

Their statements point to the fact that they had not the faintest idea of what Jesus was saying. Every word of Jesus was always pressed down into the dust by these people. They could never perceive intuitively for once. They could only think of earthly bondage and freedoms. As mentioned earlier, sinning leads to a propensity to continue to sin in the process described above. It is this propensity, like all propensities that is tantamount to slavery. And as slaves, our lives are not worth much. These people liked to claim that they were descendants of Abraham, but as Jesus said, they did not act like him. In fact, they acted contrary to what Abraham stood for.

John 8:42-47 Jesus said unto them, If God were your Father, ye would love me: for I proceeded forth and came from God; neither came I of myself, but he sent me. (43) Why do ye not understand my speech? even because ye cannot hear my word. (44) Ye are of your father the devil, and the lusts of your father ye will do. He was a murderer from the beginning, and abode not in the truth, because there is no truth in him. When he speaketh a lie, he speaketh of his own: for he is a liar, and the father of it. (45) And because I tell you the truth, ye believe me not. (46) Which of you convinceth me of sin? And if I say the truth, why do ye not believe me? (47) He that is of God heareth God's words: ye therefore hear them not, because ye are not of God.

The scribes and Pharisees, through their enslavement to the intellect have become Lucifer's servants. As a result, they could not bear to listen to Words that proceeded form the Luminous Heights. The darkness cannot bear the Light. It tries to hide or escape. These people have become Lucifer's seeds and can only act according to their nature, which is to oppose all that is of the Light.

Those who are children of God will hear His Word and those who are of the devil will listen only to the devil's commands. Through their behaviour and attitude towards the Word of Jesus, they marked themselves out as belonging to the darkness. No other proof is needed. After all, in the Judgment that is the yardstick that will be used: people will be judged according to their attitude to the new Word, either accepting It, in which case they are saved, or rejecting it in which case they will have to face the night of horror.

If the seed within these people was of God, then they would listen to Jesus but this was not the case as they opposed and antagonized Him until finally they found a way to be rid of Him.

John 8:48-51 **Then answered the Jews, and said unto him, Say we not well that thou art a Samaritan, and hast a devil? (49) Jesus answered, I have not a devil; but I honour my Father, and ye do dishonour me. (50) And I seek not mine own glory: there is one that seeketh and judgeth. (51) Verily, verily, I say unto you, If a man keep my saying, he shall never see death.**
Jesus was not referring to physical death as it should have been surmised by now. He was referring to the fact that those who believe in Him and act according to His Will would act in such a way as to escape spiritual death. We all must die physically. Physical death is universal to all but not spiritual death. The latter is the fate of those who continually reject the help that God has always sent them for their salvation.

Avoidance of spiritual death requires that we live a pure life so that we can free ourselves in time from the sphere of matter and avoid going through the same disintegration to which all matter is subject. All that has been created in the World of Matter must one day undergo disintegration for the purpose of renewal. If there are still human beings on the particular celestial globe who had not purified themselves enough before the arrival of this time, they would have to undergo the same fate as the celestial body. Their ethereal bodies will be dragged through the mills of disintegration and the suffering engendered by this experience leads to loss of consciousness The spirit germ returns to its former state of unconscious formlessness.

The accumulated experiences of millennia, which he possessed within him and the form that his spirit may have acquired up till then is reversed. His personality up till then would have been found to be useless. He has developed his personality in the wrong direction and as such is not useful for the upward swinging of the Universe. It must be ground to dust. This is the self same process on earth whereby people lose consciousness when subjected to the most intense pain. Only in the case of the spirit, there is to be no awakening for such an individual. The ethereal form is ground to dust but the spirit reverts to being a spirit germ.

John 8:52-53 The Jews said to him, "Now we know that you have a demon. Abraham died, as did the prophets; and you say, 'If any one keeps my word, he will never taste death.' (53) Are you greater than our father Abraham, who died? And the prophets died! Who do you claim to be?"

Again the pride "we have Abraham as our father". Their gazes, just as is the case today on earth is turned downwards towards only the material. They had no spiritual understanding whatsoever, as can be surmised from their words. It was like with every discussion Jesus had with these people He managed more and more to expose their ignorance and hollowness. How these people could claim to be spiritual teachers and guides baffles the imagination. They are absolutely spiritually dead and no further proof of that than their own words is needed for this conclusion to be drawn.

John 10:1-5 Verily, verily, I say unto you, He that entereth not by the door into the sheepfold, but climbeth up some other way, the same is a thief and a robber. (2) But he that entereth in by the door is the shepherd of the sheep. (3) To him the porter openeth; and the sheep hear his voice: and he calleth his own sheep by name, and leadeth them out. (4) And when he putteth forth his own sheep, he goeth before them, and the sheep follow him: for they know his voice. (5) And a stranger will they not follow, but will flee from him: for they know not the voice of strangers.

This is the description of spiritual highway men who hijack many souls on their way to the Luminous Heights. People that are perhaps not sufficiently alert with their spirits will be misled by the teachings of these highwaymen who work for the darkness. They are the ones who come in through the back door and lurk in the dark because they cannot face the Light of Truth and will never agree to an objective examination of their teachings. They shroud whatever they teach in some form of mysticism whereby only the initiated are admitted.

The real shepherd, however, has all knowledge because of His connection to God. He has nothing to fear and as such declares His Teachings openly. He addresses all human beings and all He desires is that human beings approach His Words with open unbiased minds, as that is the only way that they can help themselves.

Those who keep their intuitions open will hear this Voice of the true Shepherd. It will be a familiar sound to them because the Words of the Shepherd are natural and are from God and just because every human being bears within himself the recognition of God, His Words will sound familiar. They will follow this Shepherd, that is, those whose spirits are open. Not so, however, for those who in the meantime have chosen to have another master. The Voice of the Redeemer will not be their master's voice and they will not follow Him. In fact, like ravenous wolves they will seek to attack Him. These people will only listen to the voice of their master, who is Lucifer.

Those, however, who belong to the Lord or the true Shepherd need not fear the spiritual highwaymen. Their open intuitions will never allow them to fall into the hands of such. Theirs will be unfamiliar voices to them. They are spiritually alert enough to wave off such people. Therein lies their protection. Everyone else will fall victim to these highwaymen and will follow them since they are simply following a voice that they are familiar with: that of the darkness. They wished for nothing else. The misplaced fear that people have today for the so-called false prophets are not justified. It is all a question of opening one's spirit and it will be easy to recognize which teachings are true and which are not.

In the final analysis, this time, we must look for the right new Teaching that Jesus promised us and it is our duty to go out there and investigate. At the same time, we must not say that we have it all in the Bible and that we need nothing else. Those who say this have not read their Bibles at all. They are lazy servants who face the *too late*.

Jesus Himself promised the new Teaching through the Spirit of Truth and they would contradict Jesus because of their unwillingness to make the personal effort towards their own salvation. The words **"Albeit when the spirit of Truth will come and He will teach you all things"** will rise up before them in the last days and they will be forced to mourn the loss of so much time.

John 10:11-13 **I am the good shepherd. The good shepherd lays down his life for the sheep. (12) He who is a hireling and not a shepherd, whose own the sheep are not, sees the wolf coming and leaves the sheep and flees; and the wolf snatches them and scatters them. (13) He flees because he is a hireling and cares nothing for the sheep.**

With the analogy of the good shepherd, Jesus has declared here that if need be, He was willing to lay down His Life for the preservation of His Word among mankind so that we might continue to have It for our spiritual progress. He was willing to do whatever it takes. This is not to say that He was destined to die and that His death will carry away anyone's sins but that if it came to it, He was ready to defend His Word and Its preservation on earth so that those who believe might continue to have It. He was ready to face the darkness head on, even if it meant the destruction of His physical body.

Spiritual highwaymen and false teachers do not care about the preservation for their word or the human spirits they preach to. They only want the temporary earthly gain. They will never risk their lives as they have no one else's interest at heart.

John 10:14-18 **I am the good shepherd; I know my own and my own know me, (15) as the Father knows me and I know the Father; and I lay down my life for the sheep. (16) And I have other sheep, that are not of this fold; I must bring them also, and they will heed my voice. So there shall be one flock, one shepherd. (17) For this reason the Father loves me, because I lay down my life, that I may take it again. (18) No one takes it from me, but I lay it down of my own accord. I have power to lay it down, and I have power to take it again; this charge I have received from my Father."**

Again Jesus emphasized that He was prepared out of His Own volition to lay down His Life for the preservation of His Word. He was not going to allow those who could only kill the physical body to stand in the way of redemption for mankind. That is the sacrifice that He was prepared to make. His Love for mankind allowed Him to make this greatest of Sacrifices.

The Gospel of John is particularly useful in regard to the exposition of the identity of the Son of Man.

The Son of Man

John 14:15-16 **If ye love me, keep my commandments. (16) And I will pray the Father, and he shall give you another Comforter, that he may abide with you for ever;**
John 14:25-26 **These things have I spoken unto you, being yet present with you. (26) But the Comforter, which is the Holy Ghost, whom the Father will send in my name, he shall teach you all things, and bring all things to your remembrance, whatsoever I have said unto you.**
John 14:30 **I will no longer talk much with you, for the ruler of this world is coming. He has no power over me;**
John 15:26 **But when the Counselor comes, whom I shall send to you from the Father, even the Spirit of truth, who proceeds from the Father, he will bear witness to me;**
John 16:7-15 **Nevertheless I tell you the truth; It is expedient for you that I go away: for if I go not away, the Comforter will not come unto you; but if I depart, I will send him unto you. (8) And when he is come, he will reprove the world of sin, and of righteousness, and of judgment: (9) Of sin, because they believe not on me; (10) Of righteousness, because I go to my Father, and ye see me no more; (11) Of judgment, because the prince of this world is judged. (12) I have yet many things to say unto you, but ye cannot bear them now. (13) Howbeit when he, the Spirit of truth, is come, he will guide you into all truth: for he shall not speak of himself; but whatsoever he shall hear, that shall he speak: and he will shew you things to come. (14) He shall glorify me: for he shall receive of mine, and shall shew it**

unto you. (15) All things that the Father hath are mine: therefore said I, that he shall take of mine, and shall shew it unto you.

Jesus could not be referring to Himself when He mentioned the Spirit of Truth or the Comforter. It is generally agreed that here the Holy Spirit is meant. What is, however, not clear is how the Holy Spirit is to manifest. The conventional explanation is that He had already appeared when He descended on the disciples at Whitsuntide allowing them to speak in tongues. The prophecy of the fulfillment of the Comforter, of the Spirit of Truth that the verses above refer to, according to present belief has already been achieved through the descent of the Power of the Holy Spirit two thousand years ago on the disciples.

If we look at these verses carefully, however, it is clear that this is not the case. Jesus here promised a personal fulfillment. He said that the Holy Ghost will *teach* us all things and will *bring* things to our remembrance. This looks very much like a personal fulfillment. It looks very much like the Holy Ghost will come personally to teach mankind and bring the Teachings of Jesus to our remembrance.

He went on to say that the "ruler of this world is coming". Obviously here, He could not be referring to Himself in the third person. He was referring to the same Holy Ghost. The Holy Ghost, according to this verse is not some amorphous power but a Personality. If He is the ruler of this world, then He must be personal and not some amorphous force. He said that this ruler of this world, the Holy Ghost has no power over Him, which indicates that this Holy Ghost and Jesus are equals.

He also said that this Holy Ghost or the Spirit of Truth will bear witness to Him, Jesus. It is obvious that to bear witness to Jesus has nothing to do with the interpretations which have become prevalent. This has nothing to do with human beings at all. We attach too much importance to our roles. It is easier for us to understand this verse if we accept that the Holy Ghost is a Personality. An amorphous energy cannot bear witness to anyone. It is only a person who can do this. If, therefore, the Holy Ghost is a Personality, then it becomes clear that in fulfilling His Mission, this Holy Ghost will take of the Teaching of Jesus, will remind us of It and by so doing will bear witness to the authenticity of Jesus' Message.

With His impending departure, Jesus tried to assure His disciples to take heart. His departure will be painful for them and subsequent follow-ers but He was not going to leave us alone. He was going to pray God to give us another like Him, Who will abide with us forever. Jesus' Mission was to be a short one and for us not to be abandoned to the whims of the darkness He was going to ask God for **"the Ruler of this World"** to be sent to us to remain with us for ever. This obviously, if properly thought out will never be an impersonal fulfillment.

He continued that this Comforter will reprove the world of sin, right-eousness and Judgment. This goes more than ever to show that the Comforter, the Holy Spirit or the Spirit of Truth is a Person Who will come to judge the world. Jesus used the pronoun *he* and obviously an amorphous energy cannot judge the world or reprove it of sin. It has to be someone who will come personally and carry out these duties. These duties, which Jesus mentioned cannot be carried out through any other means than the appearance of an individual with the requisite qualities for these. He went on to say that *he* will guide us to all truth, *he* shall not speak of his own accord. This is clearly a person. *He* will guide, *he* will show and in the process *he* will glorify Jesus.

These are fulfillments for the end time when a Comforter will come for the Judgment. Hand in hand with this Judgment, as Jesus has indicat-ed is a remembrance of His Teachings. Jesus will be glorified and His Teachings will come to life once more. This Comforter will teach us all things. He will show us all things. He will take what is of Jesus and teach it to us. He will also hear things of His own accord and show it to us. This is clearly the prediction by Jesus of an individual who will come person-ally and teach the world: *a World Teacher*.

He will teach us all things. He will be able through His Teachings to answer all our questions, no matter what they are. He will also bring the Judgment and reprove the world of its sins. Jesus went on to say that He could tell us many things but we were too immature to understand them at that time but that when this World Teacher comes, everything will be revealed by Him.

He has identified this World Teacher as the Holy Ghost. But not the Holy Ghost as convention understands It. This indeed has been a tragedy of immense proportions. Jesus asked His disciples to tarry in Jerusalem and the spirit will be sent to them. **Matthew 24:49 "I am going to send you what my Father has promised; but stay in the city until you have been clothed with power from on high."** Indeed it was and they were filled with power as never before and this allowed them to achieve things that had never before or since been achieved by human beings. This event however, was the descent of the *Power* of the Holy Spirit on the disciples and not perhaps the descent of the Holy Spirit Itself. In fact, this verse goes to prove, contrary to popular belief that what the disciples received was not the promise of the Counselor, but power from the Holy Spirit. This has nothing to do with the Coming of the Spirit of Truth which Christ promised for the end age. Not even Jesus used the word Holy Spirit; He used the expression **"clothed with power."**

In the book "In the Light of Truth: The Grail Message" by Abd-ru-shin, we learn that the descent of the Power of the Holy Spirit is a yearly event in which the Holy Ghost pours down the Power for the renewal and sustenance of the whole of Creation and its creatures. Jesus knew about this specific day and time for this happening which had always been and still is today. The momentous events surrounding the death of Jesus made the disciples especially open to this Power, which otherwise would not have been so. Their spirits were open and they absorbed of this Power of God, which worked miracles in them.

This event was an entirely different fulfillment and has nothing to do with the verses quoted above. The events at Whitsuntide did *not* reprove the world of sin, did *not* bring a new teaching that reminded us of Jesus, did *not* bring the Judgment. Nothing that Jesus said would happen happened after this event had taken place. Why do we then insist on placing Jesus' predictions of the end time on the events at Whitsuntide? It is indeed baffling. It is lack of understanding, and since the interpreters could not help themselves they demanded blind faith. Otherwise, it is difficult to imagine that this mistake has gone on for this long. This Comforter, the Son of Man then brings the Judgment.

PART V

THE TRIAL OF JESUS

1

His Arrest and Trial

The role of Judas has often been disputed. If indeed Jesus' death was in the Will of God, then Judas was a useful instrument to that end and in the Laws was not to be accounted guilty. He should have been declared a Saint because he played a vital role in the achievement of something of vital importance to mankind. It is illogical that the Christian Church had not declared this man a Saint. If they were to carry their argument of a propitiatory sacrifice to its logical conclusion, then there is nothing left but to canonize Judas Iscariot.

The illogical way in which the events surrounding the Life of Jesus has been handled by the Christian religious authorities is ever again brought to the fore. They are at a loss and it is only the demand for blind faith that has kept them going. This demand for blind faith will not take them much further anymore. Now, all must be revealed so that at last mankind will breathe a sigh of relief and worship God with a free mind and complete conviction based on knowledge.

Here, we do not have to do anything more than to examine the Words of Jesus Himself as to the Will of God in regard to His crucifixion. Not a Word of the Scriptures need be changed.

Matthew 26:24 **"The Son of man goes as it is written of him, but woe to that man by whom the Son of man is betrayed! It would have been better for that man if he had not been born."**
With His own words Jesus condemned the traitor Judas. He said that woe unto him by whom He is betrayed and that it would have been better if Judas had not been born. No clearer words could be said as to the opin-

213

ion of Jesus and the Will of God on this matter. If what Judas was doing was in the Will of God, then Jesus would never have uttered this statement. His views on what Judas did, and consequently on His death has now been made clear with this statement. It was clearly an act that went against the Will of God. The fact the He said He was going as it has been written is a sad testimony to the fact that the prophecies of Isaiah, in spite of their intentions to induce man to change his ways in time so that these dreadful actions would not take place had clearly not worked. His saying this is not proof that God sanctioned or approved of His death.

He broke the bread and served the wine as a token that He was willing to shed His Blood for the preservation of His Teachings. He was prepared to die so that we would continue to have His Message and by so doing the Way would remain open for the remission of sins, but only for those who follow this Way. Since He was the Word of God Incarnate in flesh and blood, those who absorbed the Word of God within themselves and acted accordingly have drank the Blood of Jesus and eaten His Flesh.

This is an act that takes place in the entire Creation and Jesus confirms this by saying that He would drink this wine anew with those who find their way back to Paradise through His Word.

Matthew 26:36-39 **Then Jesus went with them to a place called Gethsemane, and he said to his disciples, "Sit here, while I go yonder and pray." (37) And taking with him Peter and the two sons of Zebedee, he began to be sorrowful and troubled. (38) Then he said to them, "My soul is very sorrowful, even to death; remain here, and watch with me." (39) And going a little farther he fell on his face and prayed, "My Father, if it be possible, let this cup pass from me; nevertheless, not as I will, but as thou wilt."**
The fact that Jesus was very sorrowful at His passing further proves that His death was not willed by God. He knew that His death was not lawful but an arbitrary act through the will of men. He knew that His Mission among mankind was being cut short through this wanton act of wickedness. Jesus would never have been so sorrowful and heavy if He knew that by dying He was achieving something great for men, especially considering the love He had for us. He would have embraced death joyfully.

He would never have lamented. People have explained this away by saying that it was the weakness of the flesh of Jesus that was taking over. No! It was not a question of the flesh but sadness and sorrow at this dastardly unnecessary suffering that was going to be wrought on Him.

The proof of this is Jesus asking God to let the cup of suffering pass Him by. If He was dying and taking away the sins of men, He would never have prayed thus. His perfection through the Will of God would never have allowed Him to say such a prayer, and as mentioned above, He would have been all too happy to carry this cup. The fact that He did not want it and rejected it and even prayed God several times that the cup be taken away is proof that He did not want this and that his death was not to achieve what mankind in their indolence have come to expect. It was proof that whatever was happening was happening only through the free will of men and God does not interfere with the free will of men.

The question of watching and praying and the spirit being willing but the flesh weak had nothing to do with Him. He was addressing Peter saying that their spirits indeed wanted to keep watch with Him but their flesh was weak, which prevented the possibility of keeping watch. Certainly, Jesus was not referring to Himself but this has been taken as proof by some people to say that Jesus' flesh was weak and this is the reason for the appeal to God.

Matthew 27:3-5 When Judas, his betrayer, saw that he was condemned, he repented and brought back the thirty pieces of silver to the chief priests and the elders, (4) saying, "I have sinned in betraying innocent blood." They said, "What is that to us? See to it yourself." (5) And throwing down the pieces of silver in the temple, he departed; and he went and hanged himself."

Judas realized what he had done; filled with dread he committed suicide. Judas was obviously far more clear-sighted than the majority of the believers today. He immediately realized that the betrayal, arrest and the crucifixion of Jesus was not in the Will of God and his role in that was contrary to this Will. He knew that he had betrayed the Innocent One and said as much. Why do we insist on portraying this event as necessary and willed by Jesus and God Himself?

215

Matthew 26:51-54 **And, behold, one of them which were with Jesus stretched out his hand, and drew his sword, and struck a servant of the high priest's, and smote off his ear. (52) Then said Jesus unto him, Put up again thy sword into his place: for all they that take the sword shall perish with the sword. (53) Thinkest thou that I cannot now pray to my Father, and he shall presently give me more than twelve legions of angels? (54) But how then shall the scriptures be fulfilled, that thus it must be?**

This is one of the verses quoted to justify the teaching of a fulfillment of the prophecy and the propitiatory sacrifice. As mentioned before, what people did not understand they added their own thoughts. This has led to the various inconsistencies and contradictions. This is obviously a contradiction. How are we to explain it? All that can be said is that we should take a hard look at the Words of Jesus and the consistent thread through it all and make up our minds as to what to believe. The disciples more than once have demonstrated their ignorance of the Word of Jesus and their lack of understanding could be regarded as primarily responsible for some of the contradictions. This last verse is meant to be quoted to convince us that Jesus wanted this to happen. It is, however, just one verse in the whole body of the Word of Jesus that asserts the contrary.

Matthew 26:63-66 **But Jesus held his peace. And the high priest answered and said unto him, I adjure thee by the living God, that thou tell us whether thou be the Christ, the Son of God. (64) Jesus saith unto him, Thou hast said: nevertheless I say unto you, Hereafter shall ye see the Son of man sitting on the right hand of power, and coming in the clouds of heaven. (65) Then the high priest rent his clothes, saying, He hath spoken blasphemy; what further need have we of witnesses? behold, now ye have heard his blasphemy. (66) What think ye? They answered and said, He is guilty of death.**

They had their excuse. They had played their last trump card. After empty platitudes which was leading nowhere and after the stepping forward of many false witnesses to no avail, they were offered with the one thing by the darkness which was certain to put Jesus under immense pressure. There was no question of His denying His Origin and as discussed earlier, He preferred to die than to allow His Message to run to sand.

Pilate obviously knew that Jesus was not guilty and was prepared to release Him, especially with the warning from his wife **'not to have anything to do with that innocent man'**. The people, however, were obdurate and they demanded that a criminal be released to them in place of One Who had done so much good in their community.

The surprisng thing about Jesus' trial was that his enemies had absolutely nothing to go on. They had nothing on Him and it was all blind fury and hatred.

Matthew 27:22-23 **Pilate said to them, "Then what shall I do with Jesus who is called Christ?" They all said, "Let him be crucified." (23) And he said, "Why, what evil has he done?" But they shouted all the more, "Let him be crucified."**

Luke 23:13-25 **Pilate then called together the chief priests and the rulers and the people, (14) and said to them, "You brought me this man as one who was perverting the people; and after examining him before you, behold, I did not find this man guilty of any of your charges against him; (15) neither did Herod, for he sent him back to us. Behold, nothing deserving death has been done by him; (16) I will therefore chastise him and release him...."**
John 19:12 **Upon this Pilate sought to release him, but the Jews cried out, "If you release this man, you are not Caesar's friend; every one who makes himself a king sets himself against Caesar."**
The series of quotations above goes to show that there was absolutely no reason for demanding the crucifixion of Jesus other than hatred and jealousy. The blind demand for His death is obvious from here. No single trace of objective reasoning. They just wanted Him dead. Pilate asked them several times what Jesus had done, but instead of giving any reasons, they raged the more.

He asked them several times 'What evil had he done?' Instead of answering, they shouted all the louder that a riot was even going to take place. These were mostly ordinary people who probably knew nothing of the issues, but they just allowed themselves to be incited by those who thought they had a reason for demanding His death.

Matthew 27:29-31 **And when they had platted a crown of thorns, they put it upon his head, and a reed in his right hand: and they bowed the knee before him, and mocked him, saying, Hail, King of the Jews! (30) And they spit upon him, and took the reed, and smote him on the head. (31) And after that they had mocked him, they took the robe off from him, and put his own raiment on him, and led him away to crucify him.**

Matthew 27:39-44 **And they that passed by reviled him, wagging their heads, (40) And saying, Thou that destroyest the temple, and buildest it in three days, save thyself. If thou be the Son of God, come down from the cross.**

It is pertinent to remember here that the soldiers and most of the people who mocked Jesus had not the faintest idea of the issues. Some did not even know Jesus at all. It was all fun, and unfortunately mankind has not changed in this regard. The penchant for mocking what we do not understand is still very much with us with their disastrous consequences. It is all a senseless sham. They thought it was all funny, but they would have to account for every action and word.

2

Crucifixion and Death

It is also pertinent to examine the crucifixion and death of Jesus through the eyes of the Scriptures in order that we may arrive at a new understanding of the events surrounding His death.

Luke 23:28-31 **But Jesus turning unto them said, Daughters of Jerusalem, weep not for me, but weep for yourselves, and for your children. (29) For, behold, the days are coming, in the which they shall say, Blessed are the barren, and the wombs that never bare, and the paps which never gave suck. (30) Then shall they begin to say to** the mountains, Fall on us; and to the hills, Cover us. (31) For if they do these things in a green tree, what shall be done in the dry? Jesus told the people that they should not feel sorry for Him but that they should feel sorry for themselves because what they had done will exact a terrible revenge that they would wish for death. *Are these the words of someone who came to die and take away our sins?*

He would never have said this if His main aims were those that had been set out by conventional teaching. What humanity had done would bring upon them such a fate that they would wish that they had never been born. Weep for yourselves and your descendants, since they had already cursed themselves by saying to Pilate that 'His Blood be on us and our children'. He who after reading this statement from Jesus still insists that His main Mission was just to die and carry people's sins away will fulfill the Words of Jesus in **John 15:22-25 If I had not come and spoken to them, they would not have sin; but now they have no excuse for their sin......(24) If I had not done among them the works which no one else did, they would not have sin; but now they have seen and hated both me and my Father.** He went to say that if men could behave in this bestial fashion in the time of plenty, then what will the situation be during the time of Judgment, when through the effect of the natural Laws disasters accumulate, leading to a severe scarcity of resources. We would probably tear ourselves apart.

Luke 23:34 **And Jesus said, "Father, forgive them; for they know not what they do."**
Is this the statement from One Whose Mission was for a propitiatory sacrifice? Would He ever have said this prayer of intercession that God should forgive us if His Mission was as we insist on representing It? It was a prayer said on our behalf to intercede for this dastardly crime committed against Him. There is no other way of looking at this. There is no way that this can be glossed over. From these statements alone we can conclude that Jesus' death was not in the Will of God and that His death did not and does not carry away humanity's sins.

Some people might ask that if it was not according to the Will of God then why did He die? The answer to that is that the Will of God manifested in Jesus' determination to lay down His Life, no matter what it took, even physical suffering and death. The Will of God manifested in the fact that His Word, in spite of all the attacks of the darkness must still be established here on earth. That the road to salvation of human beings must remain open in spite of humanity's will to the contrary so that those minority as seeks the Creator might continue to have His Word to cling to. It was that Will that commanded Jesus to do whatever was necessary for the preservation of this Word. This Jesus said as much in: **John 10:17-18 "For this reason the Father loves me, because I lay down my life, that I may take it again. (18) No one takes it from me, but I lay it down of my own accord. I have power to lay it down, and I have power to take it again; this charge I have received from my Father."**

The importance of the preservation of His Word was so great as we see in the prayer that He said not only for His disciples but for also those that are to come. He said a prayer for those people in the future who would come across His Word and believe thus: John 17:20-23 **Neither pray I for these alone, but for them also which shall believe on me through their word; (21) That they all may be one; as thou, Father, art in me, and I in thee, that they also may be one in us: that the world may believe that thou hast sent me. (22) And the glory which thou gavest me I have given them; that they may be one, even as we are one: (23) I in them, and thou in me, that they may be made perfect in one; and that the world may know that thou hast sent me, and hast loved them, as thou hast loved me.**

So it was according to God's Will that His Word be preserved. It will be preserved in spite of all the evil will of mankind and all the attacks of the darkness. Even if they threatened Jesus with physical death. We must realize that the intention of the darkness was to make certain that the Will of God was not established. It was hoping that by threatening Jesus with physical death, He might flee and abandon His Mission. By so doing, Jesus' Message would have completely run to sand and the darkness would have gained a final victory. With Jesus standing His grounds, however, the darkness was utterly vanquished since the Word that the darkness wanted to prevent its establishment would now be preserved because Jesus was not going to abandon His Mission, but on the contrary was prepared to do the ultimate. The last trump card of the darkness had not worked. With this determination from Jesus, the seed was planted and there was nothing anymore that the darkness could do about it. This seed was destined to grow as history proves.

What about the unrest in Nature? And what about the curtain that was torn? Are those evidences that God was happy with His Son's death? The tearing of the curtain that veiled the Holy of Holies has been interpreted by convention as meaning that now the connection between mankind and God was complete and that it symbolized an admission into God. *Nothing could be further from the truth.*

The curtain was torn in anger by Luminous Hands because after this dastardly deed, the pure worship of God was no longer to take place among mankind. Mankind had rejected God and the Word brought down in order to show us His true Worship. The Holy of Holies was no longer necessary because the pure Worship of God that was to take place through Jesus had been rejected. The Holy of Holies was rendered superfluous. Of what use was the Holy of Holies if those who would go there to worship had rejected the very God that this was supposed to be dedicated to? With this act of murder, the Jewish people had lost their heritage. Their religion and as such all their symbols as from then on meant nothing.

What is this talk of a reconciliation with God when He had already signified the cleavage with mankind? Mankind's opinions count for nothing. The upheaval in nature could be viewed in the same light. This was a crime against the Will of God and the darkness that physically came over Golgotha is the earthly manifestation of the ethereal darkness that streamed over mankind with this deed. This darkness separated mankind all the more from the enlightenment of God's Light. We should never try to deceive ourselves and must make the effort personally to try to understand these events for ourselves. Adopting the opinions of others in this most important of matters places us at the risk of spiritual death.

3

Resurrection

Resurrection of Jesus in the physical body is the prevailing concept that we have today. Let us, however, examine the words of the Scriptures to see for ourselves whether indeed Jesus did resurrect in the physical body.

John 20:13-14 They said to her, "Woman, why are you weeping?" She said to them, "Because they have taken away my Lord, and I do not know where they have laid him." (14) Saying this, she turned round and saw Jesus standing, but she did not know that it was Jesus.

John 20:15-18 Jesus said to her, "Woman, why are you weeping? Whom do you seek?" Supposing him to be the gardener, she said to him, "Sir, if you have carried him away, tell me where you have laid him, and I will take him away." (16) Jesus said to her, "Mary." She turned and said to him in Hebrew, "Rabboni!" (which means Teacher). (17) Jesus said to her, "Do not hold me, for I have not yet ascended to the Father; but go to my brethren and say to them, I am ascending to my Father and your Father, to my God and your God." (18) Mary Magdalene went and said to the disciples, "I have seen the Lord"; and she told them that he had said these things to her.

It is obvious that Mary Magdalene who knew Jesus very well would undoubtedly have recognized Him under normal circumstances. The same thing happened with the disciples on the road to Emmaus when Jesus spoke with them for a long time without them recognizing Him. Yet, they were His disciples, lived with Him for years and undoubtedly under normal circumstances would have recognized Him.

It is obvious that Jesus was not in His customary physical body; that we can safely surmise because if He had been, He would have been recognized at once. Jesus was not recognized by those closest to Him because He was not in His physical body. For those who are familiar with what constitutes man on earth, these events should already be clear.

Man on earth has not just the physical body with him but also the coverings of all the layers of Creation within him. If he drops the physical body, he is left with the densest layer after this, corresponding to the layer that he finds himself. If he still finds himself on earth even though he has died then the outermost layer will be the form of medium gross matter, what has generally been called the astral body. This body is different form that of the earthly body. It is lighter and finer. Jesus, having dropped His physical body at death was left with nothing else but His Astral body or the body of medium gross matter. His body was therefore lighter and finer than His customary physical body. It was different and this is the reason that He was not recognized by anyone.

Luke 24:36-37 **As they were saying this, Jesus himself stood among them. (37) But they were startled and frightened, and supposed that they saw a spirit.**

John 20:19-23 **Then the same day at evening, being the first day of the week, when the doors were shut where the disciples were assembled for fear of the Jews, came Jesus and stood in the midst, and saith unto them, Peace be unto you. (20) And when he had so said, he shewed unto them his hands and his side. Then were the disciples glad, when they saw the Lord. (21) Then said Jesus to them again, Peace be unto you: as my Father hath sent me, even so send I you. (22) And when he had said this, he breathed on them, and saith unto them, Receive ye the Holy Ghost: (23) Whose soever sins ye remit, they are remitted unto them; and whose soever sins ye retain, they are retained.**

John 21:4 **Just as day was breaking, Jesus stood on the beach; yet the disciples did not know that it was Jesus.**
The ability of Jesus to make sudden appearances in rooms which doors were locked was another issue that has not been properly explained. As

mentioned above, the body of medium gross matter, which is lighter and finer is the kind of body that can penetrate through the material substance of this earth. Jesus' body, now lighter and finer could penetrate and enter into rooms without opening doors, things that He could not do when He still had His physical body with Him. Jesus therefore, could not have had His physical body with Him for these reasons alone.

Jesus entered a room where the disciples were gathered. They thought that they saw a ghost and were startled. This alone is enough to explain the condition of the body of Jesus after He had left His physical body. Many of us have heard stories of ghosts, or even experienced them and our experiences correspond to these experiences of the disciples.

Some sentences have found their way into the Scriptures, probably in the zeal of the disciples, or some other people to show that Jesus was with His physical body. It is important to note here that Jesus would not have made special efforts to prove His physical nature after He had laid down His physical body. All He had to do was convince His disciples that it was Him, *whatever body He was in*. Some verses went so far as to say that Jesus ate broiled fish and things like that. He had no need to do that. It was not necessary. He did not have to prove His physicality to anyone. But somehow this found its way into the Scriptures. It is left to the individual to examine the words. It will not be difficult to recognize that which man had inserted deliberately to cause confusion.

The question of His appearance to Thomas is not difficult to explain: John 20:27-28 **Then he said to Thomas, "Put your finger here, and see my hands; and put out your hand, and place it in my side; do not be faithless, but believing." (28) Thomas answered him, "My Lord and my God!".**
Jesus commanded Thomas to believe, to open his spirit. It was this condition of Thomas opening his spirit that made it possible for him to feel the marks on Jesus. Jesus had no need to say these things if these marks were ordinarily physically visible. There would have been no need for that because being physical everyone could see them with or without faith. However, with the ethereal marks that Jesus bore on Him, something more was needed to recognize them and this is the reason that Jesus

asked Thomas to have faith and not doubt. Doubt is the work of the intellect. It closes down our spirits. Faith, however, opens up our spirits to the wonders of Creation. Thomas opened himself and he was allowed to behold the marks of Jesus and even more to feel them. Of course he felt these marks with his own ethereal body, which we all have with us on earth.

At that moment, Thomas' body of medium gross matter was able to feel the marks on the medium gross matter body of Jesus. He was then able to transmit this perception to his consciousness. Many of us have perceived pain or feeling or pressure from our body of medium gross matter. This is the case with phantom pains where people who have had a limb amputated still feel as if the limb was still there, and sometimes can feel some pressure there. The body of medium gross matter is the counterpart to the physical one and the removal of some member of the physical one does not at the same time remove the member of the medium gross matter one. It is therefore the same process, whereby Thomas used his medium gross matter hands to feel and this feeling was transmitted to his earthly consciousness.

Thomas therefore, through his faith was able not only to feel the ethereal marks of Jesus but also to transmit this perception to his day conscious brain, something which under normal circumstances could only take place when dreaming.

Jesus' ascension could be described along the same lines. His body was now lighter, finer and it is this kind of body which has the quality or capability to ascend up to the realm which corresponds to its weight. Physical bodies cannot and do not ascend. The Law of Gravity keeps it down because the weight of a physical body corresponds to the material weight of this earth. This is the reason it stays anchored here.

Other bodies, however, be they those of medium matter and so on are no longer held by Law of Gravity as it applies to the earth, and as such can ascend to places in the Beyond which correspond to their weights, unless such souls are earthbound, in which case they are held down here by threads of fate. There in the Beyond, they can go no further until through inner experience, they change and as such become lighter as a consequence. They then rise again and so it goes on until they reach their destination, which is Paradise. In the case of Jesus once He began to ascend, He shed all the bodies that He had acquired on His way down until He was absorbed back into His Origin and held there.

4

Conclusion

Disciples' Culpability

It is generally known that the disciples did not understand their Master at all on many issues and in some cases filled their lack of understanding with their own understanding and thoughts. There are so many instances in the Bible where Jesus was clearly not happy with His disciples' spiritual dullness and He often upbraided them.

People try to defend the disciples by saying that the Holy Spirit descended on them and as such all that they said was of the Holy Spirit and that it was impossible for them to make mistakes. Firstly, the Holy Spirit does not occupy people's bodies. People are not possessed by the Holy Spirit as if now the person is now no longer himself, and has been crowded out of his physical body and the occupier of that physical body is now the Holy Spirit. One can receive the power from the Holy Spirit as has already been discussed but the degree to which this power is effective in each individual depends on that individual. Even those who are fully open to the power of the Holy Spirit as is humanly possible are still open to errors in transmission because of the problems and chasms created through the overdevelopment of the intellect to which all men are subject.

The Holy Spirit does not repair defective memories, especially when it was many years before Jesus' Words were written down. The Holy Spirit gave them the power so that they might accomplish all they did, in the fortification of their faiths, in the miracles that they performed and in their ability to face all opposition with boldness and conviction and also in the force of their words. Whatever they had forgotten, they had forgotten and what they forgot, they tried to replace with their recollection, which is never the same as the actual words. Are we then surprised at the many inconsistencies and conflicting details?

In any case whether the disciples misrepresented their Master's Words or not, the onus is still on us as individuals to personally examine these words in the Scriptures with an open mind and intuitive perception. It will not be difficult to separate what is real from what is not. This discovery will be a shock and probably even depressing at the outset but at the same time, it will be freedom and a fresh breeze for those who truly want to be Jesus' servants.

A

Aaron 8
Abd-ru-shin 22
abomination of desolation 8
Abraham 22
Alcimus 8
Alexander Jannaeus 9
Alexander the Great 7
Alexandra Salome 9
amorphous energy 207
Angel Gabriel 176
Annunciation 21
Antigonus 9
Antiochus IV Epiphanes 8
Antipater 10
Archelaus 11
Aristobulus 9
Assyrians 6

B

Babylon 6
Babylonians 6
Beatitudes 43
Bethlehem 21
betrayal 40
Birth of Jesus 21
Blood of Jesus 214
Book of Life 133

C

Caesar Augustus 10
Caesarea 17
Caiaphas 36
cerebellum 100
Childlikeness 138
cold calculating intellect 76
Comforter 207
Coming of the Son of Man 170

P

R

S

spiritual arrogance 56
spiritual bondage 35
Spiritual highway men 205
spiritual Messiah 35
suspended animation 154

T

Talmud 17
Temple of God 184
Ten Commandments 6, 58
the Adversary 39
The Law of Sowing and Reaping 107
the Maccabee 8
The tares 112
Thomas 224
Torah 17
Tribulation 167

V

vineyard 148
Voice of the Son of Man 193

W

Whitsuntide 207
Word Incarnate 183
Word of God 178
Word of the Scriptures 213
Work of Redemption 137
World of Gross Matter 79
World of Fine Gross Matter 79
World of Heavy Gross Matter 79
World of Medium Gross Matter 79
World Teacher 208

Y

youth of Nain 74

Z

Printed in the United Kingdom
by Lightning Source UK Ltd.
9401600001B